The SCORPION and the FROG

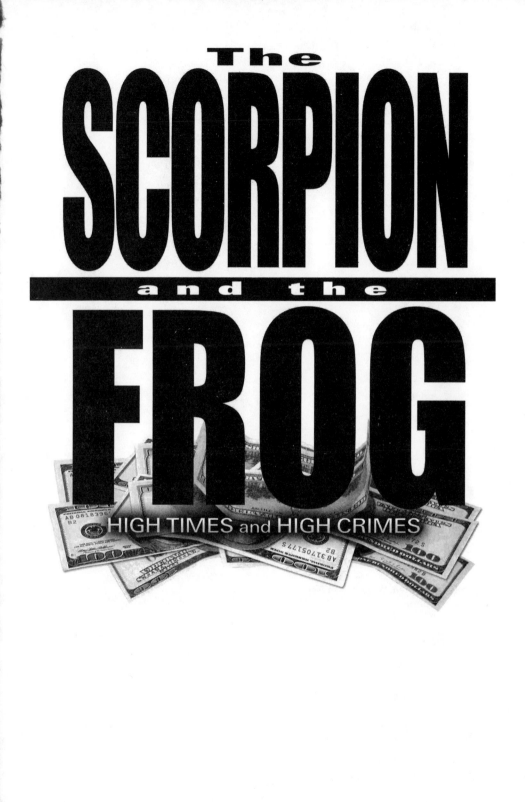

HIGH TIMES and HIGH CRIMES

ISBN: 1-893224-26-0

Library of Congress Cataloging-in-Publication Data Available

Design: Kerry DeAngelis, KL Design

New Millennium Press
301 North Canon Drive
Suite 214
Beverly Hills, CA 90210
www.NewMillenniumPress.com

10 9 8 7 6 5 4 3 2 1

The SCORPION and the FROG

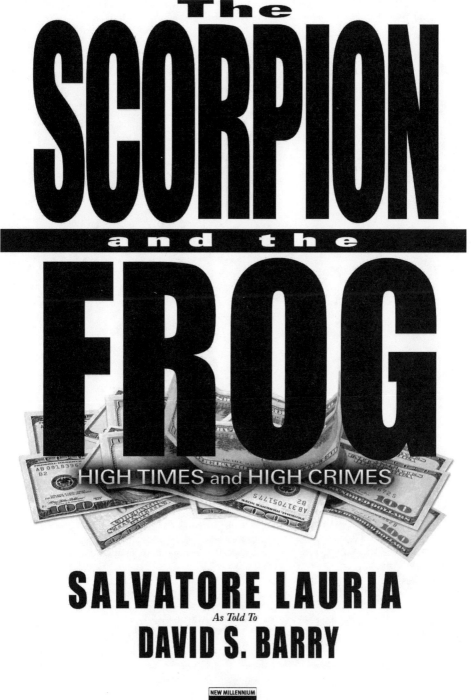

HIGH TIMES and HIGH CRIMES

SALVATORE LAURIA
As Told To
DAVID S. BARRY

NEW MILLENNIUM PRESS
Beverly Hills

INTRODUCTION

Writing Sal Lauria's story was a walk on the literary wild side that did not end when the book was finished. There was plenty of adventure in the research I did to vet the criminal life story Sal told me. I spent hundreds of hours reading Justice Department strike force complaints, indictments, court rulings and sentencing reports. I combed organized crime reports by the FBI, the New York State Attorney General's office, sanction records of the Securities and Exchange Commission, NASD on unlawful trading practices. I read hundreds of newspaper and magazine articles about stock fraud, organized crime family racketeering on Wall Street and other trading areas.

Every one of the stories Sal told me was verified by public records that I tracked down in my research. Some of the research trails were easy to follow, like looking up major news stories and working backward. Others were obscure, like discovering an e-mail posted by one of Sal's cohorts wheeling and dealing in energy futures in the former Soviet Union. This book took me through research not only of US organized crime family operations but also of organized crime run by Israelis and Russians. The tension in the story is the crossover of brutal mob intimidation and retaliation tactics in the fields of stock trading and money laundering. The book took me through stories of rock stars, socialites, dope, sex, and murder.

When the book was finished, a new adventure began. It started when Sal, through an attorney, filed a motion to block publication of the book on the grounds that his life would be in danger if names weren't changed from real names to pseudonyms. Though every one of the referenced mobsters had been identified in major news stories before I signed on to the project, Sal did not want his name and his book to repeat the identification.

Almost all of the cases against the 19 men indicted with Sal for the major stock-trading swindle related in this book had been resolved with plea bargains before I began work on the book. But the legal drama of the book, for me, was just beginning. I was questioned about my part and my experience and recollections of writing the book in depositions by attorneys for Sal and for New Millennium, the publisher.

Then the case went to court. I had the first-time experience, after years of reporting on criminal trials as a journalist, of testifying in one, as a witness. I was questioned by New Millennium's attorney and by Sal's attorney. I was also questioned by the judge. Unlike a trial on TV, there was no audience and there was no press. That didn't lessen the tension of being sworn in and testifying under oath. The courtroom proceedings that involved me were in December, 2002. Little would have surprised me more than to hear, nearly a year later, that the case had been settled and the book was being published.

—David S. Barry, Aug. 11, 2003

There's a folk tale about a scorpion and a frog. They meet each other by the side of a riverbank. The scorpion needs to cross the water and asks to ride on the back of the frog.

"I can't carry you on my back. If I do, you'll sting me and then I'll surely die," says the frog.

"But I need to get across the river and I can't swim. If you give me a ride, I promise not to sting you because if I did, I'd die," says the scorpion urgently.

The frog ponders the matter for a moment, and then decides that what the scorpion says makes sense. "All right. I'll carry you," he says, and the scorpion hops on his back.

The frog enters the water and swims. Halfway across the river he suddenly feels a sharp sting followed by the scorpion's venom entering his bloodstream. "You fool!" croaks the frog. "Why did you do that? Now we'll both die."

"I couldn't help myself," the scorpion replies. "It is my nature."

PROLOGUE

On March 2, 2000, the U.S. Department of Justice released this information:

19 DEFENDANTS INDICTED IN STOCK FRAUD SCHEME THAT WAS PROTECTED AND PROMOTED BY ORGANIZED CRIME

Loretta E. Lynch, United States Attorney for the Eastern District of New York, Lewis D. Schiliro, Assistant Director-in Charge of the Federal Bureau of Investigation in New York, and Howard Safir, Commissioner, New York City Police Department, today announced the indictment of nineteen defendants, including six members and associates of various Organized Crime Families of La Cosa Nostra, who are charged with participating in a large-scale stock fraud and money laundering scheme between 1993 and 1996. Seventeen of the nineteen defendants are charged with racketeering.

The charges in the indictment center on the activities of two brokerage firms with offices in downtown Manhattan: White Rock Partners & Co. ("White Rock") and State Street Capital Markets Corporation ("State Street")[1]. The indictment alleges that the principals of White Rock and State Street, together with other brokers and brokerage firms, planned and carried out a series of fraudulent securities schemes and then laundered tens of millions of dollars of illicit profits.

As alleged in the indictment, the schemes were led by the defendants JOHN DOUKAS and WALTER DURCHALTER, together with Gene Klotsman, Salvatore Lauria and Lex Tersa, who collectively controlled White Rock and State Street (the "White Rock and State Street Partners")[2]. The White Rock and State Street Partners secretly acquired large blocks of stock and warrants in the following four companies: Country World Casinos, Inc. ("Country World"), which was based in Colorado and was purportedly attempting to develop a casino in Black Hawk, Colorado; Holly Products, Inc. ("Holly"), which was based in

---

[1] White Rock and State Street ceased operations in late 1996. U.S. Department of Justice.
[2] Klotsman, Lauria and Tersa have previously pleaded guilty to RICO charges in connection with their activities at White Rock and Street. Ibid.

Moorestown, New Jersey and was in the business of manufacturing tables and cabinets for the gaming industry and custom-built equipment for hospitals; U.S. Bridge of New York, Inc. ("USBNY"), which was based in Queens, New York, and was a subcontractor on public infrastructure projects in the greater New York area; and Cable & Co. Worldwide, Inc. ("Cable"), which had offices in New York and New Jersey and designed and imported men's footwear which was sold to department and specialty stores in the United States.

The indictment alleges that the White Rock and State Street Partners were able to acquire secret control of these securities through undisclosed financial arrangements with the following defendants: ABRAHAM SALAMAN, a stock promoter who provided the Country World stock; LARRY BERMAN, Holly's chairman and chief executive officer; and JOSEPH POLITO, Sr., an associate of the Gambino Organized Crime Family who was the president and principal shareholder of USBNY.

All of the defendants in the indictment have subsequently pleaded guilty to the charges.

Organized Crime Grows Up

In the lurid light of the Enron investment scandal, which may reach more than $1 billion swindled or stolen from unwitting investors and pension holders, the $40 million cited by the Justice Department as the dollar amount of the fraud described in this book does not stack up as a big heist. In fact, one individual alone—the president of Enron—made off with $62 million for himself, all of it taken when he knew the stock was tanking and the investors had no hope of saving their investments. By the standards of its time, however, in the mid-1990s, a $40-million swindle was a large one: in fact, one of the biggest recorded as of that date in 1995 when the government first made its case.

This story is told by Sal Lauria, one of the perpetrators. His insider's look at this sophisticated new era born of crime, born of the computer age and radical stock market innovations, is unique.

His and his fellow swindlers' robberies and thefts were not accomplished through stickup men with automatics, hired drivers, safecrackers, or any of the familiar means of force and vice characteristic of old-fashioned crime. This stock fraud scheme was a rip-off accomplished not in the old-fashioned way of extortion, armed robbery or various old-fashioned modes of theft. Nor was it based on methods of coercion or the implementation of fear of reprisal that characterized the Mafia enterprises of old. There were, to be sure, instances of each of those tactics, but the grand scheme of the fleecing of so many billions of dollars involved nothing more threatening or frightening than the behind the scenes manipulation of stock prices and the deception of unsophisticated investors.

The men responsible for these heists came from varied backgrounds. Some were part of the criminal organization known as La Cosa Nostra. Some were friends of members of that sinister clique. Others had no prior involvement with organized crime, but became part of these schemes because like so many street hustlers of their time, they were out to make as much money as quickly as possible and they were not particular about how they made it or who they hurt in their pursuit of the big score. They found that on Wall Street in the 1990s, more money was being made hand over fist by more people, in greater quantities than ever before. The way to make it even faster was to break the law and swindle the investing public. From 1990 through 2000, there were 4,531 IPOs on NASDAQ and 720 on the New York Stock Exchange. More money was being swindled than ever before, and by the end of the millennium it would cost investors trillions of dollars. This investment playing field was so immense that there were not enough law enforcement officials to keep an eye on all of it.

In the 1950s, the most notorious bank robber in American history was a master career criminal named Willie Sutton. When asked, on the record, why he robbed banks, he answered very simply: "Because that's where the money is." In the 1990s, Wall Street was where the money was, and organizations that had previously focused on stealing money, by force, threat, or theft—and sometimes all three—were drawn to Wall Street. They saw brokerage houses as the places to go to take money out of the booming stock market. They had seen prosecutor-Mayor Rudy Giuliani close down garbage collection as a mob enterprise, clean up much of the construction industry and shut down a great deal of the prostitution business. Wall Street seemed to be the place to go. It was the new frontier that still had the wild, wild West, gunslinger mentality for those so inclined.

In the beginning, Sal Lauria was just another hard-working Brooklyn guy running a tile-laying business in the 1980s, making money but working very hard for it. In 1990, he saw Brooklyn friends from his own neighborhood living the lifestyle of New York chic: fast cars, private parties in the Hamptons, designer labels, ritzy condos in Soho, and trendy nightclubs in Tribeca.

Sal's friends were living the good life of the American success story, 1990s style. His friends were from Brooklyn, guys who spoke of themselves as being "from the neighborhood." Some were connected to the Mob. But the lifestyle they enjoyed was nothing like the *Godfather* image of black Cadillacs, white-on-white shirts, greased hair, ringside fight tickets, high-roller accommodations in Las Vegas, and VIP treatment from the maitre d's in Miami Beach.

This was Ralph Lauren, Rolexes, Porsches, BMWs, Lexuses, Ferraris, skiing in Aspen, and clubbing at hot New York spots written up in *New York Magazine* and *Vanity Fair*. This was jetting to the French Riviera and popping champagne corks with CEOs and international socialites. All these Wall Streeters who fleeced so many people out of so much money knew they were breaking the law doing it. But few of them, especially Salvatore Lauria, had any idea how serious the crimes would be considered, and how much retribution they would face from the law enforcement agencies once they caught up with them.

This is Sal's story.

CHAPTER ONE

WHITE ROCK. IND   Mar. 2, 2000
United States District Court
Eastern District of New York

United States of America   Indictment
- against -   Cr. No. CR-OD 0196
FRANK COPPA, SR.
ERNEST MONTEVECCHI,
    Also known as **"Butch"**
DANIEL PERSICO
JACK BASILE
ROCCO BASILE
LARRY BERMAN
JOHN CIOFOLETTI
JOHN DOUKAS
WALTER DURCHALTER
    Also known as **"DUTCH"**
EDWARD GARAFOLA
DANIEL LEV
EUGENE LOMBARDO
EDMOND NAGEL
ALFRED PALAGONIA
ALEKS PAUL
JOSEPH PAUL
JOSEPH POLITO, SR.
LAWRENCE RAY
ABRAHAM SALAMAN
GIUSEPPE TEMPERINO
    Also known as **"Joseph Temperino"**

The Grand Jury Charges:

At all times relevant to this indictment, unless otherwise indicated:

1.   The BROKERAGE FIRMS
      A. WHITE ROCK and STATE STREET CAPITAL

1. White Rock Partners & Co. Inc. White Rock was a broker-dealer of securities, registered by the National Association of Securities Dealers (NASD). White Rock bought an existing broker-dealer and commenced brokerage operations about February 1994, with an office at 17 State Street, New York, New York.

2. White Rock was originally a partnership owned and operated by the defendant **WALTER DUR-CHALTER**, also known as **"Dutch,"** and unindicted co-conspirators **"Gene" Klotsman**, **Salvatore Lauria**, and **Lex Tersa**. In July 1995, the defendant JOHN DOUKAS acquired the partnership interest of DURCHALTER, who left the firm. DOUKAS then owned and operated White Rock along with Klotsman, Lauria and Tersa. DOUKAS, DUR-CHALTER, Klotsman, Lauria and Tersa are sometimes referred to herein as the "White Rock Partners."

3. In or about September 1995, the White Rock Partners renamed White Rock as State Street Capital Markets Corporation ("State Street"). State Street continued the trading of securities that had been conducted at White Rock. In or about June 1996, State Street moved its office to One World Trade Center, New York. State Street was a partnership owned and operated by the defendant **John Doukas**, **Gene Klotsman**, **Salvatore Lauria** and **Lex Tersa**,

(sometimes referred to herein as the "State Street Partners" and collectively with the White Rock Partners as the "White Rock and State Street Partners"). State Street ceased operation in or about September 1996.

State Street Partners on the French Riviera: Four O'clock High

August 1996. Hotel Biblos, St. Tropez, France.

The four o'clock afternoon ritual actually began at lunch time in the Val Rouge, a small restaurant that would have seemed like a quaint country bistro almost anywhere else. But being in the village of St. Tropez made the Val Rouge qualify as one of the most exclusive watering holes on earth. The town had been the home playground of Brigitte Bardot, and it was in St. Tropez that Picasso had sketched a profile of her, a minor masterpiece reflecting her beauty and privilige. St. Tropez is close enough to Cannes to be convenient to the guests at the Cannes Film Festival, and far enough away, and sufficiently more exclusive, to hold back people who haven't yet reached the lofty financial status required for St. Tropez.

The favored means of arriving there are in the private jets parked at Nice airport and the seagoing yachts moored offshore within sight of the restaurant. Several of the yachts were mini-ocean liners seven or eight stories high with helicopter pads and cranes to lift aboard cigarette power boats. The yachts provided every imaginable luxury accommodation for the pampered guests. They were owned by new and old money billionaires: Arab oilmen, European or English aristocracy, and Russians who had emerged from the collapse of Communism as business magnates.

There was no hint of this opulence in Val Rouge's decor or menu. It had perhaps ten tables and a square bar on the beach and offered simple Sicilian country dishes served in an unpretentious manner that nevertheless delighted the millionaires and billionaires who dined there. One could see the wealth on the diners' wrists:

Cartier, Rolex, Audemars Piguet and Briguet watches. Rings, bracelets, necklaces and earrings sparkled and glowed with the unmistakable hue of quality jewelry that often represented hundreds of thousands of dollars worth of precious stones on diners' necks, ears and wrists. My watch that summer was a Briguet that retailed for $186,000, more than the sticker price of the Ferrari parked at my home in the Hamptons.

I was an Italian-American who had been raised on Long Island and in Brooklyn who had risen to become a millionaire on Wall Street in half a dozen years. And the watch? I had learned it was necessary to convert large amounts of cash into gemstones in order to move it out of sight of government regulators. A rude term would be to call it money laundering, and three years later that would be the charges made on my business partners and me.

Spectacular as the jewelry was at Val Rouge luncheons, it drew little attention because it was what everyone there was used to seeing. But there was plenty to look at besides jewelry. Local boutiques sent models to show summer fashions during lunch, and diners often arranged to have an outfit for their female guests wrapped and delivered to their table, before the meal was over. The astronomical prices on the Val Rouge menu were largely irrelevant to the clientele. They were either too rich to care, or regarded showing up for lunch there as an important statement of success and financial well-being.

I was in St. Tropez with my cousin Sal, two partners in my Wall Street brokerage firm—Gene Klotsman and John Doukas, whose nickname was The Duke. We had also brought along Danny Persico, a boyhood friend of mine from Brooklyn. His last name figured in Federal Organized Crime Strike Force investigations of the leadership of the Colombo organized crime family. Danny was not along on business. We were treating him to the trip because he was a friend who had done us favors, and I wanted him to enjoy some of the rewards of our success.

The Cristal champagne that we drank went for $300 a bottle. Our lunch tabs could run to several thousand dollars. No matter how much we might spend, others were spending more, and the only way to impress anyone in St. Tropez was to be with someone who was considered important. When I had showed up, Gene was already there, spending time with the Princess of Seville, whose official title was the Duchess of Seville de Barbone, and with one of our new "beards," Dan Tellach. A beard is a stand-in, used in a stock—or any other—deal to conceal the real owner or operative.

The day's fun really began with the Four O'clock Ritual, which was kicked off by the Val Rouge house band that I called Big Soul, playing a keynote song. Then the Val Rouge regulars would count down the seconds to four o'clock, just like New Year's Eve revelers counting the seconds to midnight. Only this was in French, and it was a short count. Already in the hot, intoxicating rays of the French Rivera sun, beautiful girls had gathered on the sand:

"Un, deux, trois…" Then there was nothing but the sounds of corks being popped from expensive champagne bottles. At the end of the countdown, bikini-clad young women there for the occasion unhooked their tops and threw them onto the sand. As the tops flew off and the champagne corks popped, the men cheered, the music played and suddenly there was dancing on the hot sand with eager, topless girls. Sometimes, we bought and opened a case of Cristal champagne just to spray people for fun, like grand prix racecar winners, joining the rest of the wealthy in their club ritual.

The dancing turned into a party that would go for three or four hours, ending at sundown. Then everyone would meet at midnight at Le Cave, the only club in town, and the party would continue. I became friends with a guy named Eric, the head of security at Le Cave, a hot club, who also worked at Val Rouge. His friendship was a ticket to the VIP sections at both places. The next morning, the Val Rouge would again look like a quaint, quiet, over-priced beachfront bistro. And every afternoon, just before four o'clock, the song would begin anew—"Un, deux, trois…."

We loved the Four O'clock Ritual and the partying that followed it. I had learned early that part of the game of making major league money on Wall Street was partying hard at night. But not even the world's most hedonistic and exclusive merry making was enough to distract me from the unpleasant truth that our business was in trouble. We were under financial siege in the form of attacks from short traders, the predators of the brokerage business. These pillagers, in effect, wager that the price of a stock will go down, and then by various means they purposely drive it lower and lower, making fortunes for themselves as it loses value. We were fighting to hold up the price of a stock we had taken public and had a big position in. I could see that it was a losing battle.

But there were even worse things to worry about. Our company had become a target for gumshoes from the SEC—the Securities and Exchange Commission—the IRS and the FBI. And it could go from worse to cataclysmic. We might be in the sights of somebody's revenge plans in the Mob. The Duke, Gene and I, and Lex Tersa, a Russian business partner who had stayed behind in New York, had all ascended the financial pyramid very quickly, and some of the people who had helped us on the way up didn't think we had treated them as well as they deserved.

We knew our offices were not safe from snoopers. We had found electronic eavesdropping devices which were one or two generations more technologically sophisticated than those usually planted by the FBI or the SEC—that meant competitors, the Mob, or someone else. There was a Federal investigation underway into illegal stock manipulations called Operation Street Cleaner. Overall, I had the feeling we were being set up. The handwriting I saw on the wall said "Mene, Mene, Tekel"—our days were numbered; we had been found wanting.

The *New York News, CNN, Business Week,* and other media outlets were reporting investigations into and/or indictments of such brokerage houses as Hanover Sterling, D.H. Blair & Co., and Stratton-Oakmont. The FBI was drawn by the scent of organized crime on Wall Street, and eventually they would be drawn to us more forcefully. The terrible truth was that my partners and I had inadvertently opened our business door to members of the Bonanno, Colombo, and Genovese crime families. Yes, all three.

The SEC was studying the "pump and dump" schemes and other forms of stock manipulation that were standard practice in companies like ours (as well as in much bigger, more respectable houses who would fall under the prosecutorial gun later). The IRS was investigating money laundering, which was another shady aspect of our business. The knowledge on the Street that undercover investigations were everywhere made for a very uneasy business climate. So many people were turning state's evidence that there were incidents of violence based solely on suspicions, some of which were unfounded. Typical was an incident that had occurred September 25, 1996 at a company called Diamond Capital, Inc. Diamond was one of my trading enemies and a major force in short trading, which they did under the guise of handling over-the-counter stocks. Diamond manipulated stock in a broadcasting company which brokers thought was legitimate. The brokers had no idea that a Mob-controlled firm was juggling the stock price, and that Diamond was jeopardizing legitimate dealers' trades.

According to Complaint No. 10530 filed with the First Precinct of the New York City Police Department, three brawny men walked into Diamond's offices, one of them making certain that a handgun was visible in the belt of his pants. The complaint said "At that point they asked the victim what he was trading in. Then they slapped him in the head and stated again, 'What the fuck are you trading in?' Then he slapped the victim in the head again." Before the men left, one of them warned, "Don't fuck with our stock." Reported in *Business Week*, this story led to other brokers coming forward with their own tales of threatened violence and intimidation.

But it was the Mafia's trespasses into territory that had not heretofore been Mob-connected, firms that did not involve men and women who had knowingly sought help from the Mob, as I had done, or gone into partnership with organized crime, that intensified law enforcement interest.

Sure, I knew it was time to get out of the business. Before I had left New York for France, I had set up a bailout plan. I was ready to leave the partnership and move with my family to Monte Carlo. But as the days passed, I wasn't really ready to carry it out. I was too infatuated with the luxury of my $10,000 a month Manhattan penthouse, my summerhouse in the Hamptons, my $2,000 Ermenegildo Zegna suits and my $186,000 Briguet watch.

My partners and I were literally making millions. We had started cutting legal corners to make even more, ever faster. I knew on a gut level that I was breaking the law, but I wasn't willing to face it. I loved my wife and daughters back home in the Hamptons but not even love of family was enough to make me confront the reality that I was courting prison time.

Lulled by the balmy breezes of St. Tropez or under its jewelry store shop window of stars, I could delude myself into believing that I could keep the business going and survive, that I could keep flying high without crashing, that I could keep playing without getting burned by the law or the Mob. Part of my mechanism of denial was that the players I had come to meet in France were doing things that were perfectly legal in Europe. Our business in St. Tropez involved conferring with the front-men, the beards, who we used to buy and sell stock or to handle our Regulation S purchases and sales.

Regulation S, which we called "Reg S," is a loophole around the rule that requires maintaining ownership of stock in an offering like an IPO for 13 months before selling it. Under Reg S, if an offshore company owns the stock, it can be sold after only 41 days, a circumstance that completely alters the structure of the manner and time frame in which money can be made on new issues of stock. Securities and Exchange Commission regulations don't apply. So it was technically legal for our beard to buy and sell stock from an offshore location. It was also technically legal for our beard to buy discounted stock overseas to replace the private placement (PPM) stock that otherwise would have had to be held in the U.S. for 13 months. The stock, in theory at least, could not be sold without endangering the value of an IPO offering.

In August, 1996, we were in St. Tropez negotiating with our beard to handle our next private placement offering and settle accounts for a shoe deal whose IPO we had just taken public. The shoe company was financially healthy, and didn't need to go the Reg S route. Reg S could send a signal to the street that might cause the value of a stock issue to drop quickly. This deal involved a million shares of stock that we acquired with our beards at a deep discount months in advance. Our beard who was registered as our nominee owner—our mask—bought the million shares for us at $.50 a share, putting himself in for a ten percent chunk of the profit we would make when the stock opened at $5.00 and moved to $12.00 before we sold it. My partners and I would split the rest of the money. We were able to walk away with over eleven million dollars in profit.

Of course, owning stock through a nominee in that manner constitutes a form of securities ownership which by law must be disclosed, particularly in the case of securities your firm is promoting. To put it simply, we were breaking the law. By the summer of '96, the Feds were not far behind us. They were wise to our pumping and dumping, our hyping a stock with aggressive sales tactics and selling it to clients, conning them with our assurance that it would be a moneymaker.

The Feds had looked into firm after firm, and also found other consistent misleading practices. They discovered such things as unauthorized trading within a customer's account to assure desired price changes of a stock. The brokers, sometimes on their own and sometimes under orders from their employers, did not execute customer orders or failed to execute them at the time and price requested.

Brokers also deliberately misled buyers by making improper price and performance predictions. That year the SEC levied a $950 million fine—the largest fine in history and almost the full SEC budget for that year—on half a dozen big trading firms. The fine was levied for stock manipulation. Of course, the settlement did not require any of the principals to admit or deny guilt. None went to jail.

Strong-arm tactics were increasingly common means of keeping control of the stocks being traded. Most brokerage customers had no inkling that Mob-controlled firms were manipulating stock prices and threatening the control that legitimate dealers exercised over their trades. And I of course had no idea that the growing involvement of Danny Persico, along with other members and associates of the organized crime families, had reached a point where the Justice Department Organized Crime Strike Force saw my businesses as a front for Mob activity.

There was more than a little irony in that. At exactly the point where I saw my success validated by the luxury to which my partners and I were treating Danny, the Feds saw us as minor players, whose business had effectively been taken over by the people to whom we had occasionally turned to for help. We shouldn't have been so blind. Danny's uncle Carmine (Junior) Persico was at the top of the Colombo family when he and his son Alphonse "Allie Boy" Persico went to prison in 1989 on racketeering charges. Uncle Carmine would be in forever, with a 39-year sentence to start with, and then a 10-year sentence added on top of that for good measure. Alphonse, Danny's college educated cousin, got out of prison in 1994 after serving a 12-year sentence. He had directed Mob energy and resources into the stock market. It was a situation that made me particularly uncomfortable.

We had flown commercially to Nice, then hopped a chartered helicopter to St. Tropez where a driver waited in a Mercedes 600 that we had leased for our entire stay. We would have been just as well served by a Mercedes 420. Or stepped up in price and power with a 500 model. But that wasn't enough. We leased a 600—the $140,000 absolute top-of-the-line Mercedes—that is to many the ultimate statement of performance and prestige on wheels.

On our first morning in St. Tropez, Gene and I helicoptered back to Nice and flew from there to Geneva to move money in our Swiss accounts and return with enough French francs to fund our vacation. We easily accomplished our mission and were back in St. Tropez by dinnertime for a great weekend of partying with a crowd of super-rich people. One night when Le Cave was too hot from dancing, we went outside to get some air. We had brought a bottle of chilled Stoli vodka with us and suddenly we saw a silhouette lurching toward us, staggering from a night of partying, shirt open to the middle of his chest. It was "Jack the Man" Nicholson himself. He stopped and with his patented Nicholson voice, asked "How is it in there?" and grabbed the vodka from my hands to take a swig.

"It's really fucking hot in there," I replied.

"That would be a first," Nicholson said sarcastically. Then he took another swig and went inside the club. A few minutes later we followed him inside and there he was—sitting in our VIP section. We had a blast!

But the Monday after was ruined by a phone call from Lex, the partner we had left in New York to mind the store. Lex had been at work for hours when he called us with the bad news that another of our IPO stocks was under heavy attack. The attackers were short traders, intent on destroying the value of our IPO and profiting on the price drop of the stock. Our offering was US Bridge of New York, a construction-contracting firm with a good business history. We had supported a public offering by US Bridge. Now the entire value of that offering was under threat. We were long—owned $3 million on the trading desk. We had a contingency plan calling for our brokers to swap stock in the shoe company we were supporting for the less valuable US Bridge stock.

But the contingency plan had not worked. Lex sounded frantic. He had good reason. In the game of IPOs, an attack by short traders can cut the value of stock issued in an IPO from dozens of millions of dollars to pennies on the dollar in a few days. Sometimes in only a single day. Once short traders batter a new stock, its value begins to drop, and the falling price becomes a plummeting ride down, accelerating as the price falls. The only way to stave off the attack and save the stock is to feverishly buy the stock even though its value is falling.

"We're getting hit!" Lex shouted over the phone. "Stock is coming in, clients are reneging, there's stock rolling back. They told me they were going to swap like we planned, but they sold the shoe company and never bought the other...."

If Lex had been a trader, I could have directed him to take the kind of action I would have taken if I had been back there. But he had been barred from being a broker because of a felony conviction and could not buy or sell without violating the law.

"Lex, they're abusing you," I told him. "Do a meeting. Get them motivated. Tell everybody they have to buy a thousand shares tomorrow for themselves or the client."

Our business had 150 brokers, and if every one of them moved a thousand shares, that would shore up the price of 150,000 shares of whatever stock we were trying to pump on any given day. The reality was that 20 percent of our sales force did 80 percent of the business. What we needed with US Bridge was to get the brokers and the cold-callers, fast-talkers who can set up sales for brokers, motivated to get clients to buy the stock. It was not that hard to do.

The stock market was a dance that I had learned: Make the deal. Arrange for the under-the-table split. Arrange for the offshore deposits. Arrange the artificial support that causes a stock price to rise. Excite the brokers. Excite the buying public.

First, we had to orchestrate the trades so we knew where almost every share of stock was being held. Then we could arrange anything, including the freezing of accounts, even if it happened to be against the owner's desires or best interests. Anything we did to support the stock so long as such support worked was okay. Then we could motivate our "troops"—our cold callers and brokers—to do whatever I asked them, including blowing up their books if necessary.

But there was a freakish problem. Lex was the son of a Russian gangster whose greatest desire was that Lex become a respectable businessman in America. Lex had done exactly that. He had made his way into the brokerage business from the ground up, just as I had. He had earned the broker's license that put him on the road to the status his father wanted for him. Unfortunately, Lex was a hothead. He was a smart money man but he was volatile. He had lost his right to act as a broker due to a felony conviction as the result of a bar fight in a torrid New York nightspot. So Lex was legally barred from setting foot on our brokerage floor. Our solution? He worked from an office in a separate building.

Therefore, on the day of our crisis, there was no one in place to carry out the defense strategy we needed to protect our stock from the short traders. Under this kind of attack there was no hope.

This was a firefight in a financial free-fire zone, and we were getting bombarded, our flanks unprotected. The shorts' bullets and shells were massacring us. They knew our capital was too thin to protect the three stocks we were trying to support, and they had built up a cash position from which to take us down. There were millions of dollars at stake here. My partners and I had split $18 million in our last IPO, and we were expecting to make that much on this one.

I directed Lex to energize the troops, even though he was not allowed to go onto to the brokerage floor. I wanted him to do the same things I would have done. I wanted him to make the guys' competitive juices flow and to get them in the "I-can-do-anything mode," like we did to stir up the cold callers. One way to do that was to tack a $100 bill on the wall as a bonus to the first guy who sold 1,000 shares. Or offer four courtside Knicks tickets that were worth $250 a pop. It wasn't so much the value of the incentive as it was the spirit of competition and the thrill of the chase.

The one thing I wouldn't have done was what Lex did, which was to bull his way onto the floor, yell for everyone's attention and then wave a wad of one hundred $100 bills—$10,000—saying: "The guy who sells the most shares gets this!"

I was horrified when he told me he had done that. Not only would it disruptively draw attention to Lex's highly illicit presence, but waving $10,000 in cash would be an obvious red flag to everyone on the floor. It would signal to our staff that we—Lex and the other partners—were desperate. It would mean we were panicking. It would mean the stock was in trouble. It would mean our ship was taking on water fast.

And that's when I knew I definitely wanted out.

I had a fail-safe prospect at a brokerage firm run by my cousin Sal. The Duke had already offered to buy me out. His offer provided for him and Gene Klotsman to split the company fifty-fifty and allowed Lex and me to keep the money we had made on the shoe company. Now was the time to sell. I made several calls to New York, and spoke the words I had not been able to say:

"Guys, fix it. Or I definitely want to resign." In my mind it was over. Gene and Lex knew I was burned out and needed to take a break.

The St. Tropez vacation was over. I arranged for a lawyer to draft the documents to sell the company to the Duke, and then flew back to New York to assess the damage. I instantly saw how devastating it was. The Duke had come into the company when we had moved into our current office at the World Trade Center with $1 million in assets, and in one year, I had built that up to $5.8 million. Now that $5.8 million was plummeting and there was no telling how far it would fall.

I had been back there for a couple of days and I was trading, fighting, trying to keep the stocks alive. I had done a pretty good job psyching up the troops and undoing the damage Lex had done, but I was getting long—buying back a lot of stock. All the brokers who were not on vacation, or already busy cutting their immunity deals with the federal investigators, were disillusioned. We needed to buy back more than $10 million worth of stock to save the issue, and I only had five million in cash. That meant that, with margin buying, I could only go long—two to one.

I could go long $10 million with my trading account margin, but because this was shorting going on, $7.5 million is the point where you start getting nervous. And so does your clearing firm. We could have parked some stock in fictitious accounts, but the clearing firm was hip to that trick thanks to the Hanover-Sterling crash which took down their clearing firm with them. The dike was opening up. The walls were cracking, and I saw it coming. It still looked as if we could hold it together if we kept struggling even though the reality was that there was no coming back. Like so many other firms before us, we believed the trouble would soon be over. But it was not to be.

The phone rang, and the head of clearing at the firm handling our clearinghouse account told me he could no longer buy US Bridge. If he did, he told me he would lose the clearinghouse. We couldn't operate without the support of a clearinghouse; we could not openly buy the stock we were supporting. That's just what the shorts needed. This was a disaster.

Then a trader called to report that 10,000 shares of US Bridge were for sale. I told him not to buy any and "fade," which means to go just below the highest bid as the market for the stock dropped. The stock went from ten dollars a share to nine. Our syndicate and other short players had been in the field. But when they saw that I was no longer going to support the stock, they backed away, too. Those who were long sold at a loss and tried to go short and join the party on the way down. That was to be expected. I was looking at the screen, and saw that the stock had gone from ten to nine. Within minutes it was at five and I knew the word was out. The brokers were freaking out. The horrendous collapse was beginning. My head hit the desk. I rubbed my face. My phone started ringing. I let it ring. My top trader walked into my office. I looked at him and told him, "Doug, they're all in on it, from the clearing firm to the shorts. They want us out of business."

The short traders hadn't gone after our other two IPOs yet. For some reason, they were just focusing on trying to cut US Bridge down to pennies. They had it on the run and they were keeping it on the run. We were watching it all on the Quotron, a video screen that plays trading transactions in real time. Watching the Quotron on that day was like being fixated on a horror movie.

People were running around the firm. Clients were calling and yelling, "Sell! Sell!" Brokers were rushing to the desk by the tens and twenties, looking to sell their positions as the stock went on tanking. And we couldn't buy a share. We cannot buy one share internally. We could only sell it on the street to an outside market maker, and they were all going south. There was another seller out there, and our own clearing firm was also selling, trying to minimize their loss, which was a tremendous signal to the short piranhas. Our clearing firm just let the stock die, and us with it.

Once I started selling, everyone realized that the stock was going to zero, because the underwriters, the people who once were buying the stock, were now selling at whatever they could get. When the closing bell sounded at the New York Stock Exchange, US Bridge was down sixty percent. Our other two companies—the shoe company and a game company—were both still healthy but down $1 each. They had yet to be attacked and so had very little trading risk in them at the moment.

The next morning the Duke arrived before the market opened. I was waiting in his office with a contract.

"John, I'm out," I told him. "Here's the buy-out like we discussed, please sign it."

"What's the rush?" he asked. "I'll have my lawyer look at this."

"No, John, you don't understand," I said. "All our stocks are going to get hit. We have a $3 million exposure in US Bridge and I don't know how much is owed by the clients that haven't played and probably won't."

He looked at me looking out at the harbor. "Are you sure you want to do this?" he asked.

"Yes," I said without hesitating.

He signed, and now it was his company, no longer mine.

I promised to stick around to help with the day's trading, but I felt relieved to be out. Even with the collapse of the stock, the new owners would come out a few million ahead and I would be moving to my cousin's firm where I maintained a forty-percent interest.

Next day, the short traders started hitting US Bridge even harder than they had the day before. It was like bluefish churning as they fed on mackerel. We were the mackerel. All the stocks we had been supporting began to collapse. Clients were calling demanding that their stocks be sold, but there were no buyers. The book was being blown up on everything.

The Duke was busy assessing the damage, believing he could rebuild the company. But he was going to start without brokers or a client base, because what we had created was being bombed into nothing. It didn't look that bad for me. I hadn't made nearly as many millions as I had planned, but I had a few million in the bank. I still had half a dozen sports cars. I had a beach house. I had my $10,000-a-month penthouse overlooking the Statue of Liberty, and I had a firm to go to. It was August 26th and both of my daughters and I had birthdays that weekend and I was trying so hard to think of the tuna steaks I was going to barbecue.

As far as keeping important bases covered, I had tried to take care of Danny Persico for some of the favors that he did. Besides the trip to St. Tropez, we had bought him a gold Rolex, and given him ten thousand shares of all the IPOs that we did. That was at least a hundred grand each. We had never really exposed him to how much money we were making. He found out later when more of the Mob guys were involved and Danny got closer to our operations. He felt a little cheated when he learned about all that. I know that because he made comments like, "I'm probably going to do as much jail time as you, and I didn't make any money on this. I don't have the big house on the hill."

I knew there was going to be a bill to pay for any notion on the part of Danny and the Mob guys behind him that they had been short-changed. I was born in Sicily and I knew the codes, formal and informal, that drove the power of the Cosa Nostra. I had chosen to ignore reality for a time, but that time was over.

All that was in the back of my mind on Saturday. My wife and daughters stayed in the Hamptons while I drove into the city to clean out my office, secure in the belief that nothing could happen with the market closed. Then the cell phone rang as I drove into Manhattan.

"Hello, Sal," said the caller, before identifying himself as an FBI agent. "How ya' doin'? We got a Grand Jury subpoena here for you."

"Really? For what?"

"Don't you know?"

I was more frightened than any time I could remember.

"Listen," I said, barely in control. "I gotta speak to a lawyer." Then I hung up the phone. My hands were sweating. My knees were knocking in the car. I fought to stay alert to the traffic.

The phone rang again. This time it was Lex.

"The FBI was just here," Lex said. "They showed me pictures."

Lex recognized photos of Mob leaders and Wiseguys with whom we had sit-downs to straighten out problems concerning our business, and pictures of a meeting we set up to pay them to stop trading against us. The photos meant the Feds knew much more about what we had been doing than we thought. Lex and I both had apartments in Battery Park City and I told him to head up to our office and start shredding. Destroy our offshore bank account documents, I told him. Anything that had to do with offshore stuff, anything that could link us to the money.

I was thinking of business records and documents that investigators look for when they're bringing the hammer down on a company for insider trading or stock manipulation. I wasn't thinking of evidence that might go beyond stock manipulation into areas like extortion, racketeering. Even murder. I wasn't thinking about guns and papers sitting in a storage locker in Chelsea, not all that far from our office.

CHAPTER TWO

U.S. Department of Justice, Press Release, March 2, 2000 (Continued)

As alleged in the indictment, the White Rock and State Street Partners secretly acquired control of the securities in the name of various nominees including the defendant DANIEL LEV. Most often, the nominees were offshore companies controlled by the White Rock and State Street Partners. The price of the securities was then artificially inflated through the activities of brokers who fraudulently sold the stock to investors in return for received undisclosed cash payments from the White Rock partners. These brokers included the defendants JACK BASILE, ROCCO BASILE and JOSEPH TEMPERINO at White Rock, and ALFRED PALAGONIA and JOHN CIOFOLETTI who were brokers at J.W. Barclay & Co., Inc. and D.H. Blair & Co., Inc., respectively[3]. Among the techniques used to artificially inflate and maintain the price of the manipulated securities, the indictment alleges that the defendants: (a) made false and misleading statements to persuade investors to buy and then not to sell the securities; (b) purposely failed to take and execute customer orders to sell the securities; and (c) only executed a sale of a security if the sale could be matched or "crossed" with a corresponding purchase of the same security by another investor.

The indictment alleges that after the price of the stock was artificially inflated, the defendants sold their secretly held stock for a substantial profit. The proceeds from these illicit sales were then laundered through multiple transfers of funds to off-shore bank accounts by the defendant ALEKS PAUL, who then provided a corresponding amount of cash, less a money laundering fee, to the White Rock and State Street Partners.[4] Profits for other defendants were laundered through different schemes. For example, the indictment alleges that defendants JOSEPH POLITO, Sr. and EDMOND NAGEL[5] secretly divided proceeds of approxi-

---

[3] JACK BASILE also has securities fraud and money laundering charges pending against him in United States. Dionisio et al. 99 CR 589 (EDNY). ROCCO BASILE has securities, fraud and money laundering charges pending against him. United States v. Catoggio, 98 CR 1129 (S SDNY). Ibid.

[4] PAUL also has securities fraud and money laundering charges pending against him in United States v. Schwartz et al, 99 CR 372 (EDNY and United States v. Paul et al, 99 CR 261 (SDNY). Ibid.

[5] Nagel also has bank fraud charges pending against him in United States v. Gangi et al 97 CR 1215 (SDNY).

mately $380,000 derived from the sale of USBNY warrants that were deposited in an off-shore nominee's brokerage account controlled by Nagel.

The indictment further alleges that the White Rock and State Street Partners enlisted the help of individuals affiliated with Organized Crime Families of La Cosa Nostra to protect and promote their criminal activities by resolving disputes and performing other services. Defendant FRANK COPPA, SR. was a captain in the Bonanno Organized Crime Family. Defendant ERNEST MONTEVECCHI was a soldier in the Genovese Organized Crime Family.[6] Defendant DANIEL PERSICO was an associate of the Colombo Organized Crime family. Defendant EUGENE LOMBARDO was an associate of the Bonanno Organized Crime Family.[7] COPPA, MONTEVECCHI, PERSICO and LOMBARDO resolved and attempted to resolve disputes relating to the hiring and retention of brokers, the extortion and attempted extortion of participants in the scheme, and concerted efforts to reduce the price of securities underwritten by White Rock and State Street through short selling. In return for this assistance, COPPA, MONTEVECCHI, PERSICO and LOMBARDO received compensation in the form of securities and cash proceeds from the sale of securities.

Fast Times on Wall Street

On Wall Street in the 1990s, any new player in every firm I worked for had to see the 1987 movie *Wall Street*, as part of the curriculum of what I called Stock Broking 101. It was not that the movie was a masterpiece. But it was a good portrait of what we wanted from young, would-be brokers. They had to want success, want money, and want to win. They had to buy Michael Douglas's character Gordon Gekko, whose motto was "Greed is good." By way of explanation, in the movie desire for wealth and power had driven progress in America. Greed built railroads, airlines and software giants. Greed built the medical establishment that saved countless lives through new pharmaceuticals, diagnostic, and surgical equipment. Greed, the movie

[6] Montevecchi is in custody based on his conviction in United States v. Gangi et al 97 CR 1215 (SDNY).
[7] Lombardo is in custody based on his conviction in United States v. Gangi et al 97 CR 1215 (SDNY).

seems to claim, is the driving force behind much that ultimately resulted in the public good. It was a movie that figured all too mightily in my life on Wall Street.

In my case, greed led me to unimaginable success and an insatiable desire for more of everything money could offer. From almost any point in my life before I hit it big on Wall Street, the idea of driving a new Ferrari would have satisfied my quest for success. But once I made enough money on Wall Street to buy a new Ferrari, the Ferrari wasn't enough. I had to have a Lamborghini, too. And a Porsche. And an Acura NSX, as well as a house in the Hamptons, and closets full of expensive clothes.

It was a time of plenty. By 1990, when I entered Wall Street, it had been experiencing the longest sustained bull market in American history. More money had been generated for more people, at ever-increasing rates, than ever before. The success of the market fed itself. Yields that rose higher every year drew more and more money into the market. The maturing of the Baby Boom generation had brought a larger percentage of the population to Wall Street than at any previous time in history. From a tradition in which a fraction of the population held the great majority of the stock in circulation, a substantial percentage of the public was now investing in the stock market. Millions of Baby Boomers from housewives to candy store owners to schoolteachers had reached the age when stock investment was attractive, even fascinating. Their children had finished college. Their houses were paid for. Their retirement needed to be provided for, and Wall Street was the place to make money grow. They wanted a piece of the action. The market would rise ten-fold in a decade.

From the beginning of Bill Clinton's first term through the end of his second term, the American economy expanded and the stock market kept rising, drawing ever more capital into it. As the market continued rising, a technology and communications evolution was changing the shape of communications and technology profits almost too quickly to chronicle. Advances in technology meant expanding markets and expanding markets meant more money. The profit vehicle of this capital expansion was the IPO—the Initial Public Offering.

The IPO was the means by which an idea could become a company with substantial cash assets. It was the means by which privately held companies could go public through a stock offering which could multiply the company's net worth by millions. IPOs got hot in the middle of the 1990s, and the acronym became the symbol of a quick ticket to wealth. The huge profit potential of selling a business idea to Wall Street in the mid-1990s drew people from every sector of life, with money to invest, either from the household savings, or from investment funds. Some had ideas and proposals that they believed would become the next Yahoo. Others wanted to get in on the upward climb of the market, where continuing appreciation seemed guaranteed, and millionaire status was only a result of making the right stock picks.

Others, like me, were drawn to the brokerage houses on the street itself, to trade on the frenzy of the bull market. The brokers were the only ones who always came out ahead, no matter what happened, because we made legal commissions of up to five percent on every transaction. The transaction made money for the customer or lost money for the customer. But we made our five percent either way.

And some of us skimmed another 20 or 25 percent that the client would never know about and was legal if you knew how to manipulate trading. In the Wall Street feeding mania of the second half of the 1990s, faith in the rising profits in the stock market was such that many customers might not even have cared whether their brokers were skimming. Smart investment funds were returning 25 and 30 percent gains a year. Money multiplied itself. It just needed to be put somewhere.

And brokerage clients knew—or believed—that once an IPO was launched, millions could be made that first year. Millions. What counted was being in the right place to get in on an IPO before its launch. This was the magic carrot—their desire to be in on the ground floor—that we used on our limited partners to give us money to start up our own firms. It was their greed that gave us our chance at the golden ring. Ultimately, the brokers' actions would bring average Americans' wealth beyond any traditional investment competing for their money, then all too often, send their paper profits crashing when they most needed to cash out of the market. Only the brokers always came out ahead.

The typical investor did not know much about how an IPO actually worked. I was on the inside, and I saw the process from the ground up. It looked very different backstage. Think of an IPO as a Broadway play or a movie whose success depends entirely on the performance on the day it opens.

The excitement of an IPO was ignited by the belief that the stock in the new venture would automatically rise in value, and that being in at the beginning was the key to huge profits. Being connected somewhere, like being a favored client of the right kind of brokerage firm, was crucial, because the first day's offering of an IPO was pre-sold to selected investors in a legal form of insider acquisition. Some shares went to the principals in the business and would never be sold, to be used as collateral in the future. If the principals sold their stock, it indicated a lack of faith in their own company, and the value of the shares would plunge.

Some shares went to the men and women who handled the "bridge financing," providing the money necessary for last minute preparations of the IPO. The cost of such work—accounting fees, legal fees and printing expenses—could run from a quarter to a half-million dollars for a business that had already used up its cash reserves and borrowing power. Bridge financing was a loan paid back in some variant of cash and stock. The stock was supposed to be sold no earlier than 13 months after it was initially issued, an incentive for the brokerage company to try to keep the stock popular. The brokerage company would try to maintain the market price well beyond the issue cost, in order to reap a substantial profit at a time when the company could slowly release its holdings in the marketplace.

The remaining shares, usually 20 percent of all that were issued, were sold to the favored clients of the brokers working for the firm handling the IPO. Profits were assured because it was a "hot" deal for savvy investors who were getting in on the ground floor of the next General Motors, IBM, or Microsoft.

The truth about an IPO in the Small Cap world is that it is little more than an idea, and that they often have no inherent worth. No matter what the issue price, no matter how many shares are available, an IPO has no intrinsic value because there may be no after-market. There is a real chance that everyone who wants the stock will have bought it the first day. A few may want to get in later because they've heard that IPOs double in value and they want the profits, but for the most part, the after-market is nothing more than original share holders buying from each other to increase or loosen their holdings.

There is also buying done by people we call the "hedgies" and the "flippers." They're the ones who go after an IPO to buy whatever they can get and hold it just long enough to make a half-point a share (12-1/2 cents to 50 cents). They're people out to make a little bit of money right away. They're not interested in the long term. If the stock rises steadily and sustains its value, they've still made a little money. And if it sinks quickly, they consider themselves smart investors. To us, hedgies and flippers are nuisances, selling when everyone else is just starting to buy, so you have to buy back their stock and get rid of it right away. Otherwise their selling could drive the stock price back down or keep it at or above the issue price and everyone will lose confidence.

Bear in mind that in addition to the ten percent commissions and the three percent unaccountable fee, the brokerage house issuing the IPO probably supplied a bridge loan, or their friends did, even to a company that didn't need it. Most companies doing IPOs have already gone through their start-up loans, maxed-out their credit cards and tapped all the relatives. The bridge loan gets them to IPO day, and that gets them to the next stage. That would be the perfect time to squeeze the company for a favorable deal for the bridge investors, considering that a $300,000 bridge loan is going to return $7.5 million in profit in 13 months to a lucky individual, and repay the $300,000 at the time of IPO, with interest.

So the brokerage house would get its nominee a sweetheart deal with the company. Thus the brokers would not only get their money back, they would most likely do the bridge loan through a nominee account. That gave them undisclosed additional ownership in the company, something that was illegal but almost impossible to detect. So they got as much as 20 to 70 percent of the stock they had to hold for a minimum of 13 months. Sometimes they managed to sell at the time of the IPO and get the same price as the issuing company.

The key to a successful IPO was seeing that the stock always opened higher than the issue price. The secret was manipulation. In a typical deal involving an issue of a million shares of an IPO, we would sell the million shares to favored clients before the public offering. They didn't have to pay for it immediately. They had a week to send in their checks. If the stock went down, "flippers" sometimes didn't bother paying for the trade and their accounts went on restriction. If the stock went up, even an eighth or a quarter of a point, a flipper would pay for his purchase and take his profit.

The perfect investor was in for the long haul and would send his check immediately, or the day the stock opened. He could see he had already made a profit. What he didn't realize was that there was no buyer for his stock. It was all smoke and mirrors. In most cases, the public hadn't even yet heard of the IPO. Every share went to company people and the brokerage firm. The stock had to trade a lot and make financial news before it was picked up by some writer or analyst and got mentioned in the business papers.

But that was not the way you related things to your customers. You played a role and acted a part on the telephone. You get up, you pace. You gestured with your hands as though the client could see you. Guys climbed on their desks to make a point, even though they were on the telephone. You made the deals by believing your own bullshit. You made yourself believe it even when you knew better. It worked if you believed it. And then, of course, we made money on the way up and on the way down.

An example was my first deal. I was to do an IPO for a genius launching a fast-food burger chain in Poland. The truth was that there wasn't enough money in the hands of consumers in Poland in 1995 to support a fast-food chain. But I convinced myself otherwise and I pitched my clients on the IPO before it was issued. To make it irresistible, I'd say:

"There's a McDonald's in Russia. One store right in the heart of Moscow. You've read about it. You've seen pictures of the lines of people waiting to get in. Every day they're doing business like that. One store. That's McDonald's. Now, Poland has 14 million people, and no fast-food franchises. How can we miss? They'll have four stores the first year and fourteen by the end of the second phase. That's one store for every million people. I mean, how can it lose?"

That was my script.

The first day the stock was out we would open around five and an eighth or five and a quarter. That was where the flippers would sell to get their profit and that was when I would go for the after-market. The after-market was something we, as the brokerage firm, controlled. Remember, we owned this IPO. All the shares were going to people we sold to. We could account for every share that was being issued. The stock was going where we pushed it.

We pushed it by using the same methods that caused the flippers to sell when it moved up a notch. We called the clients and told them that it had already moved up an eighth or a quarter, or whatever, and that they needed to get some more in their portfolio. We told them it was going up so fast, we didn't know if we could get it for less than five and three-quarters or six.

If we did it right, we were generating excitement for a stock that no one else wanted. There was no real market out there as yet. It was just hype. So we bought the stock from the flippers who snuck in and the no-pays, then sold it to our clients for whatever they would pay—six if we could get it. That 75 cents difference went into our pockets as our secret bonus, all legal. The client never had to know what we paid for the stock. He only needed to know where the stock was trading at the time of purchase. In this case, we bought it at the $5.50 bid, sold it to the client at $6.00 plus 5 percent. That was 30 cents for a total of 80 cents, or fifteen percent commission, and if we gave him enough bullshit, he'd think he had a bargain.

Already we had moved the stock to six dollars on the board, even though there was still nobody out there who cared other than the people who bought the IPO originally. And remember, we were still making our five percent base every time we made any deal. Even the flippers had to pay us five percent for handling the transaction.

Now we could see how much we could move it, that is, to put it less delicately, manipulate it. We started calling clients who had already bought maybe 500 or 1,000 shares. I told them: "You bought it at $5 and it opened at $5.25. It's been on the market only a couple of days and already it's at $6. They're going crazy for it. I need to put you in for another 9,000 shares. Get you up to 10,000 before it goes much higher. If I'm lucky, I'll be able to buy at $6.50. Tell you what, let me try, and if I can't, will you authorize $6.75? I'm sure it's going to reach $7 in the next day or two, but let's keep your purchase order at a high of $6.75 and see what I can do."

Of course I'm still going to pay no more than $6 if I can get one of my other clients to sell it to me. Then I'll tell the new buyer I bought it at $6.50 and he'll think I saved him 25 cents a share.

Now the stock would be going up, and I knew by now that the ultimate economics of Poland wouldn't add up to enough disposable income to support this. But I was into it, figuring on getting roughly 25 percent of my commission as take-home pay after taxes. Half the money went to the brokerage house. Of what remained, roughly half went to taxes. When I moved a hundred thousand shares of the IPO at $5 each, I made a gross commission of $50,000. That was $12,500 for a month's work. Once I started working the aftermarket, I still got my five percent, but now I could start making my 50 cents or 75 cents a share called the "chop"—slang for a fat commission. That's what I was really looking at. That's where I got fired up.

If someone was hesitant to make a purchase, I might say, "I just dropped a brick of gold in front of you. Are you going to bend over and pick it up?"

If the stock was not having a good day, we could "paint the tape." Say the stock started the day at $8 and dropped to $7.50. If that happened, we'd save out maybe 100 shares. Then we'd wait for 3:59 P.M. and put in a buy for the piddling 100 at $8. In fact, we were buying the 100 shares from ourselves, but the next day's paper would show that the last transaction was for $8 or maybe a little more. The price wouldn't reflect the action or the real price of the stock. But the last transaction of the day was the price listed in the papers in the morning. There's a saying in the business that buying begets buying.

You want to start the day with the client feeling good about the stock. That's why we'd paint the tape even though it was absolutely illegal—we had rigged the price.

I was such a believer in the burger franchise project that I traveled to Poland to check on the first store that opened. It was in Warsaw in early 1996, and what I saw on the opening day was unbelievable. People were lined up to get in. They stretched outside the store, down the street, and around the block; thousands upon thousands of people, all wanting their first taste of American junk food. I took pictures to show other brokers and some of my clients. I really thought it would fly. I saw myself as being in it not only for the short haul, but also for the long run. I actually believed that I would be buying and selling the stock the way you might IBM. In fact, I told people to sell their blue chips to take advantage of the new fast-food franchise in Poland.

That was a scam a lot of guys used. Get a client into an IPO that's being manipulated, show them they're making money, then get them to sell their good stock that wasn't doing anything dramatic in order to buy the high flyer. There was always a market for IBM, for AT&T, for DuPont, and other stable businesses with track records. We'd turn over the blue chips for our five percent, and then get the client into our dubious IPO for another five percent plus commission.

The client would do okay if he sold right then. Of course, he never did, and when someone tried, we'd discourage it. We were just about the only market, and we sure didn't want it back in house. Eventually the unpleasant realities of the Polish economy would catch up with us. Long lines on opening day did not translate into enough daily business to keep the store open. The fact was that too few Polish citizens had the money to support even a single store and the company failed. The stock would fail. And only my fellow Wall Street brokers and I made money. I earned my wings in the small cap game expensively—with my client's money.

CHAPTER THREE

The indictment also alleges that, in connection with the USBNY fraud scheme, the defendant LARRY RAY agreed to pay $100,000 to an executive of a bond brokerage firm to insure that USBNY would be granted zoning that would enable it to act as a general contractor on large-scale construction projects. Finally, the indictment alleges that defendants JOSEPH POLITO, SR., USBNY's president and an associate in the Gambino Crime Family, and EDWARD GARAFOLA, a soldier in the Gambino Crime Family, attempted to extort money from Lex Tersa and others to recoup this $100,000 cash payment, but that defendant ERNEST MONTEVECCHI intervened in Tersa's behalf, causing the extortionate demands to cease.

The charges in the current indictment carry the following maximum sentences: as to each RICO count, 20 years imprisonment, 3 years supervised release, a $250,000 fine (or twice the gross gain or loss) and an order of restitution as to each money laundering count, 2 years imprisonment, 3 years supervised release, a $250,000 fine (or twice the gross gain or loss) and an order of restitution; as to each substantive securities fraud count, 10 years imprisonment, 3 years supervised release, a $1,000,000 fine (or twice the gross gain or loss) and an order of restitution; as to the conspiracy to commit securities fraud counts, 5 years imprisonment, 3 years supervised release, a $250,000 fine (or twice the gross gain or loss) and an order of restitution; and as to the extortion counts, 20 years imprisonment, 3 years supervised release, a $250,000 fine (or twice the gross gain or loss and an order of restitution. The defendants also face criminal forfeiture of approximately $40,000,000 in real and personal property.

United States Attorney Loretta E. Lynch gave special thanks to the Criminal Prosecution Assistance Group of NASD Regulation, and in particular to Special Investigator Linda Walters for the extensive assistance she provided to the investigation. In commenting on the indictment, Ms. Lynch stated: "This prosecution sends a strong and clear message that law enforcement will marshal its resources to combat the corruption union of Organized Crime and large-scale stock fraud. The breadth of the charges reflects the serious and widespread nature of the problem. The indictment not only targets the brokers who exploit the investing public, but also the dishonest company insiders who secretly profit from the illegal schemes, the money launderers who conceal the illicit gains, and the Organized Crime members and associates who protect and promote the illegal enterprise."

Assistant Director in Charge Lewis D. Schiliro stated: "Investor confidence in the securities markets depends on the ability of law enforcement regulators to ensure fundamental market fairness. Members and associates of Organized Crime were not the first to seek easy money by artificially inflating the demand and price for stocks. They saw an opportunity and seized it. A recurrent theme in our investigations has been that organized crime goes where the money is. We intend to be there when they get there."

Commissioner Safir stated: "I am pleased to join with United States Attorney Loretta Lynch, and Assistant Director-in-Charge of the Federal Bureau of Investigation in New York Lewis Schiliro, in announcing the indictment of 19 individuals responsible for a $40 million dollar stock fraud ring. We called this 'Operation Street Cleaner,' because it was designed to fight fraud on Wall Street, but it could just as well have been titled 'Goodfellas Meets Boiler Room.' For those that seek to use these 'pump and dump' schemes to prey on unsuspecting investors, today's indictment should serve as a stark reminder that stock fraud is a serious crime and the law enforcement community is firmly committed to shutting down these and other illicit operations used to support organized crime."

Up From the Street: A Neighborhood Kid

A year after the Polish burger-chain IPO, I was running White Rock Partners, my own brokerage company. We had a new, ninth-floor office waiting to be filled with aggressive young guys (and the occasional girl) who would call anyone and say anything in order to make the bucks they wanted to make. We had three brokers committed to the business who would need the support of ten to fifteen cold callers the moment they arrived. Cold callers are the ground troops of the brokerage business. If you want to become a broker, you start out as a cold caller, and you sit at a long table with chairs on both side and rows of phones. TV monitors provide up-to-the minute stock market information on screen, and the phones are smoking with dozens of conversations going on at once as our cold callers dialed number after number.

I was sitting in the conference room, waiting to interview a job applicant. I was wearing an $1,800 Ermenegildo Zegna suit, a tailor-made shirt and cufflinks hand-hammered from an antique gold ring in a diamond-opal setting. I wore a $200 Hermes tie and Ferragamo shoes of leather so soft I might have been barefoot, and I was thinking that the kid coming in to get a job was a lot like the person I had been three years earlier.

His name was Louie, a raw kid from Brooklyn who claimed to be 20 but was actually 19. He showed up for the job interview in a dark polyester suit that didn't fit, the kind of suit your mother bought for your first formal dance. His shoes were polished, but he was wearing a Yankees cap with the bill pointed backwards. His accent was rough. Maybe as bad as mine had been when I started out. I didn't care about his accent. We could fix that up. At the third brokerage I worked at before starting my own firm, I had a speech therapist come in every day to work on my accent. Besides that, I took acting lessons outside the office.

What I was looking for was not polish but street smarts. To find out what Louie had, I gave him the test I used to hire new cold callers.

"Sell me this pen," I said, handing Louie an inexpensive ballpoint from my desk drawer. He noticed my manicured hands. Not the hands of the laborer that he had heard I had been, like his father and brothers. My hands still looked powerful, but they were groomed. No calluses.

Louie had heard of me from people in clubs, when the guys at the door looked the other way because the bouncer was a friend of my cousin Rocco or went to school with my brother Mike. He had heard I was a Brooklyn tile guy who had made it out of Brooklyn to Manhattan and made a bundle, but had never forgotten my roots.

He had heard I was hiring, giving a chance to kids like him. And now here I was, decked out like some movie star, telling him to sell him an f-ing pen?

"You want to learn to be a broker, don't you?" I asked him. "You want to make big bucks, drive fancy cars, and get any girl you want? That's why you're here, isn't it?"

Louie blushed, and then nodded, not sure what he was agreeing to.

"If you think you can sell stock, I want you to show me by selling me this pen."

The kid stared for a moment. Then he smiled and began stroking the dark plastic of the case. He looked me in the eye.

"This pen?" he said. "This writing instrument that separates the men from the morons?" He warmed up.

"Of course you want this pen. You know what this pen says to people? It says you're somebody. It says you're educated. It says you graduated from college instead of busting your ass for some bastard who sends you out to freeze your ass off diggin' ditches in the rain and snow while he sits warm and cozy complaining he can't get decent help when you call in sick with pneumonia.

"Morons got secretaries they call to type their letters and fix their spelling. Guys with pens got the guts to stand on their own two feet. Patriotic, too. This pen was made in America. You buy this pen, you're letting some poor slob keep a job that feeds his wife and kids. And you know what else, Mr. Lauria?" Louie was smiling by then, getting into it. A natural. "You know what else?"

"What, Louie?" I asked, trying not to laugh.

"You buy this pen, one day, when I prove myself to you, you're going to use it to write me the biggest bonus check you ever gave anybody come here wanting to work for you."

"I think you may be right, Louie," I said. "At least I'm going to give you a try."

Then I got serious.

"It's not going to be easy," I told him. "You're going to have the roughest first two weeks of your life. You get through that, you're going to have to eat shit for a year. You're going to have to listen to your broker, learn from him. You'll need a little polish, but we can take care of that. Now you have any questions?"

The kid was stunned. "Uh...Mr. Lauria...Just one. Does it matter if I maybe put some things on the application that aren't...Well...."

"So what did you lie about, Louie? You got a record? Driving under the influence? Armed robbery? Murder?"

"No, no nothing like that. I never even been to court."

"So what is it?"

"That part about City College?"

"Yeah. Education—CCNY—so what?"

"I...I like only took a few courses. You know, the easy ones that really didn't....I mean, actually, I didn't last a semester. I met this girl and..."

"Spare me the details, Louie. You got the gift. You show me you've got the hunger and the drive, I don't care what education you've got. Do well here and you'll be a rich man before the kids who stayed in your class can graduate."

"Are you serious? My grandmother says I'm trying to go where I don't belong. She says people like us never work on Wall Street unless we're cleaning up somebody else's office. She says you got to graduate from some fancy school. She says...."

I smiled. I knew the public's image of Wall Street: you couldn't walk in the door without a degree from one of the top business schools in the country. I knew there were houses where you not only had to be articulate; you had to sound as though you came from money. I also knew that in the end it was all the same. Cold callers and brokers were nothing but mushrooms. The high school graduate and the Wharton MBA played on a level field when they began working the phones. They'd all be calling wealthy, powerful men and women, pushing opportunities about which they knew nothing beyond the script they worked from. And if they did it right, if their attitude said, "I know more than you do, and what I don't know, our research department does," they'd make their deals.

That's why men who ran brokerage houses considered them all to be mushrooms. You kept them in the dark and fed them shit. And if the script you gave them turned out to be true, their clients would be thrilled. And if whatever they were pushing blew up in their faces, they'd "only" make $30,000 or $40,000 that month from handling the trades.

My company, White Rock Partners Corporation was low on the Wall Street food chain, a place where a man could "only" take home a few million dollars instead of the serious money possible with the top-of-the-line places. But for Louie and the other kids like him, making it at my company was more than a dream. Making it at my company meant that one day they could be like me, spending what I could spend, living the way I lived. That was the attitude I wanted in rookies.

Ultimately, who the cold callers and brokers were, what they knew, where their parents came from, where they went to school still ended with them working the phones, dialing name after name from lists which, if you were lucky, had been bought on the black market. A street mushroom with a gift of gab was better than a pedigreed mushroom that couldn't sell ten dollar bills for five bucks. And on Wall Street, there were more of the latter than any outsider ever imagined.

"Like I said, you got the job, Louie. Now shut up and get out of here because I've got other guys waiting to see me. Get here early Monday and I'll put you with one of my best brokers. He'll teach you what you need to know. You listen. Work your ass off. There's no limit to what you'll make down the road."

The kid stood up, awkward, and shook my hand, confused about what just happened. He hadn't expected Wall Street to start out this way, but who cared? If what he had heard was true, one day he'd be able to buy everything he'd ever dreamed about owning.

"Oh, and Louie, just one other thing," I said as he was walking away.

Nervous, the kid paused in the doorway and looked back. "Yes, Mr. Lauria?" What was I going to tell him: the deal was off, and it was back to Brooklyn to sell shoes?

"Lose the baseball cap."

CHAPTER FOUR

Coming to America: The Dream Prevails

The traditional image of the Italian immigrant family coming to America has been one of people leaving harsh circumstances in Italy for the hope of a better life in the United States. My family was not poor but there was poverty all around us. My grandfather Sal owned a small sweater factory and one of my uncles was proprietor of a café. In the summer I worked part-time for my uncle as a pizza delivery boy, loading pizza on a tricycle and pedaling from home to home filling orders. I was so little I had to look around the pizza boxes to steer. People would call out and wave when I pedaled past and everybody knew who I was.

In 1961, the year before I was born, my grandfather decided the future was in America. He closed the sweater factory and moved to New York and because he didn't speak English, he had to start out shining shoes on Wall Street. But in a year of shoe shining he saved enough money to buy a wreck of a house in a blue-collar neighborhood. The house needed carpentry, plumbing, wiring and painting, and the work took a long time. When it was finished, my grandfather sold it at a profit and bought another, which he renovated, and sold, again for a profit. After several renovations he was able to buy a nine-unit apartment building in the Bensonhurst section of Brooklyn, and rent two units at reduced rates to two aunts who had married and moved to New York.

I was born in Sicily in 1962, and my first ten years were divided between Campobello di Licata, Sicily, which I remember for its vivid beauty, and Milan, where I was raised. I have childhood memories of watching dubbed James Bond movies, watching Clint Eastwood in spaghetti Westerns like *A Fistful of Dollars, A Few Dollars More*, and seeing Errol Flynn playing Robin Hood. Robin Hood became my hero, which may not have been helpful to my childhood. As a boy I was drawn to trouble, cutting classes in school and borrowing mopeds for joyrides, without telling their owners. In 1971 when I was nine, my father followed his father-in-law's move to New York, and stayed with a brother-in-law on Staten Island to save enough money to send for me, my mother Maria and my two sisters.

My mother worked for a dry cleaner the year my father left and she put me and my sisters in a convent school for the summer, hoping it would keep me out of mischief. It was an unhappy experience because it was a school with some very mean nuns. I got in trouble repeatedly and was treated very badly for it.

On our last week in Italy, I went to say goodbye to my schoolteacher. I had skipped class so much he was surprised to see me when I showed up after school. I told him I had come to tell him that I was going to America and wouldn't be seeing him any more.

"America," said the teacher, rather wistfully. "Yes, there is opportunity there."

Then he reached into his wallet and gave me 20,000 lire, the equivalent of maybe $10. "Take this," he said. "And remember that in America, the streets are paved with gold."

I know now that he was trying to tell me that everything was possible in America. The future was very limited in our community, even though almost everyone was educated and everyone worked. But the type of success that could come for anyone in the United States did not exist in the suburb of Milan where we lived. Of course, being a kid, I took my teacher's metaphor literally, and expected to see streets actually paved with gold. I was disappointed when I saw asphalt. But as it turned out, my teacher was right. America was a place where I had opportunity for wealth beyond my most extravagant hopes.

My father found work doing ornamental iron welding and my sisters and my mother and I joined him in 1972. I was happy to be with cousins who were bilingual, because I spoke almost no English. That was a hardship for me at PS 46, the school on Staten Island where I started out. PS 46 was a bilingual school, but the problem for me was that the other language besides English was Spanish, not Italian. I was a total outsider and being very small for my age made it worse. For speaking only Italian well and being small, I got picked on. Kids who spoke English beat me up because I spoke Italian and the

Hispanic kids beat me up because the white kids beat me up.

Before the end of our first year in the US, my father progressed from ornamental iron welding to a better-paying job for a hydraulic systems manufacturer. He bought us a house in a development in Patchogue, Long Island. By then my English was good and I was able to keep up with the kids in my class. Like my classmates, I had a pronounced New York street accent. We lived in a modest three-bedroom house in a blue-collar neighborhood where most of the homeowners were older than my parents, with children in their late teens or already out of high school. There were quite a few Vietnam vets in the neighborhood and there was a lot of dope. Some vets had come back to the states with a taste for the killer marijuana available in Saigon, like Hawaiian Thai sticks and Acapulco Gold. There were blue-collar, Vietnam vet, and hippie subcultures among men entering jobs such as construction work that would play an unfortunately large part in my teenage life.

For better or worse, I never applied for American citizenship. Oddly, it never seemed to matter. My papers were all in order, and as I failed and prospered, crossed social and geographical frontiers, however much I became Americanized, I doggedly maintained my Italian passport.

Danny

Danny Persico and I met by chance on a playground where we each had gone to escape grown-ups. It was a schoolyard within sight of my grandfather's apartment house in Bensonhurst, where my parents and I visited every weekend. Sunday dinner at Grandpa's house gave my cousins and me a chance to go across the street to play in a neighborhood where I fit in, and where the kids knew who my family was.

Danny Persico wasn't first-generation Italian, but he had been taught to respect the old country, and the fact that I was from Sicily made me trustworthy, like my cousins, who were already his playmates. My cousins and I were "zips," which was a term of respect for kids who came from the "other side." It meant we had clout. Even grown-ups treated us differently from other children.

Danny's family accepted me for the same reason that the children did. The Persicos were rich from both legitimate and illegitimate businesses. They were in the building trades where there was about as much extortion as there was construction. In addition to supplying services and influencing several unions, the Persicos were said to be a Mob family that could squeeze exorbitant fees out of anyone moving supplies from the docks to the building sites.

They also made loans to neighborhood business owners who couldn't borrow from banks. Sometimes the loans were at interest rates that were higher for a month than banks charged for a year. Other times, the interest was even higher: a piece of the business. The Persicos also ran legitimate enterprises, like the limousine company one of Danny's uncles started with five limos and built into a 50-car fleet serving a variety of lucrative locations. One Persico family member invested in Manhattan and other boroughs when values were low, buying buildings before prices soared. Apartment houses provided legitimate income sources that helped hide illegal profits.

After Danny and I became close, I was invited to his family's 100-acre farm compound, where there were three mansions, each for a different brother, a caretaker's house, and a racetrack for a family member who raised thoroughbreds. I learned that Danny had an uncle and other family members in prison, but we never talked about it. And as a youth, I don't think Danny knew that in his family, homicide was a routine option in day-to-day business dealings. For them, it was no different than a bank employee utilizing foreclosure for an unpaid mortgage loan.

Danny's family was part of La Cosa Nostra, and they, like other members of the Mafia, made money from extortion, loan sharking, and skimming from gambling operations. Though the Persicos may have earned more from legitimate investments such as real estate than their organized criminal activities, crime was definitely a family business, and when the time was right, Danny would be introduced to that world. But boys Danny's and my age—pre-teen—were allowed to be kids for a few more years.

Once Danny and I were at the table with the men, all of us having spaghetti. They were talking about Al Sharpton, who was leading protest rallies on the street in Brooklyn, and they were really upset, saying, "Can you believe they're doing that, going rallying in the street in Brooklyn?"

I spoke up, not knowing any better, and said: "That's what we should do. We should go rally on the street in Harlem!"

Danny and I didn't know about their business deals, the ongoing criminal investigations, the beatings, and the murders. Even if we had, it would not have affected our friendship. Danny had seen men, old and young, who had been kind to him while he was growing up, suddenly go off to prison. He had seen the sadness and the anger over their disappearance. He had watched his father, his brothers, and other men eat dinner together, talking of everything and nothing, then having the women and children withdraw while they smoked cigars and spoke of weightier matters. Danny knew his thoughts on the matters were not welcome. A time would come for him to join the men. Then his heritage would be discussed and expectations for the future explained. But for the moment, he was to lead a normal childhood, unaware of the surveillance cameras, the wiretaps, and the Federal officers who shadowed family members once they left the sanctuary of the one 100-acre estate.

As schoolboys, Danny and I were friends who looked forward to my weekly visits to my grandfather's house, which was when we could play together. Once I was old enough to drive, Danny's home in Brooklyn was always one of my first destinations. What neither of us could imagine is how much each would impact on the other's destiny. Within a few years, Danny would both help save my life and come close to destroying it.

Long before that came up, however, I moved in the direction of destroying my own life through drugs. It began in junior high, when I started smoking marijuana as a way of being accepted by my peers. I felt different in my neighborhood and among my classmates as an Italian-American whose family had less money than those of most of my classmates. Our family car was older. My sisters and I didn't wear the clothes everybody else did, or have the toys and possessions they did. That was tough for us, being new to the area.

Smoking pot was a way to acceptance, even if it was from kids who were often seen as losers. It also carried with it the excitement of something completely foreign to my family's culture. My parents knew nothing of drugs. Wine was part of our cultural heritage, drunk with every meal, even by children. But when I came home glass-eyed and stoned, they had no idea what it meant. They didn't even know what pot was.

Marijuana did more than get me stoned. It brought out an entrepreneurial spirit that spurred me to go into business. I began buying pot by the ounce and selling enough to make a profit on top of what I smoked. I'd roll 20 skinny joints, put them in a cigarette box and sell them on the bus on the way to school. That was before my neighbor Timmy and I decided to walk instead of taking the bus so we could smoke on the way to school and arrive stoned out of our mind. I don't know how we even functioned.

Drugs and people who used them began to dominate my life. At first I limited my partying to what we considered relatively harmless drugs. I would use profits from dealing to buy expensive clothing like the leather jacket The Fonz wore in the TV show *Happy Days*. My friends wore those jackets too, and we would take the train into Manhattan to go to clubs with lax ID checks. In Manhattan we began trying THC, mescaline and lesser drugs without anybody getting addicted or showing a problem.

I developed a multi-tiered marketing program for marijuana and went from buying ounces to buying pounds. I could get 2000 one-dollar joints out of a pound that cost me $400, and by the 10th grade I was totally into selling drugs and totally out of school. I partied a lot, got into cocaine, and went to hip clubs in Manhattan like Max's Kansas City, and CBGB's. I was listening to Berlin, Blondie, Iggy Pop, Billy Idol, Sid Vicious, Led Zeppelin and White Sabbath, up until Saturday night. Then it was disco, because disco was where the finest girls were.

My marijuana sales force was providing me a good income without my having to do much. I had essentially cut tenth grade and barely got my promotion to the junior class. The only way for me to graduate and receive a diploma with the others would be to double my classes during senior year, which the school principal thought was beyond me. I proved him wrong by studying hard, earning a "B" average, and then doubling my class load senior year, taking eight full classes every day. I had no free time, but I passed.

I had also drastically reduced my drug use. The organization I had built up made me enough money to buy a one-year-old Datsun 280Z. My parents didn't understand how I was able to swing it. I told my dad I had bought it used for two grand when I had actually paid eight or nine thousand dollars for it. Once I had the car, I would drive to Brooklyn to meet Danny and my cousins at the school playground. Even as a teenager, Danny stood out. He was a six-footer, weighed about 175 lbs, with dark hair and dark eyes. He had good taste in clothes and was always impeccably dressed, wearing an alligator belt, perfect slacks, Ferragamo shoes and a nice watch. Everybody knew who he was when we went out. But when we would go to the clubs, cruising for girls, I would pick up the tab. Thanks to my marijuana sales business, I could do that.

When I wasn't going to Manhattan, I was enjoying Long Island as a rock-and-roll community for young adults. It was also a mostly male experience. The rock clubs would have like five chicks wearing spandex and maybe 200 guys who were there for the music. Brooklyn, like Manhattan, was involved with disco, and in the clubs you saw older types who looked like John Travolta in the movie *Saturday Night Fever*. They had the swept back, slicked down hair, and the ponytails. And there were guys my age who wore good slacks, shirts, and shoes for an expensive, casual look to make the girls think you had money. We went where the girls were, and clubs divided up the week so there was rock one night, punk another, and disco a third. Some guys would go to everything because each night drew a different type of girl.

A few of us decided to start our own social club. We all had part-time jobs and could afford the $20 or $30 per month each to rent space for couches, a TV, pool table, arcade style games, food, and beer. It was a place to talk, smoke weed and hang out. It was also a lifestyle from which I would soon turn away. My cousins were exploring the party scene in the Hamptons, where my parents home was 20 minutes away, giving them a place they could go to on weekends all summer. I left the Brooklyn and Manhattan club world for the

Hamptons, and got deeper into the drug culture.

At the same time, I knew I would need college to get ahead in life even though I had no idea what I wanted to do. I started at Suffolk Community College and got straight A's. Then my dad got me a job as a machinist in the plant where he worked, learning to build aircraft parts at $7 or $8 an hour. That was more than double the minimum wage and the company helped me go to Farmingdale University to study engineering. The company was involved with computer-assisted design and production and I was being trained as a programmer. I commuted every day with my father and my uncle and I was approaching graduation when I realized I didn't want to go on. I decided to quit the company, and leave Farmingdale to major in chemistry at Stony Brook University. By then I had a Toyota Supra, which, along with my income, enhanced my appeal with the girls. I hadn't realized when I decided to go there that Stony Brook was known as a party school, but I was, to my detriment, happy to find that out once I was there.

At Stony Brook I backed off on my studies, focused more on partying, and cocaine became a bigger part of my life. Freebasing was just becoming popular and there was a lot of demand for coke, so I switched from selling pot to selling coke and got addicted to it. If I had been spending time in Brooklyn instead of the Hamptons, Danny might have been a voice of reason at that point in my life. Danny disapproved of drugs, partly as a result of the 20-year to life sentence his younger brother Teddy got for drug sales. The harsh sentence reflected a hatred by the Federal authorities for the Persico family and an effort to stop them any way they could. Danny was against both using and selling narcotics and he would have given me a very hard time about destroying myself with drugs. But Danny and I had gone in different directions. Between college, my manufacturing job, my drug dealing and partying with my cousins in the Hamptons, I left Brooklyn behind. Our friendship was never forgotten, just placed on hiatus for what would be five critically important years for both of us.

At 23, I was a bone-thin 90 pounds. I had reached a height of 5'10" through growth hormones, but I was living in an ever-increasing drug-induced haze. Smoking cocaine, and other drug abuse had damaged my liver and weakened my immune system. Drugs had dominated my life to the point where I had no interest in anything else. I remember looking at myself in the mirror and seeing a skeleton, and that's when I went to my mother and asked for help. That night my mom and dad took me to Mission Pines Rehab Center, which had a clientele ranging from teenagers to men and women of prominence. My roommate was a state senator addicted to gambling. There was a woman who was a soap opera star who combined drug addiction with physical fitness. And there was an adolescent ward with several highly aggressive older teens.

After 35 days in rehab, I was out, and I realized I needed to completely change my lifestyle. Everything about Long Island reminded me of drugs and my drug business, and most of my friends were drug users or small-scale dealers. To escape that, I went to stay with my sister Donna in Brooklyn and got a job working for her husband Danny, who ran his own ceramic tile business.

I moved into a $300-a-month apartment in Bensonhurst and collected $300 a week off the books from my brother-in-law's tile company. It was hard work under primitive conditions and I was seriously out of shape. The first day I hefted a 90-pound cement bag on my shoulders, my knees almost buckled. After a couple of days, I was expected to lug two at a time, one on each shoulder, like the rest of the guys. Carrying buckets of wet cement upstairs was even tougher than hauling bags of dry cement, but I pushed myself until my muscles ached, sweating, covered with grout and cement dust. I had to prove I was there because I could do the job, not because I was the boss's brother-in-law.

The first time I had to use the bathroom, I asked where to go, and another worker handed me a closed spackle bucket. That was the bathroom. Crude. And I went to college, for Christ sake! But I used the bucket like everybody else. And I applied myself, learned to work with the mechanic, learned to handle the tile, learned to handle the tools. I had always been good with my hands, always liked building things, and found I had a knack for laying tile.

Being a tile man was good for me. The hard work put me in the best shape of my life. The tile business could be extremely creative and artistic when the customer wanted specialized tile designs, and I was determined to become the best tile man I could be. I worked for my brother-in-law for three years, mastering every aspect of a job, from the initial sales pitch to planning, costing, obtaining materials, organizing the crew, working the equipment, and installing whatever was desired, including elaborate designs.

Then I decided to go into business for myself and I turned to Danny Persico for help with the capital to get started. I invited him to be my partner, knowing his family connections would help us get work. He agreed to invest $5,000 in start-up capital in exchange for a percentage of each job. The percentage was around ten or fifteen percent whenever there was enough to share. It wasn't a hard and fast deal. Danny accepted whatever payments I gave him, as income on an investment in a new company that would provide a fair return on his loan.

I had a partner. I had an investor. I was working hard to generate more business to be in a position where I could take multiple contracts and hire work crews for each job. It was 1986 and the New York real estate market was booming and my business was good. By 1988, I had 16 employees and a great apartment on Shore Road in Brooklyn, with a view of the Verrazano-Narrows Bridge. My clients included an heir to a food fortune on Manhattan's upper east side.

I did not realize that I had entered a world where business ultimately transcends friendship, but that became apparent as time went by. The jobs Danny's family were getting me increasingly became work I didn't want—jobs that were favors for someone in or connected with the Mob. One contract was with a Catskills hotel owner who was supposed to get a job done by me as a favor from one Wiseguy to another Wiseguy. The job didn't pay well but I had to take it. I hired nothing but Mexicans and cheap labor and did a cheap job. I think that's the first time I realized I was being manipulated by the Mob and I didn't like it.

In 1989, I was 27 and I fell in love with a girl named Lynn whom I had known since high school. I had first seen her at a dance with her stepsister and I thought she was beautiful. She had long, curly, dirty blond hair, and a voluptuous figure and she was so obviously out of my league that I had never tried to approach her. In high school, I had been an immigrant kid running with a crowd that had little sense of the future. I assumed that she would have just put me down.

Time passed and I began seeing her at some of the dance clubs on Long Island. Since she didn't seem to be dating anyone, I decided to approach her one night when I saw her parking her car with a valet. I was by her side all night fending off advances from other guys. It was almost four in the morning when I asked her out. I did not want the night to end.

"Want to go out for coffee?" That was best line I could come up with. We looked at each other and I tried not to let my eyes say too much.

"Okay, sure," Lynn said. "Let's go." Those were the words that started it. I was nervous, but excited as we walked to a nearby diner and sat in a booth by the window. We had coffee and more coffee, and then stopped drinking coffee and just talked. We talked until the sun came up and by then I had the nerve to ask her for a real date.

"Come out with me tomorrow night and we'll into town and go clubbing," I said, "town," of course, meaning Manhattan. I knew the clubs and I told her where we'd go.

"I'll take you to the Red Parrott, to Max's, Visage, and some good places," I said. "We'll really go clubbing right." She smiled.

We were standing on the street outside the diner on Sunrise Highway and commuter traffic was just beginning. It was still too early for people going to work, and we were in that magic time zone between the end of night and the beginning of the workday. The city was just waking up. We were in Long Island and I was telling her about Manhattan.

"Okay," Lynn said. "That sounds great. Can you bring a friend? I'll bring my girlfriend Linda."

Making it a foursome would make for an easier first date, and I said I'd bring my friend Bobby. I went off to work at my tile business that day with a glow on. Bobby had a Lincoln Town Car and agreed to play chauffeur to make it a seriously special evening.

We picked up the girls and began the evening at my apartment. Bobby did a maitre d' act there, putting a towel over his arm to serve wine from an ice bucket, while I showed the girls the view of the bridge, the river and the city lights winking like a field of diamonds.

Then we went clubbing and had been to two or three places before we hit a club at 56th Street and the West Side Highway called Visage, where we were going to meet Danny and his friends. Visage was a happening place with a futuristic décor. There was a small, square pool in the floor like those in lavish villas, and under the previous management of the club, there had been house mermaids cavorting in the waters. Music pumped and pounded. The vibe in the place was electric and everybody was modishly dressed, some guys wearing white, some girls wearing white, some guys still decked out disco-style with chains and open shirts.

That night was a going-away party for Danny Persico's brother Teddy, who was going to turn himself over to the law the next morning to begin a 20-year prison sentence. Danny was in his customary impeccable clothes and you would never have guessed he was a major Wiseguy. Some of the guys with him looked more like what they were—soldiers and hangers-on of a dominant Mafia crime family.

"Danny, this is Lynn," I told him. Danny was gracious and respectful in a way that immediately impressed Lynn. He never projected the power and toughness that was there.

"Don't believe anything he's told you about me," Danny said.

"It's all been good," Lynn told him with a smile.

"Even more reason not to buy it."

Our first date was going well. I would have enjoyed the meeting of the girl who was going to become my everything and my best friend, except that I could see a major problem with another crew of Wiseguys that night. I recognized the kind of eye contact and body language that signified trouble, and it looked as if it might be soon. I was trying to talk to Lynn and act as if everything was fine, and still stay alert to these other guys.

Nobody else in the club was aware of anything potentially dangerous. People were drinking Stoli, smoking, talking, laughing, flirting and posturing. Then there were words between Danny's guys and the other mobsters. Danny's brother Teddy was in the center of it, and all of a sudden it turned violent. There were arms flailing, grunts and movement that was not supposed to be happening. It was like something you had seen in movies but it took a moment to grasp the reality of what you were seeing. Then one of the guys with Danny stuck a chrome-plated .380 automatic in my hand. He wanted it off him if he got into a fistfight and I slipped it into my pocket before Lynn noticed.

I wanted to get the girls out of there before they panicked.

"Bobby," I said, trying to sound a lot more calm than I was, "take the girls out to the car."

"We're going to another club," I told Lynn. "I'll be with you in a minute."

The place was erupting as the girls rushed out the door. Fists began flying, bodies were moving, and beer bottles were being smashed. There was chaos as it widened into a brawl. It was a crazy scene and the bouncers immediately started trying to push the fight outside. Then the shooting started. I had passed the gun back to the guy who had slipped it to me and I was already on my way out the front door when I heard shots. Pop, pop, pop, pop. Like firecrackers, only I knew they weren't. I whirled, and I saw guys shooting, and I saw people going down. Then I got outside and ran to the car. Even outside, I was worried. Those were my friends in there. I found out later that people were wounded by gunshots from both sides, but luckily nobody died.

Bobby had the car waiting just down the street and I jumped in and he pulled away.

"What was going on?" Lynn asked me anxiously.

"A fight started," I said. "We had to get out."

"We heard firecrackers," Lynn's friend Linda said.

"They weren't firecrackers," I said. They got the point.

It was my first real date with the girl I was going to marry. An insane evening, but I guess it worked. We continued dating and when I got the hotel job in the Catskills, I asked her if she would visit me on weekends because I would have to live on the site for the three months it would take to do the job. She agreed. I don't think she fell in love with me very quickly. I was always in love with her, but I think at first she just liked me. I was different, and European, and then after a while I guess I got to her, and she fell in love with me.

During the two years we dated before getting married, the New York real estate market took a dive and the tile business fell off dramatically. I could still earn a good living, but only if I acted as boss, salesman and one of the laborers. By my fourth year running my own business, I was sick of the hard physical work. My hands resembled lobster claws and I couldn't caress Lynn's skin without thinking they must feel like sandpaper. I wanted a business where I could sit down in a nice office and not have to shower off the cement dust before I went out to dinner.

Then my cousin Sal, who was working on Wall Street, invited us to a party in Southampton. Sal had grown up in Sicily. He lived in Brooklyn, and this summer he was sharing a house in the Hamptons with a bunch of stockbrokers and their girlfriends. Ricky, Dicky and a guy named Lex Tersa were all guys from Brooklyn, like Sal, but every car in that driveway was a BMW, a Porsche, or another luxury car. Sal had just bought a BMW 325 convertible, and I was impressed. I lived near him in Brooklyn, and I knew he had worked as some kind of mail courier before going on Wall Street. He had moved up to being a cold caller, which paid $200 a week—about what I made in a day. He had once told me that if I wanted out of the tile business, I could join him as a cold caller. When I had asked him how much, and he said "$200 a week," I didn't even bother asking what "cold caller" meant. I told him, "No shot, I couldn't even pay the rent with that. You live home with mom. I don't."

But that was when he started out. Now he was driving a BMW, and so were all his friends. Wall Street. I wanted what these guys were getting, so I asked Sal:

"Do you think I could make it on Wall Street?"

"Yeah," he said. "You have larceny in your blood, you'll do okay."

Living on $200 a week would be tough. But if starting as a cold caller was the way to become a broker like Sal, that was what I wanted. Some of the guys who were brokers had gone to college and some of them hadn't. At the time, I had all the mannerisms of a Brooklyn guy, on top of a Long Island accent, which was even worse. But I didn't sound any different from the other neighborhood guys at the party, and they were all working on Wall Street.

The next day I called Danny to tell him I'm leaving the tile business. "I'm going to try this thing on Wall Street."

Lynn asked how we'd manage on the $200 a week until I could get my broker's license and I told her we would move into my parents' basement to save rent money. With her job as office manager for a car dealership, we could survive. I would take the train, commuting two hours and twenty minutes in each direction, then walk from the station to the office. It was a big risk. It meant giving up a comfortable lifestyle for complete uncertainty, betting that I would like the work on Wall Street, pass my broker's exam and get licensed. If it didn't work out, it would take months to get my tile business back up and running.

We knew we were taking a gamble, and we knew we had no way of knowing how it would turn out. What we could not imagine was that we would soon enter a world where having too much was not enough, and a mere millionaire was held in disdain for not trying to increase that, hundredfold.

CHAPTER FIVE

The Grand Jury Charges, continued:

4. The business of White Rock and State Street consisted primarily of the sale of stock and warrants in small and start-up companies. White Rock and State Street frequently underwrote initial public offerings ("IPOs") by which stock and warrants in formerly privately owned companies were first sold to the public. White Rock and State Street also participated extensively in the trading of securities after they were first sold to the public (referred to herein as the "aftermarket" or "aftermarket trading.") White Rock and State Street also took part in offerings to the public of stock and warrants subsequent to an IPO, known as "secondary offerings" of securities.

5. White Rock and State Street held themselves out as legitimate brokerage firms, although they were in fact operated for the primary purpose of earning money through fraud involving the manipulation of the price of securities. Among the securities fraudulently sold by the White Rock and State Street Partners to the public were stock of Country World Casinos Inc., ("Country World") and stock and warrants of Holly Products, Inc. ("Holly"); U.S. Bridge of New York, Inc. ("USBNY"), Cable & Co. Worldwide, Inc. and Fun Tyme Concepts, Inc. ("Fun Tyme").

My cousin Sal had been working at Gruntal & Company at 605 Third Avenue in Manhattan but he had already left for a job at Shearson Lehman by the time my interview came up. Sal told me to go see a guy at Gruntal named John Doukas and I wore my best suit. The 605 Third Avenue office was on the third floor of a massive high rise and seemed to exude old money, the Ivy League, and proper breeding. The reception area had mahogany furniture and the company name was in gold lettering on a classy white background.

I was relieved when I got past the receptionist and saw Lex, Ricky, and Dicky, the brokers from the house in the Hamptons. When they looked me over, they told me I couldn't go to the interview in the shirt I was wearing. My suit was a custom-made Bill Fiovante. A client of my tile-laying business had given me the suit as a thank you present for the job we had done marbling his Park Avenue apartment. The shirt I had chosen to wear with my suit was too casual they said. I had to have a white shirt. They took me out to buy a white shirt and then said I looked okay for the interview.

Gruntal was a mid-size, mid-tier stock brokerage firm that was part of a national chain. I didn't know much about it at the time. I only wanted to become a broker there. If I had considered what Gruntal was, I could easily have felt intimidated at the idea of coming in to sell myself to a place whose clientele was a cross-section of wealthy, influential American investors with degrees from major universities, men who read the *New York Times* and the *Wall Street Journal*.

I had never even bothered to look at the *Wall Street Journal*. I just came for the interview with my good suit, a new shirt and a lot of attitude. I might be a rough-sounding guy whose accent was Brooklyn over Long Island, but I had already run a successful business and had 16 people working for me when I decided to give it up and apply for a $200-a-week job as a cold caller at Gruntal. I went into the manager's office and John Doukas, whom I would come to know as The Duke, was not at all what I expected. True, he was dressed in a way that told me he was making a lot of money. But he was missing several fingers on one hand. His other hand was a prosthesis and he had one glass eye. There were two stories about this. One was that he had been disfigured in a motorcycle accident. The other was that he had lost the fingers in an explosion when he was a kid trying to blow off the change box from a pay phone.

Either way, he was a disconcerting sight when I walked in. He looked me over.

"'So you're Sal's cousin," he said. "Know anything about stocks?"

"No. Not a clue."

"That's okay," he said. "You ever cold call before?"

"No," I said, wondering what cold calling was.

"What makes you think you can do this?" the Duke asked.

"Well, my cousin always said I was a good bullshitter, so I think..."

"Okay. That's a pretty good response."

I was wondering what was with this weird-looking guy. I was basically being a smartass, because, let's face it, what did I know about the business? I just knew my cousin Sal wasn't any brighter than I was, and he was the one with the BMW and the condo.

"So do you want to be rich?"

"Absolutely," I said.

"You got the job."

I didn't think I was qualified for whatever the job was. It was obvious I was being hired as a favor for my cousin. I understood that. I asked when I could start, and he told me right away.

Cold calling was, as I have said before, bedlam. Here it was dozens of guys on phones in a huge room that was almost half a football field wide, with desks everywhere. The desks were for the brokers and each broker had four or five assistants calling for him. You could hear dozens of phone conversations all the time and the din was constant. The only hint of privacy was when a cold caller went under a desk to simulate the quiet of a private office.

I had never seen or imagined anything like this, but I didn't have time to think about it. The one thing I figured, from the looks and the voices of the guys making calls, was that they didn't know any more about Wall Street and the stock market than I did. I turned out to be right about that. Gruntal gave us a script to use for our calls, along with cards listing the Dunn & Bradstreet ratings of the people we called. The D & B ratings told us the people had money and our job was to find how much they had invested in the market, and whether it was enough to make them worth pursuing as potential investment clients. We were looking for people with at least one hundred thousand dollars in the market, and our script might go like this:

"Hi, I'm contacting you on behalf of Gruntal and Company, which is one of the top brokerage firms on Wall Street. Next time we have a great idea from an educated point of view, we'd like to call you back and share a minute with you. Would that be okay?"

If you were lucky, the guy might answer by saying something like, "Well, sure, I'm always interested in a good stock." At that point you just start grilling him. "Well, how much do you have in the market?"

But it didn't usually go like that. Cold calling was about dialing, dialing and re-dialing all day long. A conversation where the person you dialed answered with interest was a triple play, if not a home run, because most of the times you dial, you didn't get through. The number didn't answer, it was busy, you got a recording, it was a wrong number, or you got a receptionist or a secretary. You had to get past the secretary to speak to her boss and if you managed to do that, there was a fifty-fifty chance that once you started making your pitch to him, he would hang up on you. Slam! So what did you do? You hung up with a smile and dialed another number. Smile and dial. Rejection was always your friend because each rejection put you that much closer to the next Yes!

To beat the odds, you were supposed to make 300 dials a day, and that was what we did. The AT&T Merlin phones had lights on them that showed whether you were on a call or not. A green light meant you were on, red was off. The brokers and bosses yelled at anyone whose phone was red, and they'd yell at you if your ear wasn't red at the end of the day. They wanted to see cauliflower ears from constant phone pressure. Once you spoke to a potential client who passed the first muster, and you had a full conversation with him, you would send him a packet of information on Gruntal with the business card of the broker you were assigned to. You were expected to do five packets in a day, out of 300 dials. If you got 10 in eight hours, you'd had a great day. Then your broker made the follow-up call to the people you'd sent packets and cards to. Maybe three out of ten of those follow-ups resulted in accounts being opened. Three out of 300 calls! One percent! But those three were where the money started.

On my first day, I was determined to master the pitch, to find a way to be relaxed, enthusiastic, and to generate an attitude that would make the potential customer want to take a chance on me and Gruntal. I concentrated so hard on doing it right that I read the script and the cards without thinking that they included information like whether we were calling someone at the office or at home. I just glanced at the card when a man answered the telephone, and I said:

"Hello Mr. Home Phone...." Of course, everyone could hear what I was saying. They broke up and I never got a chance to make my pitch.

I was assigned to a broker named Brock Samith, a guy from Tennessee who had made his fortune in New York without losing his Southern accent. Samith, in his soft Tennessee drawl, told me right away that I had a speech problem. He said my Brooklyn-Long Island accent needed work, and the way to do that was speech therapy. I agreed, and resolved to find an acting class to further improve my delivery. I was bent on succeeding at this, and there wasn't any choice but to do what my broker told me.

For us newcomers, there was a good deal of hazing, like telling us that there was a box of "Up Ticks" we would need to get from the trading desk. The Up Ticks were for when the stock goes up, and the "Down Ticks," kept in a different box, for when the stock went down. One new cold caller was given a key and told it was to the New York Stock Exchange that was across the street. It was 9:29 and he was warned to race right over to open it because there was only a minute before everyone expected to begin trading.

My broker Brock had his own peculiar habits. Every day he'd send me down to the street to buy him a Coke and a bag of Skittles for his sugar and caffeine fix. He'd give himself a sugar high and get on the phone to pitch whatever he was pushing with total commitment. Brock would get such a sugar boost, that his enthusiasm, with his soft Tennessee accent, was infectious. He sounded like he really believed in what he was selling and people bought it. I figured out right away that people don't buy the stock; they buy the conviction of the person pushing it.

Brock was making serious money. In the Midwest, a stockbroker thinks he's making a good living when he makes $150,000 a year. Brock was making a hundred grand every month, almost all of it from commissions on stock trades he made. Most of those trades came from accounts brought to him by his cold callers, who, like me, were making $200 a week. One way the broker would compensate you was to give you $25 to $100 for every account he opened with your lead. It doesn't sound like much, but it was off the books, and when you were making $200 a week, it meant a lot.

Brock was genuinely obsessed with the market, buying $50,000 to $80,000 in stock options every month, showing that he actually believed in what he was doing. As for me, I believed in the money I saw him making, even though all I was getting was $200 a week. And I stopped worrying about how much I didn't know about the stock market. I realized I had always been a salesman, whether it was working the high school drug trade or hustling new business for my tile company.

I rose to the challenge of cold calls and I was good at it. Two weeks into the job, I loved it. I figured out that what I was doing was a form of show business. I found a place to take acting lessons, and speech lessons. And every night Lynn would help me with my homework for the broker's exam. I would study early in the morning and she would ask me questions while I was in the shower. At 28, I was almost ten years older than most of the cold callers, and I was totally committed. My cousin Sal was doing so well he had already sold his condo in Brooklyn and bought one in Soho. That just fueled my desire to make it from Brooklyn to Manhattan like him.

I was one of the Bull Market babies of Wall Street, entering the business in the longest Bull Market in history and the biggest run of IPOs in the history of the market. Everyone was investing in the market and prices kept going higher. Since the crash of December, 1987, when the market dropped 500 points in one day, the market had started a run from a low of 1,616 to 2,600 by the time I started in 1990. And it would run to 11,000 within a decade.

There were old timers warning about the past, but no one was listening to them. We had 401(k) retirement plans. We had guys who used to play the numbers or buy lottery tickets putting money into mutual funds. You'd go into a deli and the guy behind the counter would be talking about price-to-earnings ratios and blue chip stocks. The waitress at a coffee shop would be discussing whether or not she should still put money into Microsoft. It was like everybody had expendable income and everyone was taking it to the market.

The big companies were trying to hire the well-trained college graduates they always wanted. If you went to Wharton, you'd have job offers before your senior year was half over. But graduates of the big business schools were mostly going to companies that used them for serious money management, the kind of work most people think is done by the typical broker. However, those weren't the guys making most of the sales. The majority of sales were being made by guys who maybe had no college or just went to a junior college, and that included most employees of companies that wanted the Wharton graduates. And more firms than you might think were hiring kids out of high school who just had a gift of gab.

Everyone wanted to make their fortune. The college graduates thought about making their millions and then living off the interest. The kids working with me wanted to make their millions and spend them. I came to see that they wanted to make $1 million and spend $1.2 million. They all had the same hungry outlook—look good, dress good, party hearty, and live for the moment. They believed in excess, whether that meant buying cars, gambling in Vegas, or paying for hookers.

But the customers couldn't tell that because the broker was just a voice on the telephone and it wouldn't occur to the client that the voice might belong to some kid who was being an actor. It was really like doing improv every day. Every morning we'd be given the name of a company to pitch with a script to follow. Then we'd get on the phones and play the role of someone who knew enough about stocks, and the company we were pushing that day, to convince people to buy. It didn't matter that we knew nothing about the market—only about that one particular stock. If the stock went up, the client loved us. If it went down, sometimes the client accepted the loss because he felt the broker also suffered. He didn't think that we would make money either way because our commission came from the trade.

Of course, that was after you became a broker. As a cold caller, you only made what your broker fed you on the accounts you led him to. The story in the office was that you put in six months as a cold caller before you were eligible to take the broker's exam, and for those six months your only extra income was what you got back from your broker on accounts you brought him.

That is, unless your broker encouraged you to actually make sales, the way Brock did, before you were licensed. It didn't take Brock long to decide he could trust me and teach me the business right away. His way. As soon as the office manager left the area, Brock would let me call qualified leads on the West Coast where the working day still had two or three hours to go. I wasn't calling big customers. My leads were men and women who would buy stock in quantities of perhaps a hundred shares, not regular traders in any way that brought meaningful commissions.

I'd sell them in Brock's name and that was usually no problem. Occasionally someone would have talked to us both, and would remember Brock's southern accent. That could get pretty funny, but Brock didn't care if I lost the sale. The whole thing was illegal and it was just meant to give me some experience. And, if I got lucky, it would pay off for him, too. The action, seemingly innocent, was my first bending of the market's rules.

By the time I was making sales calls in Brock's name, I was dressing sharp, unlike the other new cold callers. The classy-looking cold callers made fun of the others, the ones with really bad ties, by asking: "Did that tie come with a sandwich?" referring to the deli across the street that sold ties, two for $5, along with pastrami sandwiches. There was also the Lehman Brothers' handshake, which involved two brokers passing each other and stopping to talk, each reaching to casually turn the other's tie, and check the label. We snobbish cold callers felt we had to look rich to be comfortable talking to rich people on the phone, so we spent as much as we could on good tailoring. We were playing roles, and how we dressed made a difference in the way we felt. I used to stand up when I called, and move a lot, gesturing with my hands as if I was in the room with the person I was talking to. You learn to shut out distractions and focus on your conversation. Your whole goal is to qualify the guy, and when you were selling, you just keep talking, working the guy until he buys or he slams down the telephone on you.

I'd be calling in Brock's name, doing my best imitation of his southern accent, and get some guy in Texas. His D & B report told me he had money. But what I really needed to know was what kind of player he was. He might be a "piker," which meant he was good for less than $100,000. Or he might be a "whale," which was over $1,000,000. I had to try to find out what he was worth and at the same time, sell him on a stock. You wanted to get him in a "yes" mode and the secret was to never stop talking except when you asked for the order. Then there was silence as you waited for his response. You never hung up first with a potential client. You wanted to be the last one talking, right up to his hanging up. If you hung up, you lost. If you kept talking, you might get him.

It was a bizarre game. I'd talk in Brock's accent, and sometimes I'd be getting nowhere, and I was getting tired, so I'd hand the phone to one of the guys sitting around me. First Rocco, another cold caller, then Bob Peters. He'd start talking, keeping up the same pitch, working the guy. So long as he didn't hang up, we weren't going to stop. Some of the pitches lasted for hours. I would pretend to be this guy with a Southern accent, but it was just me, the Italian kid who learned English in Long Island. Then I'd give the phone to a kid with a thick Brooklyn accent who sounded like a street hustler. And if he couldn't land the guy, and if I was busy, he'd pass the phone off to another cold caller, maybe someone who sounded like he went to school in New England.

The amazing thing was that most of the people we called, they didn't know the difference. They'd hear three or four different voices, each of us claiming to be the same person, and they just kept talking as though it was the same person on the line. I began to realize that qualifying a customer didn't matter. It was a waste of time. It took as long to qualify as it did to pitch, and the results were the same. Qualifying just took extra time. What really helped was microfiche which brokerage houses like Lehman Brothers or Merrill Lynch used to keep really valuable information about clients.

If you were determined, the way I was, you could find someone at one of the big firms willing to make copies of their records for you, or maybe just sell you the old microfiche when they updated everything. You could pay a couple of hundred dollars for a whole bunch of microfiche information, or for $1000, you could buy a whole drawer full of microfiche. That's what I did. I figured it was a good investment, and it was. It didn't matter if the information was a year or two old as long as you had investment history to go with names and phone numbers. Once you had investment history, you could pitch the guy. You'd always use the same kind of ruse, whether you were a broker, or a cold caller like me whose broker was letting me pitch in his name. The thing was to act like you'd already talked with the person you're pitching.

"This is Brock Samith from Gruntal and Company," I'd tell the guy. "You remember that we talked several months ago, and you told me that you had IBM and Microsoft and…."

He wouldn't remember, but how could he be sure we hadn't talked? I wouldn't give him time to go into that in his mind, because I'd mention some of the stock he was holding. If the microfiche was current, I could tell him everything he had up to the day the copy was made. More often, the microfiche information would be older, but that worked, too. With older information, you knew what he had, and he figured there was no way you could know that unless he really did talk to you. There was another thing working here, too, which is that men who invested serious money in stock with a broker were likely to pay attention when they were on the phone with that broker. Or with someone who they thought was the broker. It was like talking to your doctor or your attorney. It involved attention and respect.

I'd talk a game to whomever I had on the phone, gearing my gab to the stock the person had, his job, and what part of the country he lived in.

"You've got some good tech stocks," I'd tell him. "But you

know what you don't have? You don't have any Lucent in there."

Then I would go into a pitch about Lucent Technologies, because it seemed to fit. Of course, before I did that, I was flattering him on having the stocks he owned, making him feel smart. And when I suggested Lucent to him, it was almost a done deal as soon as I got the words out.

With someone else, I might recommend medical stocks. I always told them what they didn't have and approached them that way. I always knew who I was talking to because I'd spent hours at home at night writing down names and details from my microfiche. Lynn would help me. I'd take them into work with me and I got so good at it that I opened up 40 accounts for Brock, just working part time at night for him. And all the money went to him.

Forty accounts was the number of accounts you were expected to open before you were considered eligible to have a desk. But I was going beyond just opening accounts. I was actually making sales in my broker's name, which was totally illegal. But the longer I worked, the more I found that it was going on to a greater or lesser degree at lots of brokerage houses.

That's not to say that all brokers allowed their cold callers to sell. Some brokers followed the rules exactly. Others waited until they had a private office, so the office manager would not know they were permitting it. But the fact is that most managers would overlook it even if they knew, because the manager got a big override that represented two percent of the total gross of the branch office. So it was in his interest to have the gross up. That was the same thing with a big Shearson-type brokerage, a Gruntal, or a Merrill Lynch. The office manager got two percent of the total gross of the branch. He wanted production up because he got a nice check at the end of each month. The forty accounts I opened for Brock were making a small contribution to the gross at our office, and before I was a broker, I was already being a broker. I knew how to close a guy. I knew how to press his buttons and trigger the sale.

We were supposed to have been cautioned against illegal activity by seeing the movie *Wall Street*, which, along with much else, dramatized the pitfalls of insider trading, and by reading the book

Think And Grow Rich by Napoleon Hill. Both were among the requirements for Gruntal new hires. We were expected to be inspired by
Hill's book and cautioned by *Wall Street*, in which a young broker
used insider knowledge to help a "whale" make a large sum of money.
The broker was corrupted by the demands of his client, eventually
stealing information that was illegal to use. But the message that really came across, from what we saw and what we experienced, was that
the real sin was not insider trading to manipulate profits. The sin was
getting caught, and having to give the money back.

Frankly, thinking about the proprieties of regulations was just
not part of the climate. Particularly considering that manipulating
stock prices was exactly what we were up to. This was a time when
you could call a guy and sell him 100 shares of a stock at $10 a share.
Then, because a lot of other people were making the same small
buys, the stock might go up half a point—50 cents a share. You'd call
him right back and tell him the stock was on the rise.

"You've got to buy while it's on the upswing," I'd say. "There
are people out there who would kill to buy a thousand shares for the
price you paid this morning. I'm telling you, buy another 1,000 shares
before it goes any higher."

So now the buyer was in for $10,000. Or maybe he bought
10,000 shares if he had the million dollars, which was my mission to
find out. And all the other brokers in the office were saying the same
thing to their clients. If you've got forty or fifty brokers working the
same stock the same way at the same time, you were going to have
trading, and the stock was going to go up, maybe another half a point,
and you were a big hero to your client. Of course, it was only moving
up because you and everybody else were pushing it. If someone
wanted to unload, there wouldn't be many buyers and the stock
would probably go down. But this was a bull market where a couple
of points made you a winner. The customer would hold on, adding to
the portfolio, bragging to his friends about the killing he was making
in the market, bringing more people into the game.

The first trade was often small or done without commission.
The idea was to sell the customer something—maybe 100 shares
unless you knew he was a whale. A thousand shares was a good buy

for the first time. Sometimes you'd give a guy that first trade for free. You wanted him to trust you. You wanted him to make some money with you. You knew that a lot of clients had several different brokers, and you wanted to get him thinking only about you. That was why when the broker did a follow-up, that first sale wasn't always that important. What was important was establishing a relationship.

As hard as we worked, it wasn't all business all the time. Except for me at 28, the old man of the bunch, most of the cold callers were barely out of their teens. Everybody was there to make a buck, but everybody was also basically a kid, and when some of the brokers were out and the manager was gone for the day, we would use the phones for fun. We had the number of a pay phone down on the street that we could see from the office window and sometimes when we could see people standing near it, we'd call the number and make believe we were a radio station.

"You've just won!" we'd tell the person. "You know about our Manhattan Has A Heart promotion, of course. You know about the bag of money we hide in different places in the city, and then surprise people who happen to be passing by? Well, you're tonight's winner, and the bag of cash is in the bottom of the trash container right there at the corner of Third Avenue. Congratulations! You go get it while we wait on the line. We'll be wanting to get your name and address for our files. But we'll do it off the air. No sense in the IRS getting a share of your winnings, is there?"

By this time the person was going crazy. Usually he or she would drop the phone and rush over to the garbage can. You could see them being very careful at first. They would move whatever trash was there, trying not to get too dirty. Then pretty soon they were tearing through it, tossing the trash onto the street, bending over the can, practically falling inside trying to find the money that wasn't there. And we were upstairs, watching, laughing our heads off.

Or there might be a delivery van parked there. If there was, we'd tell the person who answered the pay phone that there was a camera in the van that was his prize for answering our call. Then they'd run over to the van, knock on the door, and ask for the camera. The delivery guy would be like, "What? Are you kidding?"

Another thing we did involved two restaurants across the street from us. One was a Chinese restaurant and the other a pizzeria. We would call up the Chinese restaurant and pretend we were the pizzeria and tell them they had rats and start complaining about how filthy their place must be. Then we'd call the pizzeria and pretend to be the Chinese place. There was a conference button on our telephones, and we'd link the two calls. Pretty soon they were running onto the street with meat cleavers, yelling at each other, wanting to fight, and we'd just sit by the windows and crack up.

CHAPTER SIX

Grand Jury Charges, (continued)

B. Other Brokerage Firms
The White Rock and State Street Partners entered into agreements with brokers at numerous other brokerage firms in furtherance of the fraudulent sale of securities. These other brokerage firms included J.W. Barclay & Co., Inc. ("Barclay"), A.R. Baron & Co., Inc. ("Baron") and D.H. Blair & Co. Inc., ("Blair").

7. Barclay was a registered broker-dealer of securities, licensed by the NASD, with an office at 23 Broadway. Barclay commenced operations in or about March 1989 and is still in operation. The defendant JOHN CIOFOLETTI was a registered representative of Barclay from about October 1991 through February 1998.

8. Baron was a registered broker-dealer with its principal office at 153 East 53rd Street, New York, New York. Baron commenced operations in or about April 1992 and ceased doing business about October 1996. Unindicted co-conspirator Andrew Bressman was a principal and registered representative of Baron and owned the firm together with others.

9. Blair was a registered broker-dealer of securities licensed by the NASD, with an office at 44 Wall Street, New York, New York. Blair commenced operations April 1975 and ceased doing business about August 1998. The defendant ALFRED PALAGONIA was a registered representative of Blair from approximately January 1990 to February 1998.

An End to Cold Calling

After eight months of cold calling and late afternoon trading under Brock's name, I was ready for a second shot at my broker's exam. The first time I had failed by one point. The second time I passed, and I saw it as a passport to a new life and riches. I knew I had the art of the Wall Street bullshit down. I had learned how to get past secretaries, get to customers and sell them. Now all my sales would be legit, and instead of doing them for Brock Samith, I would be doing them for myself, and making real money.

There was always a party when a cold caller passed his exam, and the party for me was at a place called the Rio Grande at 39th Street and Third Avenue, near Gruntal. Lex, Ricky, Dicky and Brock were there, without wives and girlfriends, along with a lot of cold callers and assistants. It was a boisterous club, with music, women, lights, drinking, laughter, and drugs. I had been living almost like a monk for the months I had put in cold calling, commuting and studying for my exam. Now I could party, and the fact that I no longer did the drugs made it even better. Two or three glasses of wine coupled with the high of success were all I needed to have a good time.

Passing the exam meant that Lynn and I could leave the basement apartment in my parents' house and get our own place. The gamble I had taken in shutting down my tile business to try out as a cold caller had paid off. The changes were going to be much bigger, and happen much faster than I could have imagined.

In the midst of the party Lynn and I were invited to join a deal that several brokers were putting together to buy a nightclub. They invited me in for half a point, which was $12,500—five percent of the total cost. Most of the players were in for several points each. But they had been brokers for a while and I was the new kid on the block. They knew I had been working the last few months for $200 a week, when most of them earned that much an hour. That was why they suggested I come in for half a point.

I had no idea if the club would be a good investment. I had been to new clubs with my friends. Some opened and closed almost immediately, without finding the right mix of location, interior design, style of music, food, and drink to draw repeat business. A few became trendy, drawing celebrities and entertainment columnists, making big money for weeks, months, or even two or three years before falling back into the tier of second-level night spots shunned by locals and embraced by the "bridge and tunnel" crowd.

These were the unwanted customers from Queens, Brooklyn and the boroughs who read about the trendy nightclubs in magazines like *New York*. They came to town to enjoy what was left of the scene that sparked the very media coverage that would cause the genuinely hip and chic clientele to move on. Of course, I had been a bridge and tunnel guy myself in all the years of taking the subway from Brooklyn or Long Island to visit clubs in Manhattan as a teenager and a young adult. Now, Lynn and I were about to change our status.

That night at the party, being invited to invest was not about business opportunity. It was proof we had arrived in a fast-paced world of hustle and big money. I knew Lynn would look over the prospectus in the sobering light of day, analyze what was offered, and then agree to use the line of credit remaining from my tile business. She might be conservative in her thinking, but my excitement was infectious. Lynn was rapidly becoming comfortable with the idea of the lifestyle we were about to become part of, and she would understand, as I did, that a half-point investment could jump-start our future.

The nightclub investment would change our life immeasurably, but the party would change Lex's life much more. Lex was a Russian Jew whose family emigrated from Russia just before the collapse of the Soviet Union. His father was a gangster who specialized in counterfeiting and had served time in England for making and passing the British pound and dollars. He was suspected of passing other foreign currency in Russia where it was harder to detect, and he moved to America for greater opportunities in the crime that was attributed to the Russian Mafia. Call it disorganized crime.

Lex's father wanted respectability for his son and he was thrilled that Lex had become a broker. But Lex did not move far enough away from the criminal aspect of his heritage. Lynn always said he had a devious look about him, as someone you shouldn't trust, and in some ways she was right. By nature, Lex would rather go through the back door than the front door of any deal. At five-foot eight and maybe 175, he was a lot stockier than I. Like most of my friends on Wall Street, Lex was a sharp dresser. He would go to Zegna and spend $30,000 on suits. If he saw a sweater he liked, he'd buy one in every color. It was Lex who got me into collecting expensive watches. He also got me into color-coordinating cars with other things I owned, like a yellow watch I had to go with my yellow Ferrari.

Lex was a horrible driver. I never wanted to be in a car with him. I always told him jokingly that there were no professional Russian race car drivers. It was also edgy going to clubs with him, because he was a volatile guy with a quick temper.

At the party for me at Rio Grande, Lex blew up and wrecked his professional life in a few violent moments. I was outside on the veranda, so I never knew exactly how it happened. What I heard was that Lex was standing inside by the bar with a couple of girls and a broker from another office. Lex said something to somebody's girl-friend, one thing led to another, and suddenly Lex smashed his mar-garita glass on the bar. Then he used one of the glass shards like a knife to cut the other broker's face.

It took 110 stitches to sew his face back together, and he would probably never lose the scars. The rest of us had been around enough clubs to know that when a fight started, you get out of there.

"Lex, come on," we called, "get out of here!"

"No, I'm staying," Lex snarled. "I wanta' kick his ass."

"You already did. The guy's bleeding. He needs an ambulance."

"He deserved it," Lex said. His brain was fogged with alcohol and I couldn't get through to him. He was crazed, and the place was in an uproar because of what had happened. Paramedics were on their way, and so were the police.

My other friends and I were scrambling for cabs to get out before the police arrived, and we heard sirens as we left. Lex was still inside, and got arrested, thrown in jail and left there to sober up. He was convicted of felony assault, and a felony conviction cost him his broker's license. No convicted felon can even be seen coming and going from a brokerage office. Lex's career as a broker was over just as mine was beginning.

But it didn't begin the way I thought it should. I had opened the 40 accounts for Brock Samith that were expected of a cold caller prior to his becoming a broker. I had passed the exam, and I expected to begin buying and selling the next day. But Samith wasn't satisfied with the 40 accounts. He wanted me to open forty more before he would approve my change in status. John Doukas had gone to Florida on vacation when this came up, and said on the phone that we'd talk about it when he came back. I went to the call manager, Allen Underwood, who explained that Brock did not feel I was ready to be a broker. Passing the test had nothing to do with the judgment call that had to be made concerning when I could start selling. Allen said Brock and he felt that I should open more accounts for my former broker before I began doing full-time broker work.

I said no to that. I told Allen I needed my own desk and I needed to start selling. He said no, and I said I quit. Doukas called again from Florida and told me I couldn't leave. He said he wanted me to run his book, which had $20 million in it. It was an honor, but it wasn't good enough for me. I quit and called my cousin Salvatore to see where I could get another job. Sal was working at Shearson Lehman and told me to come there. Shearson Lehman was located at Fourteen Wall Street, directly across from the New York Stock Exchange and my interview there was very different from my interview with Doukas only eight months earlier.

The Shearson boss asked me what I had done at Gruntal. I told him I had opened 40 accounts and he was impressed. When I added that I had opened them in a month's time, he was even more impressed. He knew I had only passed the broker's test that week, which meant that my opening accounts prior to that had been illicit. But what I had done at Gruntal was not a problem for Shearson Lehman, and this gentleman was more interested in my success than the propriety of what I had done.

"You're pretty talented, to open 40 accounts in a month, part-time," he said. "What would it take to get you to come to Shearson?"

I told him it would take a $5,000 monthly draw, two cold callers, a secretary and a 50 percent commission. I figured while I was asking, I would ask big. He floored me by agreeing to the whole package. "Done," he said.

This was great. My own office, my own staff, and fifty percent payout. That meant that out of every dollar I earned the company in commission, fifty cents would go to me and the IRS. I was excited and as soon as we were through I called Lynn.

"Pack our stuff," I told Lynn. "We're moving. No more commuting. They just gave me a five thousand dollar check against my first month's draw, with a three-month guarantee. And I have my own desk."

We moved from a Long Island basement to a $1200-a-month apartment in Battery Park City that faced the Statue of Liberty and New York harbor and the Verrazano Bridge. It took most of my first $5000 check to cover moving expenses, the first and last month's rent, plus a security deposit. But I wasn't worried. The future looked too good to worry about. In fact, I earned $10,000 in commissions over the next thirty days. But at that moment, what counted was that I had a new home overlooking New York Harbor and the Statue of Liberty.

To this day, I still feel like an immigrant. I flew here. I didn't have the experience of traveling by ship, of standing on deck and seeing the Statue of Liberty grow larger as we came close to shore. Yet the Statue of Liberty is the greatest symbol for an immigrant coming to America. The first time I saw it, I was moved to tears. The Neil Diamond song, "Coming to America," still gets me in the heart. So here, after all this work, after giving up everything we had built together in my tile business, Lynn and I were finally able to move out of the basement into an apartment like this.

Battery Park City was on the West Side, not far from Wall Street and across the street from the twin towers of the World Trade Center. It was the nicest place we had ever lived. It wasn't that the apartments themselves were lavish or luxurious. What made it special was the view. Each morning I could get up and look out at the Statue of Liberty. Now I was from a new neighborhood; here, all my neighbors were brokers. There are important days in your business life. I'll never forget the day I made my first million-dollar sale. I'll never forget the day I opened my own office. None of those can compare with that first $5,000 draw check and the apartment that over-looked the Statue of Liberty.

My first month at Shearson, I concentrated on being the best broker I could be. I was primarily marketing pharmaceutical stocks such as the Swiss company Sandoz and the American giant Upjohn, which was in the news with products like Rogaine that helped bald-ing men and women regrow hair. I specialized in pharmaceutical stocks because I understood them. I knew it might take 14 years from the time a product shows promise until the dosage and preparation are determined, until animal trials are completed, human testing accomplished, and the drug approved for sale by the FDA. Anywhere along the way, the drug might be found to be something less than originally anticipated. Anywhere along the way, the company might find it had wasted millions on an unfulfilled promise.

I understood that the stocks would go up if an early trial lookedhopeful for a new product that might prove worthless after fur-ther testing. And I understood that the stocks would drop if a prom-ising drug failed a few months after it was announced. But this was a time when the drug companies were selling things like hair-growing products that people just had to have. The newspapers were full of stories about them. I knew the stocks would keep going up, and my enthusiasm caught on. I believed in the companies, and while I was bullshitting the customers to get them to buy, I believed the bullshit.

Success came immediately. In my first month I opened thirty accounts on Sandoz. I'll never forget that. The stock did really well and I knew I was going to make money. Plus, thirty accounts in a month was more than an account a day closure. That was pretty amazing, and everybody saw that I was a star. The word went out that I was going to be the next big producer on Wall Street.

I was very cocky. I even brought in my own espresso machine, which was popular with the entire office. But I knew that putting in the hours was the real key to success. That meant being there early in the morning to catch the owner of a business before the secretary walked in. I used the tools of calling early and calling late. Calling late, you would catch the business owners working late because guys who ran big companies worked late. And they worked early. It was their company, their money, so if you tried to call between nine and five, you got caught by the receptionist or the secretary. So you had to try to get in before the secretary arrived. That's what I did, and it paid off. I also called overseas as well, because I spoke Italian and felt I could probably get some Italian investors involved. That didn't actually work out too well, because Italians didn't take kindly to telemarketing.

I began building a "book" of clients. These were the names, addresses, and telephone numbers of customers to whom you'd sold and to whom you could go back again. They were not exclusive customers. The more successful they were, the more likely they were to have accounts with several different brokers from several different firms. All the brokers were working with a finite number of people throughout the country. The list changed as people moved up in the business world, earned more in their professions, and inherited wealth from elderly parents. But at any given time there were only so many people in the most desirable categories, and they were regularly contacted by brokers from all over the country. Because of this, each broker developed a book of clients representing the people with whom he or she had made at least one sale.

I found that some brokerage houses used four designations for the books their brokers were building. The "A" book consisted of clients with more than a million dollars in the stock market—the whales. Some were conservative, buying stock to hold for many years. Some were speculators who ordered their broker to move in and out of a position as the business changed. What mattered was that they had spent serious money on stock and could be expected to buy and sell more.

All brokers sought the "A" book listings, and people listed in the A book got called as often as two or three times a week with one deal or another. Usually the offerings were good buys because the brokers were trying to win the wealthy buyer's confidence. At other times the buyer's enthusiasm was increased by a strong broker's pitch and both found they were deluding themselves about the future of a stock. The price plummeted and the buyer stopped dealing with the broker who made the sale. An "A" book was the most volatile list a broker could have. It was also the book that could make the broker

rich. Ten "A" clients with million-dollar accounts could make a broker $500,000-plus, a year.

The "B" book represented clients with between a half-million
dollars and a million in the stock market. The younger the "B" book
clients were, the greater the potential for the future. These were the
clients who were just beginning to invest. There were older individuals who experienced windfall income from selling a business or
receiving an inheritance. Still others were newly arrived in the market, middle-aged men and women who had risen on a fast track to
success with years of ever-rising income ahead of them.

The "C" book consisted of clients who had made regular purchases but had less than a half-million dollars in the stock market.
They were the mainstays of small-town brokers, who typically netted
between $85,000 and a little over $100,000 a year. While that was considered excellent in their communities, in the league where I was
playing, there were brokers who thought $85,000 represented a bad
month's pay.

The "D" book was the book of last resort. It might be used
along with the "C" book to give cold callers a chance to practice selling during those illegal sessions when the manager was either out of
the office or ignoring what was taking place. The "D" book has the
names of people who had made a single purchase. They were mere
pikers, and the purchase might have been the buying of an IPO stock.
It might have been the purchase of a few blue chips with some inheritance money. Whatever the case, the person had not yet become a
player and might never be worth much selling time.

Because there was no obligation to buy from any one broker,
many clients constantly changed. They might like the IPO a new broker was offering. They might feel that if they spread their money
around, the brokers would work harder for their account. Or they
might have lost money and decided to leave the broker. Brokers
working in what was known as the small cap range—handling smaller money projects such as IPOs in the $5-million to $10-million
range—were always vulnerable to the failure of their stock. The stock
might start to move up quickly, sometimes showing rises of 40 to 50
percent within a few days of the IPO. That was great money in those

days before the electronic stocks went crazy. You could sell someone stock, watch it rise an eighth of a point, call him back to buy more, then see it go up maybe a quarter or half a point. By the end of the week, the stock you brought out at $5 would be selling for $8 and everyone was happy.

But there was more than money to be enjoyed. The Friday of my first week at Shearson, there was a luxury charter bus parked outside the office building when I arrived at work. From the outside it looked like the type of bus upscale tour groups sometimes rent to come into Manhattan for a weekend of sightseeing. But it was not equipped for tourists. The forty-passenger bus had televisions throughout so that movies could be shown continuously on the built-in VCR. It had a bathroom, coolers filled with wine, champagne, beer, and hard liquor. There were bags of snacks, a variety of food, and enough marijuana to make everyone on the bus high just from inhaling.

"Forget work," I was told when I entered the office that day. "We're going skiing in Vermont." I looked around. There was a clique of secretaries, brokers, and managers who all knew each other and had known me before I joined Shearson. They had decided they had worked hard enough, and since they considered me one of their own, they expected me to go too.

I called Lynn and told her what was happening. She wasn't happy, but she knew that businesses often shut down for summer golf outings, where the staff relaxes on the course. Talk comes more casually than in the office and a participant could sometimes accomplish lots. I didn't tell her that this trip looked like a plan to party and get laid.

I was right in my thinking. Friday night meant drinking, dancing, eating, and falling indiscreetly into one another's beds for those sober enough to mess around. Saturday was for skiing, though only a handful were avid skiers, like me, and sober enough to take to the slopes. There was more partying on Saturday night. Then Sunday, feeling as if I had just been spending the weekend enjoying a fraternity party with some very rich kids (I, at 29, was at least five years older than the rest of the staff), I returned home. I was casual about what had happened, letting Lynn think that being a broker and going skiing in Vermont was as innocent as spending an afternoon on the golf course. On that trip, let it be said, however, I did forge great professional relationships with my co-workers and my cousin's friend and desk-partner, a guy named Walter Durchalter, who was known as "Dutch."

The farther along I got in the world of the stock market, the more interested I got in the history of the business. I learned about it by asking people who seemed to know the details of every shrewd trade and every scam, and finding books and histories that I enjoyed digesting. One of the most interesting stories involved the name of the American who meant the most to citizens of other countries when I was a kid: Kennedy. I was born only the year before John F. Kennedy was shot in Dallas, but I grew up knowing the name as one of the legends of American greatness. It was only later that I learned how his father, Joseph Kennedy, had operated.

In 1933, just prior to being named the first Chairman of the Securities and Exchange Commission, Joseph P. Kennedy, Sr. and the men known as the Irish Mafia worked a stock manipulation scam involving Libby-Owens-Ford. Prohibition was ending and Kennedy, with his carefully controlled group of investors, each positioned in a different part of the country, spread the rumor that Libby-Owens-Ford had been chosen as the official company to manufacture liquor bottles. The orders would obviously be large, meaning soaring profits for the company. This would mean a rise in the stock price.

Through manipulation of the media and the buying, selling, and buying of the stock, Kennedy managed to raise the value slowly. To the casual observer, the stock simply reflected a solid company with a good future. Few checked to verify the liquor bottle rumors. Few checked to see where the orders for the stock might be coming from because they weren't concentrated in one area, a sure sign of manipulation. Soon many investors began buying the stock. Instead of moving at relatively small increments, large outside buyers moved it rapidly higher. Then Kennedy and his cohorts sold all the stock they owned, making massive profits, while ending the rumor mill that had artificially supported the stock. The price plummeted, especially when it was learned that there was no special liquor-bottle manufacturing deal for Libby-Owens-Ford.

Sixty years later, when I was learning the angles of what is known as stock manipulation, the problem with a small cap offering was that the companies becoming successful were still subject to rumors and gossip in the business trades. A hot IPO warranted a newspaper or magazine article, and short players betting on the stock dropping below the issue price would do what they could to plant negative information. They might tell a columnist that a CEO who was in Europe to make a deal that would boost overseas revenue was actually in the hospital with a heart attack. The columnist might or might not check the facts. Usually he would call the hospital and ask about the patient. When the staff learned that the reporter wasn't related to the person being asked about, many hospital personnel would not bother to check the records to see if the person was, in fact, a patient. Instead there would be the blanket statement, "We can only give out a patient's condition to family members." The reporter would assume the worst, and not call the company where he or she would learn the truth, and would run with a story stock buyers would consider reason to sell quickly.

Or there might be subtler sabotage, such as releasing a story that product testing was faulty or that a major client was in trouble and orders would drop. Whatever the case, the short players would count on a rash of unexpected stock sales to drive the price down to below what they would have to pay. They would sell the stock they did not yet own—as they could legally do—for $8. Then they would drive the market price down to $4.75 by the day they were obliged to cover their agreement, buy the shares they needed at the lower price and turn them over to the broker. If they maneuvered 10,000 shares, this meant that they agreed to sell their stock, (which they did not yet actually own), for $80,000. They would drive down the price through rumor and innuendo, and then buy the shares they needed to deliver to the broker for $47,500. This would leave them with a profit of $32,500. And it would create a run on the stock that would keep its price dropping.

Customers who bought the stock hoping it would rise would be so angry with their brokers that they would stop taking their calls.

They would sell, or move their portfolios. The broker's book would be "blown," and the broker would have to start fresh to find new buyers, often by leaving the brokerage firm where the book was compromised.

Large, established companies have stocks that fluctuate in value. A class action lawsuit over product liability, a one-time financial write-off reducing an expected quarterly dividend, and other factors could send the stock value down a number of points. Changes like that do not come back to haunt the broker. The company has a long-term history and buyers expect fluctuations. Most of those buyers would have purchased for the long-term, and would have seen fluctuation in the past. This is why a broker's book is most often blown with a failed IPO or highly touted house stock, where the only existing market is whatever the brokers for the single firm are able to generate.

When a stockbroker goes to a different firm he often gets cut a check, called a "trailing twelve." The check is for 30 percent of what you earned for the previous twelve months. And at the place where you start over, you can also badmouth the former brokerage outfit as though it was the fault of their investment advisers that everything went bad. Since no one knows who's doing what when they buy by telephone, sometimes that works.

It was at Shearson that I began building my first book. My cold callers were giving me good leads. My follow-up skills were unusually strong for someone so new to the business and people in the industry who heard about my sales expected me to become a top producer. That was why it was such a shock at the end of a single month's employment to be told I was personally $10,000 ahead from my sales, and that I was being let go. The company was changing hands and the star rookie was expendable. I was making money at Shearson, and my boss called me in to his office and said, "Sal, I have to let you go...."

I was shaken to my core. The $5,000 was the first real money I had earned and I thought it would never end. Nobody had told me that American Express was in the process of selling Shearson or that the deal would go through at the end of my first month. When it happened, I was in the same category as a cold caller because my paper-work had not completed the rounds of the bureaucracy. I was legally a broker, but without the finalized documents, I wasn't "official," and I was let go along with hundreds of others.

CHAPTER SEVEN

Grand Jury Indictment, (continued)

10. Between March 1993 and October 1996, the defendants FRANK COPPA, SR., ERNEST MONTEVEC-CHI, DANIEL PERSICO, JACK BASILE, ROCCO BASILE, LARRY BERMAN, JOHN CIOFOLETTI, JOHN DOUKAS, WALTER DURCHALTER, (also known as "Dutch,") DANIEL LEV, EUGENE LOMBARDO, EDMOND NAGEL, ALFRED PALAGONIA, ALEKS PAUL, JOSEPH POLITO, SR., ABRAHAM SALAMAN AND GIUSEPPE TEM-PERINO, also known as "Joseph Temperino," together with Gene Klotsman, Salvatore Lauria, Lex Tersa, Andrew Bressman and others, consti-tuted an enterprise as defined in Title 18, US Code, Section 1961, that is a group or indi-viduals associated in fact (hereinafter the "Enterprise").

11. The chief purpose of the Enterprise was to obtain money for its members and associates by acquiring secret control over large blocks of stock and warrants, and then artificially inflating and maintaining the price of these securities by means of material misrepresenta-tions and omissions and manipulative sales practices. After inflating the price of the stock and warrants, individuals employed by and associated with the Enterprise sold their secretly controlled securities to the public, generating millions of dollars in illicit profits. These profits were then laundered through numerous offshore and other nominee accounts.

Back on the Street

I took a cold look at my situation and realized that it was worse than I had imagined. Shearson had 30 days to pay my $10,000 commission and most of my $5,000 first month draw had already been spent. I was a trader out of a job, a star salesman without a company's backing or even a phone. I had gotten into debt, promising to pay people based on income I rightfully expected to make, and now there was nothing.

Once again I turned to my cousin Sal, and asked him what to do. Sal said, "Remember Dicky? He's working at a little firm uptown— Whale Securities. They'll probably give you a job."

I remembered Dicky Zalio as a tough street kid who hung out with us back in Brooklyn. Dicky had also started out on Wall Street as a courier with my cousin, and he was one of the most aggressive hustlers I'd ever seen. Before he went to Wall Street he had worked as a valet parker at an expensive Central Park restaurant called Tavern on the Green. Dicky used his position there to meet owners of Merrill Lynch and other big firms. He'd actually follow them into the bathroom and pitch them while they were standing by the urinals.

"I want to be a broker for you," Dicky would tell them, pausing as they flushed. "One day I'll be your biggest guy." And he did it.

Dicky had made himself a multi-millionaire, just like he said he would, but not in a predictable way. Dicky had plenty of drive but nobody would hire him because he was very Brooklyn. He had the gruff voice of an actor playing a mob enforcer in an old movie. To us, it was just street, but it was intimidating to a WASP or the owner of a big firm. That was why Dicky, when he made it to Wall Street, had started out at the low end of the business in a company called Cooney-Base. Mel Cooney and Sandy Base were what we used to call penny-stock criminals from the 70s and 80s, and they would give you a chance no matter what you sounded like. Dicky did well at Cooney-Base, using his drive and his street smarts to become a million-dollar producer.

When Cooney-Base was acquired by Gruntal, Dicky moved up to Gruntal, proving that his skills could overcome his diction. But that was not how he became rich. Dicky made his first million on the Street by moving from firm to firm and collecting cash payouts on contracts he signed to go to work there. Being a broker in those years was like being a ball player who was a free agent: you signed contracts agreeing to work for three years, but the agreement called for a specific cash payout, regardless of employment. Dicky was good enough that he'd get a check for like three or four hundred thousand dollars from a mid-tier firm he thought was either going to shut down or be acquired. When that happened, the contract was void and he was free to make the same deal with someone else. In one year he did this three times, ending up at Whale Securities a millionaire from signing checks alone.

Not that you'd ever know it. Dicky was a shrewd guy who kept driving a Ford well after he made his first million. Though he got so rich he finally bought a big Mercedes and hired a driver, he was one of the rare ones who saved his money.

When I called Dicky about a job at Whale, he told me he'd introduce me to the owner. He said he had heard I was good on the phone and told me to come up to the office. He said he thought they could match my deal at Shearson and said he'd like me to work next to him.

The distance he had gone from Brooklyn to success on Wall Street was evident when I arrived at Whale, which was located at Fifth Avenue and 52nd Street. Liz Claiborne was downstairs in the same building and Cartier was across the street. Class. When I reached Dicky's office, he treated me to an interview unlike any I had experienced. I walked in to see him busy with two account openers, firing one of them because he was planning to go out on his own, and throwing his desk stapler at the other. Without apology or explanation, Dicky turned to me and said he'd introduce me to Richard Stoyak, the manager. Stoyak was an old-time Lehman Brothers million-dollar club player reputed to have made the biggest single trade in Wall Street history, a $30-million order on one stock. But Stoyak was burned out and didn't want to sell anymore. That's why he was a manager.

When I told him my name and said I was looking for a job, I figured he'd ask about my background and my track record at Gruntal and Shearson. He didn't.

"So you're Dicky's friend?" Stoyak asked.

"Yeah."

"You ever kill anybody?"

I knew he wasn't serious. Or was he? I looked at him as though I was thinking about it, then said, "Not that I know of."

"You're hired."

"That's it?" I asked.

"Yeah. As long as you're not a murderer, you're fine."

Goes to show you that on Wall Street, it doesn't matter who you are or what you've done as long as you produce. As long as you don't have a bad rap sheet, like credit card fraud, you're going to get a job. Most petty crimes are pretty much condoned—DWI, drinking and driving—even manslaughter while you were driving, they probably wouldn't care. I hadn't killed anybody, so I started there the next day.

I asked for a draw of $5000—which was no problem. Then Dicky took me to meet the firm's owner, Jack Hickman, a very well dressed, distinguished-looking, small-stature guy who looked like a duplicate of Regis Philbin. He had a very refined manner. He shook my hand, told me welcome aboard, and said I'd do great there.

"Nice meeting you," he said. I was very excited. I had the job and Dicky had invited me to work in his office.

"You and me can be pals," Dicky said.

Dicky had a big heart but sometimes was so abrasive with his cold callers that I moved out to the boiler room. It was a fairly spacious room with long tables, and a Quotron every ten or 12 feet and when I started, it was empty. I found out when I began selling that Whale Securities was a decimated company, a ten-year-old brokerage firm that was almost without brokers. They had taken four companies public the year before and all their deals had been shorted down from the issue price of $5 and $6 to pennies per share. The year had been a disaster and most of the brokers had blown their books and left.

I wasn't concerned with the past at Whale because my book had not been blown. The previous brokers' customers were probably not going to be my customers, and even if by chance I got some, they would see me as someone new, who had not made the mistakes tied to the previous brokers. Yet believing this did not keep me from running scared.

We all said that in this business we could go from heroes to zeroes every month. Commissions, bonuses, everything you earn is figured on a thirty-day period with no meaningful carry-over. You fight to be the best, and when you win, you enjoy the victory for one night at the end of the month before starting over on the same track as every other broker. But getting fired because of a change in ownership showed me I had better take nothing for granted. I would have to sell as though the job would disappear tomorrow.

Putting my marriage on hold, I took to the phone as if each day might be my only chance. I would hit the phones early to reach executives before their secretaries arrived. As afternoon turned to evening, I would work my way west to California, Oregon, Washington and regions on Pacific Time where potential clients were still at their desks when it was 10 P.M. in New York City. I ate when I felt I needed a break. If I was lucky, I would eat dinner with Lynn. If not, I would go to a nearby restaurant or eat at my desk and many a night I woke up with my head on my desk where I had fallen asleep. Lynn hated the separation, but the obsession I had once had for drugs was now focused on making money. My mistress was the capitalist system that rewarded greed, and that was a mistress Lynn had to endure until I felt secure enough at Whale to give myself a more complete life.

The movie *Wall Street* had not been a cautionary tale for me in the way that the brokers at Gruntal had intended in making it mandatory viewing for new hires. Instead of admiring the one who turned in Gekko, I thought the Bud Fox character was an idiot. As far as the deal in the picture, what the hell, leveraged buyouts happened all the time. The Bud Fox character should have kept the money and not ratted out Gordon Gekko. If he felt betrayed, he should have used what Gekko taught him to buy his dad a new airline. I wanted to make $25 million on a deal myself and I saw Gordon Gekko as a role model. I wanted to be that corporate raider—the builder and destroyer of fortunes.

What I got out of that movie was the power of the money with the apartment, the cars, and the clothes as motivators. Dicky knew how to motivate the troops and he would play the theme music from

Rocky in the office every morning to psyche us up for the day. He was an incredible broker who ran his business at Whale like a military operation. So here I was: a licensed broker with a great mentor and an insider in a Manhattan investment boutique, putting what I had learned to good use.

Right after my arrival at Whale, Jack Hickman dumped a windfall in my lap: the 100,000-share allocation of an IPO, raising capital for the food company opening the fast-food franchise in Poland. The way the deal was structured, if I sold the 100,000 shares, I would get a $50,000 gross commission, out of which I would keep $25,000 before taxes. Nobody expected me to sell all 100,000 shares in one shot, but that's basically what happened.

The IPO was for a guy named Shel Robinson, a Jewish guy in his mid-50s who wore his remaining hair in a ponytail. Shel was a stockbroker's son and he had sold a chain of clothing stores for a fortune. He was worth several hundred million dollars and he would come up to Whale to take Dicky and me out for lunch and drinks at very cushy places. He sold me on the Polish burger franchise. I became convinced the IPO would succeed, and I went to work selling it to names off my microfiche. Every name I called was a "player," someone with money in the market and more to invest.

This was 1992 and the overall IPO climate was great and everybody wanted a hot new issue, so we would go in through the back door, pretending to be someone they had talked to about stocks before.

"Bob," I'd say, talking to the CEO of a medical supply company in Denver, "You don't remember me, but we spoke before. I want you to listen. I've got one of the hottest public offerings coming up that I've ever seen. It's the opening of a Burger King in Poland, which has the fastest growing economy in what used to be Eastern Europe. They're crazed for fast foods there, and anything American. How can this not be great?"

The stock was issued at 5 dollars with a $.50 commission. When it opened it went to $5.50 by 6 P.M. and we kept it there for a few days to get the loose hands out. Then we went to work on the aftermarket buying. The more people bought, the higher we could get the stock up. It was the basic law of economics—supply and demand.

I sold a thousand shares at $5.50 to a doctor. Then, when the stock hit $6, I went back and pitched him on buying another 9,000 shares. He bought it, and the stock went to $7.50. Another broker working nearby heard me on the phone, a guy who had been known as a master seller and was starting over after having gotten in some kind of trouble.

"Call the guy back," he said. "Sell him again."

Sell him again? I had just sold him 9,000 shares, which was ten times as much as I had sold him the first time. I was feeling pretty good about that, and this guy was saying call him back and sell him again.

"I'm serious," he said. "Now's the time to hit him up for more."

"What, I should try to sell him another 10,000?" I was only half-serious. The other broker had had a reputation, before his fall, so I had serious doubt about how good his advice would be.

"No, don't waste time," he urged me. "Sell him 90,000 shares. Make his holding an even 100K. Go for the big-time, kid. Always go big. What have you got to lose?"

He was right. The doctor wasn't going to cancel the order he had just made if I hit him up again and tried to sell him more. At least he wasn't likely to. The worst thing I had to fear was the idea of feeling like a fool, being turned down in trying something unreasonable. I called him back.

"Listen," I said, before he even had a chance to tell me we had already done enough business for the day. "We've got to get into this stock farther. You need to own 100,000 shares of this. You want it to be an even 100, so you're in a good position."

My mind was going along as I was talking, thinking: this guy hasn't even paid for the last 9,000 shares yet, and I'm hustling him on another 90,000! But I shut off that part of my mind.

"It's already up 50 percent from its issue price and you and I are up close to $20,000 in just two trades," I said, punching my voice up with enthusiasm. "The stock is going to take off and when it does we don't have enough. I need you to buy 90,000 shares more. If it goes to 20 and we have 100,000 shares, we'll make $1 million profit!"

There was a pause, and I kept my silence. Now my heart was really pumping. The broker at the next desk was watching and listening and waiting. I looked at him, we made eye contact, and then I looked away. Then the next thing I heard was "OK."

"Okay." The doctor was buying it! I had sold him 90,000 shares—just like that. But I stayed cool. I looked over at the other broker, and he could read it in my eyes that I had made the sale and he broke into a smile, the first one I had seen on his face. Maybe he was thinking he might make a comeback.

"I won't pay more than $9 for it," I told the doctor, all business now. "It will be hard to find that much cheap stock but I'll see what I can do, and I'll call you later with a confirmation and cost okay."

I put down the phone and looked up to see the dozen brokers that had been hired gaping with wonder and amazement at the size of the order I just closed. They cheered, and Stoyak the manager came out to congratulate me.

Ninety thousand shares at $9 was $810,000, with a minimum commission of $45,000 on that trade alone. Altogether I had earned a $50,000 commission. It was the most unbelievable rush of success I have ever felt. The floor was buzzing with excitement and everybody was pounding their phones, wanting to get the big order, too. I had just had my first whale, a man very much like the Gordon Gekko character in Wall Street. My commission, after the split with the house, was $25,000, which is $17,000 take home after taxes. In less than a month, I had brought in what the average American wage earner spends to support a family for a year.

Next, I had to go about finding 90,000 shares—ten percent of the float—which was not going to be that easy. That's when Dicky called me into his office.

"Let me show you how you make real money from this trade," Dicky said. "It's called a cross."

I thought I already had made money, but what did I know? I listened to Dicky explain the complicated game we were going to play.

"First you need to find the loose hands in your own book," Dicky said, meaning the customers who would be likely to sell the shares I had sold them.

"Call and tell them to take a profit, and then you buy them something else," Dicky said. "That way, you get two commissions: the sell and the buy. Buy all you can find from the small brokers in the firm. This way we clean up the stock before we move it up.

"Last, you sell the stock to your main client."

It sounded good to me. But I needed to know what stock I should pick for the clients that I was freeing up the cash from.

"Okay, Sal," Dicky said. "Here's the best part. I sell you some of my stock on the last deal I did at the bid so you can make the full chop on the inside and when you need the favor back some day, I'll be there for you. But most likely I'll take the stock back next month from you when we orchestrate another cross and make a shit load of commission again. Remember, Sal: Who owns the float does not fall in the moat!"

That meant that once he and I controlled all one million shares, we could cross sell all day long, controlling the price— because we were the price!

That was my introduction to serious, big-time stock manipulation. Now the quest as I understood it was to own another entire float so we could do even bigger crosses while waiting for that lucky but unlikely day that the stock would "go liquid." Going liquid means that the stock actually acquires a market value outside the artificial one we created by controlling the price. If you think about it, this is done on a much larger scale by the big firms controlling much larger floats.

I was on a roll. In my second month at Whale, my take-home total jumped to $37,000 and my third month I hit $97,000. By my fourth month I was making over $100,000, almost unheard of for a rookie.

What we did for Shel's Polish fast-food franchise was enormously successful for him, for us, for me. (For everyone but the loyal investor pool, as I explained earlier.) With my 100,000 shares in the IPO and an additional 400,000 in the aftermarket, I had half the float. And with Dicky's aggressive small-cap techniques controlling the other half of the float, we were like gold. The IPO stock shot up from its opening peg of $5 to $10, almost on cue by us, before the first burger franchise was built in Warsaw. That meant that in less than a month, we had raised six million dollars for Shel Robinson. Six million dollars! Just by talking convincingly on the phone about the value of something that was highly hypothetical. We had sold a dream! It always amazed me that people would send their money without ever seeing me.

My sales made me a new star at Whale and gave me a reputation on the Street. All of a sudden, I was being called by headhunters, almost before I could take in the magnitude of what had happened in just a few months. I was literally earning more money than I knew what to do with.

But there was more than money flowing. Bacchus, the nightclub that Lynn and I had invested in during my time at Gruntal, was opening on West 27th street, and there was a party held in celebration. The party was at a private residence in Tribeca, an area south of Greenwich Village that had once been ultra-hip and bohemian and had since become ultra-chic and trendy. Robert DeNiro was the first person in the entertainment world to settle on Tribeca as the center for his non-acting operations. He opened the highly successful Tribeca Bar and Grill, and then followed with his Tribeca Film Company, which attracted movie industry trendsetters including the director Spike Lee, who used the company for some of his casting.

Mitchell Lowe, an actor's son who had gone into real estate, bought a Tribeca warehouse and converted it into huge, floor-through apartments. He sold one to Ray Rapaglia, a legendary stockbroker who had made millions of dollars at Shearson and was one of the principal investors in Bacchus. Ray had the gift of gab and sold everything his brokerage house was offering. He made so much money that he could indulge in a flamboyantly hedonistic lifestyle and his residential suite was the ideal location for the party celebrating the nightclub opening.

Lynn and I thought we were doing well. Our apartment in Battery Park City was the nicest place in which we had ever lived. Ray Rapaglia's place was like a luxury fantasy made real. As Lynn and I rode up the unimproved freight-type elevator, we had no idea what was in store for us. The apartment opened with one of those kitchens you see in magazines, where you can have your own chef and keep him happy. There was a Sub-Zero refrigerator, a Viking stove, an island for preparation, gleaming pots and pans perfectly maintained and carefully hung. The kitchen led to the other rooms, all large, all beautifully furnished. There was the dining room, a loft-style living room, a massive bedroom and bathroom. Our apartment would fit into one room of Rapaglia's place.

Then there were the guests. We saw Robert DeNiro, Donald Trump and his bodyguard, models, actors, and Wall Street people we had read about in *People* or *Vanity Fair*. Suddenly we were part of it, and it was real. Nobody told us we were in the wrong place. No one thought we were part of the catering staff or had come in the wrong way. We were guests like everyone else and this was going to be our world from now on.

Our host Ray Rapaglia suggested that we go downstairs, and we nervously walked down to join the people whom we were both amazed to realize would be part of our new life. The whole floor was a rich man's play area. One wall contained a state-of-the-art projection television system allowing Ray to watch videos with movie theater clarity. There were pinball machines and a pool table. Waitresses in white uniforms carried trays of food and drink, taking orders from anyone who wanted something special. There was a lounge area and a bathroom.

My cousin Sal was there, along with Lex and his wife, as well as Ricky Tanzino, who had bought one of the floors and was Ray's neighbor. There were several other brokers I knew from work, and other investors who had put in more money than Lynn and I had. We joined Lex and his wife, Lori, a beautiful blonde like Lynn. The two of them attracted the attention of Donald Trump, who apparently was always on the lookout for new possible conquests. Soon, Trump's bodyguard walked over to speak to Lori and Lynn.

"Hi," he said. "You two ladies are gorgeous and my employer, Mr. Trump," he nodded back over his shoulder and paused for a moment to allow the dramatic impact to sink in, "would like your names and phone numbers."

Lynn and Lori both laughed at the same moment. You could

see from the guy's face that he wasn't used to being laughed at, and Lynn reacted quickly.

"That's terribly sweet," she said with a smile. "But we're both married, and these are our husbands." She looked at me, and at Lex, and Trump's man retreated. I watched him walk back to Donald Trump, and deliver the news. Just a statistic. I actually don't think Trump was out to breakup anyone's relationship.

"Are we supposed to be flattered?" Lynn asked.

"Look at it this way," I said. "He's got good taste and enough sense to hit on the two most beautiful women in the room. He knows a good thing. Maybe that's how he got so rich."

I'm not sure if that came out as the compliment I intended, but it seemed to go over okay. Then I walked back upstairs to use a bathroom. The door was unlocked, but when I walked in, I found one of my fellow rookies at Gruntal sitting with an actress I and just about every other male in the United States was fantasizing about at the time. She had only recently completed starring roles in highly successful movies, and she had the face and figure to draw every eye. She was sitting on the broker's lap while he poured vodka into her mouth and licked her neck whenever the vodka dribbled from her lips. An unexpected and steamy sight. I backed out hastily, and found myself in the bedroom, where Ray was almost naked with two women. It was a party, and I blurted out "Hi, Ray," as casually as I could, not knowing what else to say as I made for the door.

"Hope you're enjoying yourself, Sal," said Ray, ever the gracious host. "Would you like to join us?"

The women waited expectantly, ready either to make room on the bed for a fourth or continue pleasuring their host. I thanked him and returned to Lynn.

It was not just the women or the drugs that impressed me. New York's elite was known for excesses in the privacy of special rooms and eating areas of ultra-exclusive clubs. I knew about the high-class madams who catered to the sex-for-money tastes of Wall Street professionals. But here, I felt as though we had found a culture, a world in which we could belong.

We were Long Island kids from a middle class area, a suburban development kind of place where we'd walk to the 7 Eleven to hang out until we were old enough to drive our cars over to the L dock where everyone would go to show off their hot rods. Neither of us had ever had any reason to believe we'd see big name people except maybe sighting one in the city, or standing in line at some club while the movie stars and other celebrities went in to patronize a private room. We were ordinary people. They were the privileged elite who celebrated birthdays with their friends by taking over a fashionable Manhattan restaurant and closing it to outsiders. Now we were at a party with Donald Trump and Robert DeNiro, with models and business people. These were the people we had read about. These were the people who were photographed and written about. We had become insiders in the world the columnists and tabloid staffs could only glimpse through windows, and it was all because of the world we were in with the club and the money I was making.

The club was an instant success, largely because of the actors and models who made it hot. And because it was hot, it ended up losing money, an eventuality I was able to foresee. Nightclubs are primarily cash businesses. There are also many ways there can be legitimate losses—breakage of champagne bottles, dishes, and the like. Owners abuse their status by bringing in friends and writing off hundreds or thousands of dollars in food and drink tabs. Clubs have other problems as well. Success comes from being part of the latest trend. Bacchus opened to great success on a Thursday through Sunday night basis. The patrons were people who had been at Ray's party, their friends, fellow workers and word-of-mouth couples. When the band Metallica had a new CD release, they wanted to take over the club for an evening to celebrate the release of their new album. Actor Val Kilmer wanted the club to celebrate the premiere of his movie *Thunderheart*.

Monday is a slow night in New York. Theaters are dark Monday and most nightclubs are closed. I decided it would be smart to take advantage of Bacchus' attraction for the rock crowd, and with help from Shel Rubinson's son-in-law Anthony Winters, a rock musician who had become one of my star cold callers, I put together a plan to turn Monday into a special rock night at the club. The other investors approved the idea, which involved a theme that was a fusion of heavy metal, MTV videos, and 1930s MGM musical extravaganzas. On entering the club, you passed through a thick white curtain hung only for the Monday night events. On the other side of the curtain you were greeted by the Monday night maitre d', a midget in top hat and tails. He was an actor who had appeared in several movies, and he was hired for our club through a theatrical agency. After being welcomed by the midget, Monday night guests encountered a cauldron filled with punch, with dry ice emitting a cloud of what looked like steam, along with lava lights, and scantily-clad dancers with live boa constrictors wrapped loosely around their bodies.

The first Monday opened with what seemed like a decent buzz, but it slowed down and by one A.M. it was obvious there weren't enough customers to pay for the evening. I decided to shut it down instead of staying open till three A.M., the scheduled closing hour. I had arranged to pay the midget $250 to stay until three. I gave the instructions to the staff to close up and since I was letting him go home two hours early I hoped our midget maitre d' would agree to a pay cut. I asked him if he would consider settling for $200 instead of $250.

The next thing I know, there's a .25 automatic in his hand and he's pointing it at me. If he were normal height, the gun would have been aimed at my chest. But he was so short that the barrel was pointing at my crotch, threatening my future sex life, all for a lousy fifty bucks. I was sweating instantly. We had bouncers and a security staff that included off-duty cops trained for this kind of thing. As soon as they saw what was happening they were getting ready to jump him, which I knew might make him accidentally pull the trigger.

I carefully turned to the bartender and said, "Give him his $50." My voice was higher than I'd ever heard it. The moment the midget lowered his gun and took the money, one of the off-duty cops grabbed him. It turned out he had a permit to carry the gun. Given his size and work, he was considered at high risk for being mugged. The cop just fieldstripped the gun, taking it apart and handing the pieces back to the midget so he couldn't start shooting. Then they escorted him outside.

Outside it was crazy. Someone who had left the club earlier had apparently overdosed on something and passed out on the sidewalk. Cops were out there with an ambulance and when the midget got outside he was still mad. I don't know what he wanted to do, but he walked across the street and began reassembling his pistol in plain sight of the cops. This time he was arrested and put in jail for the night. The next day the agency called and asked if we wanted our money back. That was the end of Monday night rock-and-roll at the club.

The club only stayed trendy for a year, though it remained open about six months after the patrons changed, and during that time Lynn and I delighted in our part-owner status. We could stop by the club, walk past the people waiting in line, get in, and be seated immediately at the best table available. Everyone knew our names and we enjoyed our VIP treatment. We liked the people we associated with during our time at the club, and one of the key characters we met was a broker named Al Palagonia, who was known as Big Al. Al was also an investor in the club and he had a real appetite for nightlife. He was in the club a lot, often with an entourage.

I was getting the same kind of VIP treatment at work. Willy at Whale took Lynn and me to dinner at the 21 Club in a limo and treated us to great seats at *The Phantom of the Opera*. Shel Robinson flew me to Florida for his daughter's wedding held in a mansion in the same neighborhood with Gloria Estefan, Vanilla Ice, and pro basketball players. It was a Miami, star-filled wedding and the best man was Barry Gibbs' son Steven. Then, as a show of gratitude for the stock I had sold in the IPO, Shel flew me to Poland for the opening of the burger chain store there—from New York to London on the Concorde.

This was my first $100,000 month and I got the benefits of the 500,000 shares of International Fast Foods—its symbol was FOOD. I knew the Concorde as the vehicle of the super-rich, the ultra-achievers, and people so successful that their first names or their faces are known worldwide.

Here I was, a Milanese street kid, flying on the most expensive, fastest, highest-flying passenger plane in the world. I was up in the stratosphere, looking down on the earth like it was a globe. In my heart I had always known this would happen to me. I had always had big dreams, and now they were all coming true.

In Poland we went straight to the burger store for the final preparations. When we got close, the electricity in the air reminded me of the buzz of a rock concert crowd before a major performance. I described a little of it earlier—a line eight people-wide stretched at least a quarter of a mile from the store, a response to our intense marketing blitz. The street was closed, balloons floated in the air. Giant Coca-Cola bottles marked the site. Police were out in force but didn't seem necessary. It was an orderly, family crowd in the heart of Warsaw. There were elderly people and small children and there was no shoving. Everyone was well mannered at what was obviously a major event for them.

I watched with fascination as the food was sold. I had never seen anything like it, but one day in Poland was enough for Shel. We were in the Warsaw counterpart to New York's Fifth Avenue or Beverly Hills' Rodeo Drive, but the big-money neighborhood in Warsaw was more like a high-ticket shopping mall, if even that nice. Shel wanted a "decent" hotel so we flew back to London. I dropped the pictures at a one-hour photo place, and we checked into what Shel considered a civilized hotel room.

I was overwhelmed. The "room" was a massive suite with every luxury, including my own butler and pre-printed business cards with my name and suite number. All I had to do was ring to get food, drink, have my shoes shined and my clothing cleaned and pressed—24 hours a day. It was lavish service I had never before encountered, and I loved it. Then we flew back to New York on the Concorde.

On the flight back, Shel talked about his life, about his successes and failures. I told him about growing up in Sicily and Milan and coming to America. He was more than twice my age, and his adventures had made him a very rich man. My life had just begun, and he had given me my first real success. Shel told me the story of the scorpion and the frog. I didn't know why. I just listened, not sure what his meaning might be. All I knew for certain was that Shel was "the man." I was going to stick with him, work with him, and learn from him. He was my Gordon Gekko, truly my whale.

Then there was some unexpected music. As we talked, one passenger uncased a guitar and began playing and singing. I thought I recognized the voice, and looked over and saw I was right. It was George Harrison, one of the surviving Beatles and he was singing a duet with Elton John.

We landed in New York at nine A.M. and I went right to Whale by limo and dropped the pictures I had taken on Dicky's desk so he could see what a success the opening had been. All of us, Willy included, were certain we had a winner. But Dicky and I were what was called the axe in the stock: we had all the public stock, which means we had to buy it when it was for sale, moving it among our clients. Other brokers were willing to support it to a certain extent but eventually they would all sell it back to us and it was far from being liquid yet.

When Shel set out to do another round of financing, he knew he had my momentum and enthusiasm behind him to rally everybody in the firm on the next big winner: our junk bond offering to raise money to open up the chain of 14 franchise burger joints in Poland ahead of schedule. It only took us two weeks to raise $11 million for the secondary deal. We sold it based on our enthusiasm and the photography of the mob scene in Warsaw, and Shel had $17 million to finance his Eastern European restaurant chain.

It made me the acknowledged leader of the rookies with my own office, my own cold callers, and a secretary. I was developing an alliance with up-and-coming younger brokers and becoming close friends with a guy named John Sciascia. John was a hotshot broker, the only one who could beat me in a contest Whale ran to see who could open the most accounts in a month. The prize was $5,000 and John won it by opening 149 accounts to my 147. John was a truly gifted liar who could sell anyone anything, even after a stock dropped. He was also incredibly handsome and we used to call him the Velcro Man because of the way pretty girls stuck to him at the clubs we went to. He was a real party guy.

Another influence was Radcliff Bent, Caribbean by birth and black as night with the private-school accent of someone who was raised in houses his parents owned throughout the world. He sounded Ivy League and took advantage of that. He explained that his first name was pronounced like the famous women's counterpart to Harvard.

"Radcliff," he'd say in his marvelous accent. "Like Harvard, sir."

Radcliff had a telephone manner that not only made you trust him, but also made you think he was a genius and probably related to some guy who ran a major corporation. He oozed success, not from luck but from learning about all the businesses whose stock he was selling. His clients felt he was sharing his wisdom with them, and that trust enabled him to work only two or three hours a day. Despite the short hours, it was rare that he went home with less than $10,000 to $15,000.

There were other characters. Terence Pfizer had been involved in the big Milken scandal, and had cooperated with the authorities. Mason Sexton was an eccentric who used astrology to predict the market and made a big reputation for predicting the crash of 1987. After that, he began marketing his predictions in a newsletter that sold for an outrageous subscription fee to people who were also his customers. He taught me many of his theories, and while I never figured out if the guy believed in his system or was just another hustler, some of his ideas worked or at least lucked out. All these people gave me my first glimpse of what Wall Street was really about, through the eyes of the small cap world. It was far different from what I had imagined.

CHAPTER EIGHT

13. The Enterprise furthered its unlawful purposes by means of various criminal activities, including securities fraud, mail and wire fraud, money laundering and conspiracy to commit these offenses.

14. The enterprise was led by the defendants JOHN DOUKAS and WALTER DURCHALTER, together with Gene Klotsman, Salvatore Lauria and Lex Tersa, who collectively controlled White Rock and State Street during the periods set forth above. The defendants JACK BASILE, ROCCO BASILE and JOSEPH TEMPERINO were brokers at White Rock who fraudulently sold stock to investors. The defendant JOHN CIOFOLETTI was allotted blocks of stock which were fraudulently sold to clients of Barclay. The defendant ALFRED PALAGONIA, together with Andrew Bressman, was allotted blocks of stock which were fraudulently sold to clients of Blair and Baron. The defendants ABRAHAM SALAMAN, LARRY BERMAN and JOSEPH POLITO, SR. through affiliations with Country World, Holly and USBNY, provided "product," that is securities, for White Rock, State Street, Barclay, Baron, Blair and other brokerage firms to sell to the public fraudulently.

Further Education of a Broker:
Learning the Game's Secrets

At Whale I learned how little most brokers know about the business-es they're representing as traders. Investors like to think that brokers have access to research or up-to-the-minute information that will give them at least an informed perspective. They like to think that brokerage houses assign staff researchers to pour over technical journals or reports on the areas that the stocks are involved in. Investors would like to think, even though it might stretch the rules if it were true, that brokers had access to insider information that would put them ahead of the general public.

But the fact is, most brokers know less about a stock than the average buyer can learn from the newspaper or a corporate web site. A broker's job is to move the product, and the more successful a bro-ker becomes, the less time he has to do any market studies. At Whale, though, there actually was a source of information that was unusual and wasn't generally available. Dicky had found a night watchman in the building where *Business Week* was kept after print-ing, but before distribution to the newsstands. He would pay the guy $100 to give him a copy of the magazine a few hours before anyone else could read it. If there was a negative story about a stock, Dicky knew the price would go down. A positive story would push the stock price up. Having that slight edge improved his profits for the day.

The office I had was oversized and the space outside was tight, so I had to share it with a veteran broker named Sammy Galantz. An uncommonly skinny man, Sammy had once owned his own boiler-room operation. He had been a competitive body-builder. He had made and kept millions, then sought a quieter lifestyle because of a nagging, draining lack of energy that was finally diag-nosed as HIV. Sammy wasn't gay, and there were two stories about how Sammy got AIDS, both involving dirty needles. One was that Sammy got infected during his bodybuilding days by sharing a nee-dle with the wrong man to inject steroids. A second story was that Sammy had begun using almost anything you could swallow, smoke, or inject. I tended to believe that one because there were so many drug addicts among men and women on the Street. By the time I knew him, it didn't matter. Sammy was dying.

One of our colleagues across the hall, Joe Arsinal, got rich on just one IPO by waiting it out. He had been a broker at D.H. Blair and had done a deal there where he owned a million shares of a stock that had failed as an IPO. The stock had traded for a year at pennies. Then the company had an event that caused the stock to go to $10. Arsinal sold it over a period of a few days, bought a yellow Ferrari and drove it to Whale to resign.

Sammy wanted to score the same way and realized he had nothing to lose. He planned to leave to go on his own one more time before he died. He had already taught me the intricacies of the game, helping me to understand many legal and illegal intricacies that I could not have discovered on my own. He was going to use the tricks himself to see how much he could rake in. He didn't care if he violated SEC regulations or committed crimes, since he would be dead long before anyone might send him to jail.

After Sammy left, Jack Alaire came in with me. He was another mentor, who did a lot of business with international clients, working with Reg S stock and regularly calling money managers in Switzerland and Scandinavia. I didn't understand what he did, but I was learning. Whale was so small that individual specialists were happy to share their offbeat information.

But overall, I learned the most from Dicky. He taught me a completely different approach to the market from the one I had learned from Brock Samith in my first job at Gruntal. Samith believed in building a position. Samith would find a blue chip stock and build a big position in it, then find a NASDAQ stock with a million shares he could buy, with a 50-cent chop, meaning a percentage for him, on each share. The blue chip company could be a well-known corporation with a prominent history, like Upjohn. Brock would put together a good story to make it an attractive buy for clients. The story would be, say, that Upjohn had a new product called Rogaine in the pipeline, which was going to be a huge success, and the stock was a good buy now. His goal would be to sell a total of 200,000 shares to various clients, priced in the mid-30s, and he would get his cold callers to help do that. It takes him months to accomplish it, and during the time, he charts his progress toward the goal with a bar graph on his desk.

By the time he'd moved 200,000 shares of Upjohn to clients, he'd made $50,000 in commissions. Then, he looked for a cheap stock, most likely a small cap stock trading on NASDAQ, that paid a bigger commission. For example, it could be Rally Hamburgers, a $7 stock. Brock presented a story about why Rally Hamburgers was the stock for his clients to buy, and convinced them, again with help from his cold callers that they should sell their Upjohn and buy Rally. He made another $50,000 commission getting them out of Upjohn, but the commission going into Rally was a much bigger one: it paid him $500,000.

That's called bait-and-switch, and though it may flout the intent of trading rules, there is nothing illegal about it, and that was the approach I learned from Brock. At Whale though, with Dicky, it was a different ballgame.

"We build our own stocks," Dicky told me. "We own the float." This was the small cap world—the game of small capitalization start-ups in what is known as thinly-traded stock. This was stock that, instead of being issued in the dozens of millions like a brand-name stock, might come to the market with only a million shares issued. There are no analysts behind the issue, nobody touting it, and nobody but us floating it and supporting it. The Polish fast-food franchise was an example of a thinly-traded stock that we supported as an IPO, and in which we owned every one of the 1,000,000 shares issued.

"Owning the float" doesn't mean that you technically own every share. But it means that your company received the entire issue of stock, to sell each and every share. There are syndication rules that force the lead underwriter to give 30 percent of the float to the Street, hopefully in good hands. That means you know where every share is that's in the public's hands because you sold it to them. It's essential that you keep track of every one of those shares because anytime shares come up for sale, you have to be able to make sure there are enough buyers to support the stock at that level.

What you don't want is to see that IPO stock go back on the fully-open market. Whale couldn't tell me not to sell a client's IPO stock when the client asks me to, but there is an unwritten rule to try not to do it. With a lot of the stock, a company like Whale that issues the IPO, is also the only market. Say you took a brand new little company public at $5 a share in an IPO that raised them $5 million. They need a year or two to wrap up their business plan and be desirable. If the stock runs into trouble along the way, the company can be ruined. The rule on the street is that buying begets buying. If the public learns there are no buyers for a stock, everyone will dump their shares. So if somebody wants to sell 50,000 shares and you can't convince them to hold them, you have to find a buyer for them even if you have to go "in house" and ask the brokers next to you to go to their clients and get them to buy more.

The problem is when the owner of a stock decides to sell it through a broker not connected with your company. That broker has no reason to try and keep the price up. If it's offered at $8 a share and he sells it down to $4, he doesn't care. It's not his house that's going to have his book blown up. He'll make the deal and take the commission. For us it was so crucial to keep the price supported, we would try to avoid selling shares to someone we didn't believe was going to hang onto them, because if the shares came back on the market, their availability would threaten the value of all the other shares.

Eventually the stocks that made it for those first couple of years may become stable. They get analyst tracking and a lot of firms make a market in the stock, buying and selling it for their customers. Part of my first-year success at Whale came from the fact that Whale Securities was a boutique operation that offered what is called "bridge" or "mezzanine"—less than standard—financing to companies going public. As much money as I would make from selling IPO stock, I was about to learn about a way to make many times as much, to go from making hundreds of thousands of dollars on a deal to making millions. I was about to learn the real inside of Wall Street, the world in which insiders manipulate and profit without becoming known.

After making out on the second-round financing of Shel's Polish burger-chain franchise, Hickman handed me and Dicky a deal on a company called Saliva Diagnostics. They had a new technology to give instant results of an HIV test on saliva that would not need refrigeration. Great idea, particularly for those large areas of the world where there aren't any working refrigerators, even in hospitals. Dicky and I took the deal and did an IPO and made a ton of money on it. We each took a couple of hundred thousand out of it in commissions and things were looking great. Dicky and I are pals, just like he said we would be, and he was the only guy I really trusted at Whale. Every day we would leave the office to take a walk to the Rock on Sixth Ave and 52nd St. Dicky could smoke weed while we walked. Everybody knew about his habit, but nobody cared, since he was such a winning stockbroker. Many things were tolerated when you were a big producer.

Hickman loved Dicky and he really liked me. He paid for a masseuse to give me a massage on a day I was particularly tense. I admired what Hickman had done in his career and I appreciated the magnitude of the money being made in the small end of Wall Street. I had money in the bank and it was coming in faster than I could have imagined. The market itself was great, going higher every day. The firm had gone through its bear raid, and that was in the past. This was our run. Hickman just handed me my first deal where I would be the lead broker and I was happy. This really put me in the same league as Dicky, in only a year-and-a-half.

Then I get a phone call that would change my life. It was from Lex Tersa, whom I had hardly seen since the terrible-wonderful night of the party at the Rio Grande to celebrate my passing the broker's test, and the fight that ended Lex's career. Lex was facing prison time for that fight, with a sentencing date coming up, and he could never work as a broker again. But he was doing deals with his friend Gene Klotsman, and they had something they wanted to talk to me about.

Lex was working with Gene at a company called Westfield, which was run by a friend of Gene's, and they had a proposition for me. They wanted to know if I wanted stock in Candies Shoes, a company Whale had taken public six months earlier. The IPO hadn't been a big one but it did well because everybody knew the shoes. Candies produced what we called "fuck me" shoes. They were so cheap you could buy a pair for a special evening, then throw them away and not care. It was a good line in a market segment that always did well.

The stock was at $4 when Lex called. He said he was working unofficially, being a little vague because, as I said, he couldn't legally be involved with stock. He told me that he had 200,000 shares I could sell at $2.25, with 75 cents a share in it for me. Therefore, I could buy each share for $1.50. Of course, Lex was making money on the deal, so he had the stock for even less. This meant that the stock was being bid at $4 and Lex had 200,000 shares at $2.25—$1.75 under bid. I had a chance to sell it for $4 a share and make $350,000 on the deal. That was not going to be easy, and I figured the whole thing was illegal, but Lex told me it wasn't. He said it was Reg S stock, something I hadn't known much about before his call, though my desk partner Jack Alaire was dabbling in it.

Regulation S stock, as I touched on earlier, is stock that is considered a restricted security when issued. It might be stock owned by one of the principals in the business prior to its going public, or stock provided to the person handling the bridge financing of the IPO, or just newly issued stock of the company. Whichever, it is stock that cannot be sold in the United States for 13 to 24 months. However, under Reg S, the stock can be sold overseas, and then sold back in the U.S.

The Reg S rule was set up so companies could sell some shares directly to an investor, bypassing the brokerage firm. The regulators understood that there were times when an IPO launch was followed by a need to raise additional fast cash to keep the company afloat until it stabilized and began to grow. Reg S also gave us the ability to buy stock cheaper without going to the market and driving the price higher. But it was not meant to be abused. It was designed so a million shares of Microsoft for example, could be sold at a quarter below the market for legitimate reasons. But we brokers used it as a tool to be able to give additional financing or liquidity to companies that didn't have it, sometimes for highly doubtful purposes.

The appeal of Reg S purchases and sales was overwhelming for me. I did not yet understand all aspects of what was taking place and I did not know that money laundering was likely to be involved. What I understood was that the stock would get sold back into the United States and the money would be deposited in an account for wire transfer back to Europe after the trade passed through the clearinghouse. Now the money would sit in Europe tax-free, generally in a country picked as a haven, such as the Isle of Man, Curacao, Liechtenstein, or Switzerland. Once the stock was in the overseas account, you could sell it at the end of 41 days for whatever you could get for it. Then you would have cash back that you could disburse to the people you wanted to take care of—the people who helped you sell it. The problem was getting the cash back into the United States tax-free. I didn't know how it was done, but I understood that if I could make the deal, I would get cash out of it. Lex and Gene's plan involved a friend and former business partner who was a master of Reg S. He had set up an overseas account that he used to buy the restricted stock he owned, either under his own name, or through an overseas corporation.

At first I was hesitant. I hadn't sold much of the stock to my clients so I really didn't care if the price went down. In Wall Street language, I would have said I didn't "own" much of the stock. When I hesitated, it was because I had not sold much of the stock to my A and B Book customers. The repercussions from the 200,000 shares flooding the market which had a million shares in the float would be substantial. The stock would go down, but none of my customers had bought enough to be hurt in any meaningful way. Portfolio gains from their other holdings would more than offset any loss.

Other brokers at Whale "owned" far more shares of Candies Shoes, and some of their customers would be hurt badly by a drop in the price. I went to notify Hickman, the owner of the firm. I told him there was some stock around on Candies that we could buy below the market and put it out. I said we could buy it at $3, allotting myself another $.75 a share beyond what I was getting in the deal with Lex. I would make $1.50 a share on the deal—$300,000—just for me. And if the firm bought it for $3, they could put it out at $4, making a dollar on the trading desk for the firm—$200,000—plus a commission for the brokers who sold it. It was perfect. My mind was racing with different trading schemes. Wall Street is a land of accounting nightmares where everybody paid off everyone else and no one questioned side deals with which they were involved. I let the owner think about the offer.

To my surprise, Hickman was immediately hostile.

"No, I'm not interested," Hickman said. "I'm pissed at the son-of-a-bitch for doing this. I don't want the stock." He was talking about the chairman of Candies.

Okay, I thought, I would find someone else, and I would be more aggressive. I knew that 200,000 shares being dumped on the market with no controls, at a price well under the market value, would destroy the value of the stock. I knew they could sell the stock down to $1.50 and still make a profit, and I thought a reminder of this fate would be leverage enough to make the deal.

I went to another broker at Whale who had a big position in Candies and pitched the deal to him, telling him if he didn't buy it, he would get hit by it and hurt. By that I meant that the clients he had sold it to would take losses when the stock's value dropped because of the shares being dumped.

"You own most of it, and it's in your best interest to buy it," I told him.

He asked what Hickman's position was and when I told him Hickman wasn't buying it, he said that if Hickman had said no, then he would say no, too.

I told him that was stupid.

"You know, we could make some money here," I told him. "We could buy it below the bid if you put it out to your clients and make a buck on the inside. Or on the trading desk. And there's the regular commission on top of that!"

He wouldn't go for it. I was frustrated, but the lure of cash kept me going. I knew that if I could get a broker interested, I wouldn't have to personally take and hustle any of the stock to my clients. I would get his cash for the difference between the $1.50 and whatever price I could convince the in-house broker to give me. Finally I found the person in the form of a banker who was a new hire at the company. His name was Dan Tellach and he came from a hugely wealthy family. You know, trust fund baby, educated in England, perfect accent, perfect posture. He had the look of someone who had mastered Wall Street and finance. At lunch I told him I could get a big block of the stock and he said he was interested. I asked how much he wanted.

"I'll buy the whole block," he said.

I said I could get it for him cheap, and then told him the good part:

"I could give you green on this," I said. For some reason I felt I could trust him and added what Lex had told me, "We get paid in cash for this."

Taking cash payment for selling stock is illegal, but there it was. It seemed to make Dan hesitate, and then smile, but it didn't stop him. He said he wanted to do it, and we put the deal through with him buying the whole piece at $3.25 a share. I only gave $.25 a share, which came to $50,000 for him, and kept the difference for myself. It worked out like this: 200,000 shares at $1.50 equals $300,000—in cash. Wow! The deal had been made so casually that I didn't fully realize what had taken place until a week later, when Lex called me to come see him. He had 35 stacks of $100 bills, each stack worth $10,000. Five of the stacks were for Dan. The remaining 30 were for me.

I walked out of there with $300,000 in cash in a brown paper bag. It was as much money as if I had grossed $1,200,000 in commissions because then I'd have had to split it with Whale and also pay the IRS. This money was mine to do what I wanted with it. I hadn't bought any stock. I hadn't made any trades. I had just arranged a deal on Reg S stock that Lex and Gene came up with and that Dan passed on to his clients.

I took the money home and laid it on the bed—Three hundred-thousand dollars! When Lynn came in and looked at it she just freaked out.

"Is it illegal?" Lynn asked. She had never seen money like that before.

"Slightly," I admitted. "We have this client who can't pay straight up and can't pay the commission the right way. He has to pay in cash and this is my share."

We both understood that I had crossed a line. I had violated Wall Street rules and actually committed a crime, even though no one had gotten hurt except some unknowing investors down the line. But we knew our lives would never be the same. This was gravy on top of the seriously good money that I was making legitimately—my first year's aftertax take-home pay was around $300,000.

Since we couldn't take the Candies' cash to the bank to deposit, we bought a safe for the apartment and put the money in there. Then we set out to upgrade our lifestyle, although not in an attention-getting way. Our 32-inch color television set went into the bedroom, to be replaced in the living room with a 60-inch Sony and top of the line Sony rack stereo system that cost approximately $10,000. We redid the bedroom and bought a new couch. We bought signed Salvador Dali limited edition prints to hang on the walls, not knowing that they, like so much else in our lives, might be fakes.

We were already living well on what I was earning. We ate out a lot, and that just continued. We bought a new SUV. We were still partners in the club and continued going there. The money bought things we'd always wanted for our apartment, and we had enough cash in the safe to cover anything unexpected. And even though I had made dirty money with Lex and Gene on this, I had turned down their offer to go into business. Not only did I dislike the idea of more shady dealings but I didn't think I needed them and their manipulations. Hickman had just given me a chance to launch a recycling company IPO which I was going to handle completely on my own. I was proud of the arrangement. It was a company I was going to help take public and make several hundred thousand dollars on.

Lex and Gene knew about the deal, and they wanted me to bring the "Red Herring" for it and let them go over it with me. I was surprised. Red Herrings contain the basic information that will be in the prospectus for a deal that's going to go public. I had looked over Red Herrings without trying to make sense of them because there had been no reason to. We told our clients they were documents written by lawyers for lawyers. I was making good money selling the deals, and the inside goings-on behind the scene didn't concern me. But Lex and Gene were insistent that they had stuff I needed to know, so I agreed to meet them.

Lex said I should come over to the Hotel Pierre, a luxury hotel near Central Park in the East Sixties. He was there with Gene in the suite owned by Beno Eton, an Italian citizen who was Arabic by birth. Eton was a seriously wealthy and powerful man with a house in Houston, a two-bedroom condo at the Pierre, an apartment in Milan, and an office in Lugano, Switzerland, just over the Italian border. He operated as the American representative for all manner of individuals, several of whom had been indicted or gone to jail. He worked from Switzerland so he could do deals that would be illegal over here, hiding or manipulating money in ways that did not matter there. That's why he could move so freely around the world while people he worked with went to jail.

I wasn't thinking of the criminal acts related to Beno. I just knew the name, knew he was rich, and knew he was the kind of guy we'd all kill to get in our A Books. I told Lex I'd be over and told Lynn I needed to go out on business. She didn't like my going out, but she had gotten used to the hours I put in. Besides, meeting someone at the Pierre couldn't be anything else but business. The two-bedroom condo probably cost over a million dollars. This guy might be a part of our financial future.

I hadn't changed yet from work so I was a little grungy, but there wasn't time to change. Besides, my Wall Street grunge looked better than 90 percent of the guys on the street, so I didn't worry. I went inside, and there were Lex, with Gene, the financier Beno Eton, and his right hand man Edmond Nagel. Al Nagel was known for making a lot of money for people involved in junk bond schemes and other high-risk ventures in the Milken crowd. Nagel was an original. He had millions and lived in a Sutton Place penthouse, but he'd check wastebaskets in offices where he had meetings and if he found someone had thrown away part of a sandwich, he'd take it out of the trash and eat it.

Al would never take money from you for consulting. He was happy if you bought him a *Wall Street Journal* and took him to lunch. All he asked was to be allowed to invest in the deals he liked, and if he liked the deal it would make money for sure. That night, when I walked into this sumptuous hotel apartment with Chesterfield-style furniture along with everything indicating money, I saw Al as a player in the business to be discussed. Food arrived at 10 o'clock direct from the hotel kitchen, and it was impressive.

Another guest that evening was Abraham Salaman, a big business manipulator who was powerful and had made deals with Gene in the past. Abe was introduced to me as the "shell master," the man at the top of the small cap game. I didn't understand what that meant, but I was about to find out. My advanced education began when Lex and Gene asked me to show them the Red Herring that I had brought from Whale, presenting the details of my current deal.

Gene was the one who did the explaining and educating, conferring with Al periodically. Gene was very convincing when he was explaining intricate and complicated points, and in my experience, he was a one-of-a-kind financial guy. Like Lex, Gene was a Russian Jew from Brighton Beach. He had a whiny voice without a trace of accent and was so overweight he could be Stan Laurel of Laurel and Hardy. He always wore a bow tie and said his motto was "Dress British, think Yiddish."

Like Lex, Gene was mutually drawn to any kind of scam, and seemed to have a genius for finding loopholes nobody else could see. At least, that's the way Lex sold him to me as a potential partner. Not that Gene didn't have an impressive history in the business. He had made full partnership in a huge firm, going right to the top at 23. He had made millions, started his own firm, and sold it for millions more while he was still in his 20s. He had been married, had a child, and could have lived on the interest for the rest of his life.

But not Gene. Instead, he squandered a fortune on fast living, limos, champagne, private rooms at fancy restaurants and clubs, and hookers. Hookers were Gene's obsession and I mean obsession. He was never satisfied with one prostitute at a time. He had to have two, and they had to be beautiful, which meant they were expensive. That's also how he became an ex-husband for the third time. What was completely crazy about Gene and his hooker habit was that he loved to brag to prostitutes! He actually paid high-class hookers to listen to him boast about how much money he made, and of course they were paid to pretend they were impressed. Go figure that one. I can't.

But Gene definitely knew the game. He had won big and lost

big, having done one IPO where he ran the stock from $5 to $17 a share then got wiped out when he was shorted down to zero. So he lost all his money and his firm in one day, and to top it off, passed out at his desk from a stroke, so the story goes, and took a year off. Now Lex and Gene were working together at Westfield and they'd already made me a lot of money with the shoe deal. Gene began to show me what should be in the Red Herring for my latest venture.

He advised me that three months before I was going to take it public, a Manhattan art dealer had bought 725,000 shares of the stock for three hundred grand. It was a rich loan to the company. The stock price was 41 cents a share. At the time that I was shown what was coming down, each share was going public at $7. This meant that the holdings represented by the $300,000 seed money had a market value of $5,075,000 at the IPO price, and would be worth much more once the stock was manipulated up. That three hundred grand was, in practice a bridge loan to pay the legal fees for it to go public.

The beautiful part of a bridge loan was that you got your original money back the moment the company went public. And for that loan you were paid in stock as your interest on the loan. The risks were if it didn't go public you could lose the loan. Nevertheless, this was the way for the underwriter and his friends or best clients to almost certainly get in on a bigger percentage of the company than was allowed by the SEC.

Wall Street and American regulations only allowed you to take out twenty-four percent of a company, whether it's cash, stock, or whatever. Otherwise it was usury. But companies with ideas that looked like high-risk ventures were willing to give you 70 percent because they were so anxious to prove themselves right that some didn't care about the money. They just wanted their business to go public so they could show everyone what geniuses they were. One answer to this problem was to give the stock they could part with to a friend, a beard, and a nominee.

In this case, the art dealer presumably was the brokerage nominee, and Lex and Gene pointed out to me that what I was going to do was to raise $7 million through the IPO and foolishly give it to some CEO, "a guy you don't even know." That put my lights on fast. I hadn't thought of the deal that way, but it made sense. And it made me mad. We were talking about the IPO offering to the public; usually a fifth of the stock issued—one million shares at seven dollars per share, the other four million shares staying within the company and with the beard of the underwriter.

"You're going to support this stock for a year," Gene told me, "and the art dealer will be able to get out with 700,000 shares in 13 months. Five million dollars at the current price, but most likely higher. And all you're going to get is a commission of, what, four, five hundred thousand?"

He was right. I would just be making commission while Willy and the art dealer would get millions. And so would the CEO whose IPO it was. It made me mad and disgusted at the same time. I felt like I was being rooked, big-time, and I knew, without having to look (although I did later), that the prospectus of other deals would show that I had been suckered the same way by Shel Robinson at Whale. I saw where Robinson had been the scorpion, playing me as the frog. Now I understand the story that he told me on the Concorde.

I felt like a fool. Here I had raised ten, fifteen million for him, and what did I make? I had half a million in the bank. There were people walking around with really thick checkbooks that I created for them. I was furious, and I wished that a banker had educated me and not a Russian stock scammer.

I didn't have the time to stay angry about it, though, because at 11 o'clock, two women came to the door and changed the evening. They were blonde, Russians, stunningly beautiful, with faces and figures that I thought were perfect. Gene went to the door and spoke Russian to them and they answered in Russian, smiled, and sat down on the couch with him, one sitting on each side, touching him. You have to understand that Gene was not a handsome guy. Besides being overweight with a round face, he wore computer-geek glasses, and no matter what he spent on clothing, he always looked like one of those "before" pictures for a fashion makeover story. Here was this guy sitting on the couch with these two women looking like they were devoted to him.

I figured they were Gene's dates for the evening. If they were hookers, they didn't look like any hookers I'd ever seen. They looked like they could be walking down Hollywood Boulevard and some director would drive up and cast them in a movie. Then, without saying anything, Beno got up, went into the bathroom and turned on the shower and the girls got up and followed him. Al started to walk around the room nervously with a smile like he was going to be next, but no one would let him. It was weird. After a period of time we heard them leave the bathroom for the bedroom, and the rest of us ate, drank and talked while whatever was going on was happening in the bedroom.

"They'll stay all night if you want them," Lex told me. "Cook you breakfast in the morning."

"These girls are different from the ones Gina has," Lex said, referring to an escort service run by a woman named Gina, who catered to Wall Street businessmen from an apartment on 32nd Street. "These girls are from former Communist bloc countries who are doing what they can to survive comfortably." They were multi-lingual and extremely bright in addition to being beautiful. Their clientele were primarily brokers, and most of the girls were conservative investors in the market who relied on the brokers' tips to build their portfolios.

The women and Beno were still in one of the bedrooms when I realized it was time to go home and I stood up about the same time that Beno came out. He was flawlessly dressed, smiling, and obviously exhausted. The girls came out and sat next to Lex.

Gene held up his glass and said, "One for the road, Sal?"

He didn't mean a drink. He meant the girls, but the way he said it, I could say no, which I did, without embarrassing the girls. I went home thinking very hard about what Gene and Lex had shown me about the deals I was doing. I had earned $700,000 in total gross commission on my last deal, out of which half would go to taxes. Then there was the split with the brokerage house, which gave me a take home net of $220,000—if I did the IPO stock sales straight.

But Hickman would make somewhere between $10 million and $15 million on the same deal once he pumped up the price and sold it. When confronted by those numbers, I knew I didn't want to be only a broker in somebody else's firm anymore. The offer Lex and Gene had made for me to join them looked better and better. They had told me they wanted to use Westfield as a platform to launch their own brokerage firm and I decided to join them as a partner.

We formed it with a fourth partner named Walter "Dutch" Durchalter, who had been my cousin's desk cohort at Shearson. I hoped I might be able to stay at Whale and raise money for the new business from there, but if I couldn't, I was resolved to leave. I knew I wanted to take companies public, do the bridge financing and make millions instead of hundreds of thousands.

I had discussed it with Dicky, who told me, "You want to watch out for that guy Gene," Dicky said. "I wouldn't trust him as far as I could throw him. I don't like him, either."

That was nothing new. It was pretty much a given that people didn't like Gene. But I believed he knew things we needed, so he was going to be a partner. Instead of asking for permission to raise money for my own business, I told Hickman I planned to resign in two weeks. I knew my value to the firm and figured that if I put pressure on my boss, I might get a more flexible arrangement. But Hickman had already found out that I had started my own outfit, probably from Dicky, and he beat me to the resignation announcement.

"I heard that you want to do your own thing," Hickman said.

"Yes," I told him. "I think I'm ready for that."

"What do you mean, ready?" Hickman asked. "You've only been a broker a year and a half."

I told him I really wanted to take my own companies public. I said I thought I could raise money. He asked what it would take to make me stay. I answered:

"Hickman, I want to be you."

"What do you mean?" he answered. "You can't be me. I'm me."

"Well, I want to be you. I want to be the guy with the book."

"Well here, I'm the guy with the book," he said, "you know what I mean? You know what, Sal? You can stay here two more weeks, then I want you out. I don't want you to do something to the firm. And by the way, who are going to be your partners in this firm?"

I told him Gene.

"'Gene?'" Hickman asked. "Gene used to work here. He's going to get you in trouble, that guy."

There it was again. An echo of what Dicky had said.

I asked Hickman what he meant.

"Gene has a reputation. He's a cowboy who takes too many risks."

"Hickman, this is my chance to own my firm and be on the other side of the business," I said. "I want to take companies public."

"You've got two weeks notice," Hickman said.

I thought it was gentlemanly of him to give me two weeks rather than fire me on the spot. When a broker leaves, it's customary to divvy up his book and try to take away his clients. I gave my book to Dicky and he did not call my clients. He left them with me. When the two weeks were over, I was able to devote all my time to the new venture, which we had named White Rock Partners. The name came to me as we were driving by the offices of the prestigious Blackstone Group. We had filed papers to open a registered business but we couldn't operate until we were officially approved by NASD—the National Association of Securities Dealers.

Before we began, we had to raise capital, and we agreed to each contribute $500,000, except for Lex to whom we gave a free ride to get in because he had no book to call. Gene and I both got multiple investors—$100,000 from one person, $200,000 from another, and more from a third, until each of us had contributed our $500,000 to the pot. Dutch found a wealthy New England banker who believed in our new firm's potential to the extent that he put up the full $500,000 for one partner.

The investors all understood the same risks and possible rewards. They were each providing at least $100,000 to a trusted broker with whom they had past dealings, the money assuring them the first stock in each IPO launched. Based on past experience, they knew that a moderately successful IPO would bring them a stock value increase that could net them as much as $1,000,000 when they sold their holdings at the earliest possible time. This would be an opportunity that would not exist for other investors. Ours were located throughout the United States, and not all the past deals had been successful. But what seemed to matter was that we shared a dream, shared the greed, and these investors believed they would be taken care of because they were the bedrock of the new business.

CHAPTER NINE

"The frauds generally worked this way: (1) My other partners and I got secret ownership and control over large blocks of stock and warrants in these companies, not disclosed to the public; (2) My partners and I then made secret payoffs to brokers at Grand Liberty...and other firms, and other people, to sell this stock and warrants, and these payments were also not disclosed to the public; (3) we sold our stock and warrants at inflated prices, generating substantial profits; and (4) we then concealed our profits, and promoted the ongoing stock fraud, by wiring the proceeds of stock and warrant sales through off-shore accounts and obtaining large sums of cash, which we could then use to continue our fraudulent stock sales...."—FROM THE CONFESSION OF SAL LAURIA.

Grand Jury Indictment, continued:

The Unlawful Schemes:
From March 1993 to October 1996, the White Rock and State Street Partners, together with the defendants FRANK COPPA, SR., ERNEST MONTEVECCHI, DANIEL PERSICO, JACK BASILE, ROCCO BASILE, LARRY BERMAN, JOHN CIOFOLETTI, JOHN DOUKAS, WALTER DURCHALTER, DANIEL LEV, EUGENE LOMBARDO, EDMOND NAGEL, ALFRED PALAGONIA, ALEKS PAUL, JOSEPH POLITO, SR., LAWRENCE RAY, ABRAHAM SALAMAN AND JOSEPH TEMPERINO, and others, devised, implemented and oversaw fraudulent schemes to manipulate the price of securities of Country World, Holly, USBNY, and Cable and fraudulently induced investors to buy and hold these securities. Each of the fraudulent schemes followed a similar pattern.

The Birth of White Rock: Four Guys in a Jeep

White Rock started with just four guys with phones in a Jeep. We had $1.5 million start-up capital in the bank but we didn't have our office because our NASD license hadn't come through. Until it did, our "brokerage house" was on the four wheels of my white Jeep Grand Cherokee, rolling through the streets of the city. We'd rendezvous every morning after rush hour, connect by cell phone and I'd pick the other guys up wherever they'd parked. Then they'd get in, we'd all light up and start the day's vagabond business. I drove and Lex rode shotgun with Gene and Dutch in back.

I'd be on the phone and someone would ask where our office was and I'd look up at the street sign.

"We're located at 57th and Sixth," I'd say, since that was the intersection where we were stopped at a light. We would be talking on four separate cell calls, which must have looked odd to anyone looking at us. It may have actually sounded like an office. The Jeep would smell of cigarette smoke and sweat and we'd move all day. We'd drop off whoever had a meeting, then pick him up when he was done. I might leave Dutch with the attorney and drive Lex to a commercial leasing agent. Then Gene and I would go to Kinko's to get a presentation ready. If someone was looking for a meeting, I'd tell him we were moving downtown, and when we were interviewing employees we had to meet them in hotels until we finally lined up our space. We finally decided on the tip of the city a few blocks from Wall Street, at 17 State Street in a building where all our windows overlooked the Statue of Liberty.

As partners in White Rock, we—except for Lex—were applying to become broker-dealers. That status would let us work through stock exchanges and the National Association of Securities Dealers (NASD). We would have to meet all state and federal licensing requirements, which is why we had Gene working with the lawyers. As brokers who had studied the laws and passed our tests, we were assumed to be fully aware of the rules. That was why we were all too aware we were committing crimes with some of our deals. But the way we saw it, no one that mattered to us was getting hurt, the big firms got away with it, and if our people made a little extra under the table, they worked hard for it. So we just didn't care about the legalities.

The basics were that selling someone a share of common stock gives that person equity ownership in the company. A new technique at the IPO was to attach warrants to the common stock because they could be used to get extra money for the issuing company at a later date. A warrant gives the buyer the right to buy a share of common stock at a specific date for a specific price. When a broker sells a stock with the warrants attached, it's called a "unit." But we'd usually strip the warrants from the stock and sell them separately in order to reward the buyers: us.

Stock and some other securities can be sold either through the stock exchange or over the counter (OTC). An over-the-counter stock is sold by broker-dealers who declare themselves "market makers" for that stock. The market makers establish price quotes and declare to the public that they are ready and able to buy and sell certain quantities of the stock, or other securities, for their own account at the price quoted. The NASDAQ is one such market. It is administered by the NASD and subject to self-regulatory actions within federal laws. In a case of the fox watching the hen house, the NASD-NASDAQ trading department is responsible for the market-making functions of the broker-dealer. All of this interplay is designed to provide checks and balances, as long as the traders, broker-dealers, and oversight personnel from NASD are honest. Let any two of these groups be corrupted and the buyers are likely to suffer.

White Rock's partners and the broker-dealers that we hired used cold callers and others as a sales force for selling stock to investors. There were two ways we could legally operate. We could either buy a stock from one of our clients or sell him a stock. This is the way most people think of the market. But that was only half of it. We could also trade on what was called an "agency" basis, acting as an intermediary between the customer and another party.

This means that we could arrange to buy, say, 10,000 shares of a stock in order to sell the same 10,000 to one of our customers who wanted it at the price the owner was requesting. Or we could be a go-between and arrange a deal where a broker not connected with us could offer stock we had helped him get to a client who we might not even know. In that case we were a sort of agent for the stock, never buying it, never selling it, yet taking a piece of the action by helping the people who made the trade.

By this time, Lynn and I had two children and we had moved from our one-bedroom Battery Park apartment into a two-bedroom, then left that for a penthouse with a nanny. The year I departed Whale to open White Rock, we decided to rent a summerhouse in the Hamptons. We figured we could pay $40,000 or $50,000 for the summer but then we realized renting didn't make sense. If we could come up with $100,000 as a down payment—20 percent—we might as well commit ourselves to a half million dollars and buy a house.

A real estate agent showed us a lavish place with an S-shaped drive through pine trees that hid the house from the road. It was a combination of classic and modern, with traditional Greek pillars and a post-modern slant roof. The garage had its own lift to accommodate three cars. But these were not just any cars. In the garage was a Jaguar, a Ferrari, and a Lamborghini Diablo, which had a $300,000 price tag and a 200 MPH top speed. I'd always loved fast cars, and this did it for me. The realtor had only shown us this place to get a feel for our likes and dislikes, but I wanted it. I wanted the cars, and I wanted the lifestyle.

Then the real estate agent told me who owned it, and I knew I would have it. It belonged to "Big Al" Palagonia, a major broker and one of the full partners in the nightclub. Though I didn't know him well, I heard Al was a guy from Howard Beach, where he had been a typical Brooklyn kid who used to steal car radios and sometimes cars. Then, with no education, no college, he had become a broker and made himself a legend by making a million in his first year, when he was only 19 or 20. Al was a warm, generous type of guy who was an unbelievable salesman. My cousin Sal used to talk about him all the time.

Big Al was making $500,000 and $1.5 million dollars a month in commissions at D.H. Blair, where he had a huge corner office, three secretaries and twenty cold callers, just for himself. He had more money than he'd ever need, and he kept working and working. He was always willing to spread his money around and he was known either as an extremely generous man or a fool, depending on who was talking. He often treated friends to front row seats at Knicks games, and the Sky Box at the Superbowl. I met director Spike Lee through him on a private jet he hired to take us to Indiana to see a Knicks playoff game. Al was generous with his cars, and he'd invite me to go enjoy myself in one of them. He'd say "here, take my Lamborghini for a spin. I only have a thousand kilometers on it."

Al liked to take an entourage to trendy clubs, and he was rumored to have a huge appetite for cocaine. With the millions he was making, he could spend a fortune on drugs if he chose, which would be a total liability if he got caught. But at this point, Big Al was in good shape and this was his house. The location was prime—ninety miles out of the city in the coveted Hamptons, which had once been potato fields but long since had been converted to real estate for the wealthy. There were major movie stars and singers living out there, eating in the restaurants and enjoying the waves.

Hampton Bay was where people from Brooklyn went. West Hampton was big Jewish money, again with Hollywood people like Mel Brooks. Bridgehampton was artsy, with people like Alec Baldwin. Then you got to North and South Fork of Long Island where there was wine country in the North and a fishing industry in the South.

We would be in Quogue, an area between West Hampton and South Hampton where there were big estates built after World War II. Houses on the ocean were running about eight times the cost of the houses across the street or down a block or two where you couldn't see the water unless you walked outside. The really expensive area was Dune Road, where home sites could cost $2 million and up. Many of the homes were built on stilts to keep them from getting washed away in the violent storms and hurricanes that sometimes hit the area. Big Al's house was a short bicycle ride to the beach, so it was only worth about $700,000. There were doctors and lawyers out there. A guy who owned a big Mercedes dealership came out every weekend. Not only was the house in an affordable section, it was a great place to raise kids. They could play without getting into trouble, and we could easily take them to the beach where adults could watch them.

I called Big Al at his office, reminded him of my cousin Sal, mentioned my partnership in Bacchus, and told him I had seen his home. He invited me to his office to talk.

"I saw your house in the Hamptons this weekend and I'd like to buy it if it's for sale," I said when I had sat down in his breathtaking office.

"Everything's for sale," Al told me.

I was surprised at how fast he got down to business. I offered him $700,000 for the house as is, with all the furnishings.

"How do you want to pay?" Al asked, just like that.

"How do you want to be paid?"' I asked. This was the opener to see if Al played with cash, and had no problem with doing so. We agreed on a $400,000 sale price and $300,000 under the table in cash. The only thing I didn't get were the cars. He wouldn't part with them. That would come.

Lynn and I had enough money to pay for the house and we put the deal through. Now I was anxious to recoup. So far, the main accomplishment of our new company was creation of our own PPM—private placement—with three of the four bringing investors to back the venture. It should have taken less than a month for the licensing procedure to be completed. But Gene had a serious enemy—a member of the NASD self-regulatory board. A man named Dick Harrington had helped short players bring down Gene's previous firm, before Harrington had gone to NASD to sit on the licensing committee. Gene had called him a penny-stock criminal, and that, we were sure, caused our license to be delayed for months. Meanwhile, we were itching to get started and decided to use Gene's knowledge to do our first deal. It would be a reverse merger into a "shell." With a reverse merger, you buy a shell company, a defunct public firm. They can be bought for pennies. Then you reverse split the stock at a ratio that takes most of it off the market. For example, if there are 50 million shares out, a reverse split of 50-to-1 turns every fifty of the original shares into one of the new shares. Most of these can be purchased by the people buying the shell. That way, your business that might need several years to go public can be acquired by the shell in exchange for the new stock and become active immediately. And, presto! You have a reconstituted company trading on a public market.

Gene, with the help of Abe Salaman, found a company called Country World Casinos that seemed perfect for a reverse shell deal. It was going to eventually involve property in Black Hawk, Colorado that was going to be developed into a gambling resort. The stock was buyable at one or two cents a share, which was more than it was worth since there was no business, and no market for the stock. The original shell company was defunct, and, despite some legal issues, our venture was doable. The guy behind the whole shebang was a friend of Abe which meant we could almost cut whatever deal we wanted. So we bought what we thought was a clean shell through Abe for a fee of $23,000 from each partner.

We did a 100-to-1 reverse and then issued the new shares of Country World Casinos as a Reg S to our offshore companies. The players in this grand scheme were Abe, who sold us the shell and his partner Lynn Dixon, a man who lived in Utah where the shell was incorporated. Utah was considered the shell capital of the world because state law allowed more flexible use of shells than most other states, including New York. Also in with us was Grady Sanders, owner of the Colorado property, the man who would become chairman of the new company.

The fact that it had been through Abe and Lynn that we met Sanders, who owned the property in Colorado that was to be developed into a gambling casino, should in itself have been a warning. Grady was supposedly involved with the CIA and allegedly a top lieutenant for Howard Hughes when Hughes was out to clean up Mob influence in Las Vegas. Maybe Grady's anti-Mob connections were authentic. He was not indicted. Whatever his previous work, Grady was an amazingly vain guy. He apparently got another facelift every time his face began to sag, bag or wrinkle and by the time I met him, his skin was winched so tight that he had a permanent half smile and eyes pulled back like The Joker in Batman comic books. In fact, "The Joker" was our nickname for him. He must have been completely blind to his weird appearance, thinking he looked young and handsome. He didn't.

Grady needed capital to develop the Colorado property,

which made a perfect setup for a shell and a Reg S deal. The land was like much of Colorado, surrounded by snow-capped mountains, a river once used for panning gold, dense forests and abundant wildlife. It had a beautiful view, plenty of room for parking and an access road that could be widened inexpensively. A casino on this property would attract gamblers without driving away any non-gambling family residents who could enjoy the nearby hiking, skiing, and other forms of recreation. The land was worth $12 million to $16 million without anything built on it. Many of the buildings in the area had historic status, and it was the last piece of property on which a casino could be built, the last piece that wasn't protected in some way.

The deal seemed perfect to me. I believed in the potential of the gambling business. I had been to Las Vegas and Atlantic City and had read that Donald Trump was increasing his holdings in both cities.

"Casino gambling's a growth business," Trump told me. "It's an important area to get into."

Colorado already had enough legal gambling so that it was obvious a casino could be profitable. At the same time, gambling was still new to the state and tourist and local visitor use of the casino areas was still growing. I was so excited that I planned to fly twenty of my stockbrokers to nearby Beaver Creek and rent an entire floor at the Hyatt there. However, I learned that things hadn't been done as Grady claimed, and before that promotional trip, I called him and told him to rent some tractors to put around the property to make it look like something was going on.

The junket was a success. My brokers enjoyed the vacation and we had a boys' night out for everyone to go skiing. Some of the guys knew what they were doing. Others were beginning, and when I got tired of going down the slopes, I sat back and watched the amateurs falling down. Some guys drank too much and began chasing women whose sweaters bulged in the right places. Some of the girls were drunk enough to go along and everyone came back fired up to sell the stock.

The deal was to back the Grady project into the shell, and then do a Reg S with the money going to Europe. That would give

Grady a dollar a share for every share sold and since the stock would be free-trading within 41 days, we had Grady give us 90 days to make our side of the deal good. We paid him with a note—promise to pay—so we basically got the stock for free. This involved three million shares, and there would be three million available to prepare the land and make sure it met Environmental Protection Agency (EPA) standards. Then everything would be set for the second round of financing in the form of a secondary offering.

The Reg S offering would assure that there would be plenty of money—approximately $20 million—for us to be able to take beyond what was legal if we could manipulate the stock to seven dollars per share. That was why we contacted Beno Eton to act as our beard in Europe. He would park the Reg S stocks through many of his offshore accounts and issue the notes.

As front for the deal, Beno was to receive 10 percent of the profits. So ultimately, we would pay one dollar for stock that would be sold for six dollars through brokers currently allowed to do business. We couldn't do it ourselves because we were still waiting for approval. Each broker we could find would make between one dollar and two dollars per share of stock. The remaining money, between $3.50 and $4.00 per share was for us, to be split among the partners. We each expected to take in three to four million that we would hide in overseas bank accounts.

The selling arrangement was made by using every contact each of us had on Wall Street. We needed legitimate brokers willing to take several hundred thousand shares each to sell to clients in their book. Lex found a Russian kid named Eric who wanted to buy a few hundred thousand shares. Dutch had a friend named John Ciofoletti who owned his own firm J.W. Barkley, with two other partners. Ciofoletti, whom we called "The Brow" because of the way he looked, at first wanted to buy a few shares and ended up buying a million. The Brow's firm would eventually do another deal with us on a gaming company, so this was at the start of a mutually profitable relationship.

Gene got a commitment of a few hundred thousand shares from a man named Henry Boxer, a convicted stock scamster. For myself, I turned to Big Al, who I was sure would be interested in picking up a million shares of Country World at four dollars each when the stock was selling at six dollars. Then he could sell the one million shares at six dollars, pocketing two million on the deal plus commissions.

At best, the SEC considered this outsourcing of stock illegal. And if that wasn't enough, there had been cash under the table too—what I was doing. Our clients became brokers and they had their clients. We were considered promoters of the stock. Later there would be issues of conflict of interest raised in regard to some of the actions that were common on the Street. But then, the deal I offered Al for handling the stock was legitimate in the sense that the company had a shot and was not a total scam. After all, MCI at one point was a cash deal, and so was Acclaim Entertainment. And a host of now-legitimate companies like Candies had cash promoters running around offering cash under the table.

The problem was that Big Al's firm would not allow him to take so strong a position in the stock. So, rather than give up the money, he brought in a friend who used to work for the same firm and was both willing and able to buy the stock. That was when I met Andrew Bressman and Roy Ageloff, two friends of Big Al who owned their own firms. Al suggested that I go visit Roy at his company Hanover-Sterling and say he told me he might be interested in the stock. I did.

Roy's office was on Water Street, across from the South Street Seaport and a block from Wall Street in an impressive building. But the class and prestige stopped at the outside door to Roy's business. I knew the type of players I was dealing with the moment I saw Roy's firm. It was typical Brooklyn gangster-style, a place run by a Mob-backed hustler who had failed the broker's test seven times before deciding to hire a guy to take the test for him. It was obvious Roy had spent zero money on furnishings. It was as though he had gone to a sale of used government office furnishings. No color, no personality, nothing to inspire an investor's confidence. Instead, it was like the worst excesses of a boiler room operation.

The commissions would be "rips." A $20 stock might have a

$2.50 commission. And the place had a history of manipulating a stock from $5 to maybe $20 or $25, and then finding ways to make money on it. I didn't know it, but Roy was thinking that the layoff from Al was just another scam. I should have known, because I knew his type: a street-savvy Jewish guy who thinks he's Italian—one of those wannabes.

There were two Italian goons who met visitors and checked them for weapons, tape recorders or a wire before letting them see anyone. The Italians were Mob guys. You could smell it the minute you got in the room. If you were Sicilian, you knew. They were Brooklyn types: lots of gold chains, pinkie rings, the whole vibe.

I greeted the goons politely. "Hi, my name is Sal," I told them. "Al sent me." I might as well have been talking to animals in the zoo. They motioned for me to stand still and hold my arms out.

"We gotta frisk you for a wire," one of them said as they patted me down.

"Hey, I'm clean, guys," I said. "I'm a Wall Street guy."

They didn't care. The house rule was: you walk in, you get frisked. Period. No exceptions. Then Roy came over, looked at me without a word of greeting, and led me to the fire escape. No greeting, no explanation. No need to say, hey, the place is bugged, the Feds are listening to everything anybody says in here, so I'm not gonna open my mouth in here. We walked to the fire escape, an indoor area with concrete walls and steps. Once we were on the landing, Roy shut the door and finally broke his silence.

"So, whaddya got kid?" he asked, without bothering to indulge in any verbal foreplay.

"Big Al said you might be interested in buying a position from me," I said. "I'm willing to pay exceptional commissions on it."

"What do you pay?"

"I've got stock at six bucks," I said. "I could give it to you with two in," meaning a $2 discount per share."

"Okay, I'm interested," Roy said. "I'll buy it."

"You need to hold it," I told him. "Understand?"

He nodded yes and we made a deal for him to buy 200,000 shares at $800,000. I left, thinking that, for all his posturing, he seemed like a pretty nice guy. Walking out of Roy's office I ran into Rocco Basile, who had been a cold caller with me at Gruntal.

"Rocco, you're looking good. The word is you're doing good."

"I'm doing okay," Rocco said.

"You know, both us, you and me, started out at Gruntal as cold callers. We've come a long way." Rocco agreed.

"I hear you're doing as well as Big Al," I said, knowing that would spark his competitive spirit.

"Better," Rocco said. "I'm out-producing Al. Ask anybody."

I told him he should come say hello to me in my new firm up the street. My motive was to get him over there and then sell him on coming to work for me. Little did I know how much that visit was going to cost me. He said he would, the way people do when they're just saying it.

I did the trade the next day and then the problems began. The stock started coming back to us immediately and I had to buy it back and support it during the selling period. We didn't know what was happening at first except it was obvious that someone was dumping it. It was coming back fast. The truth was, Roy had dumped it without even keeping it 24 hours. I called him, infuriated.

"What the fuck are you doing with my stock?" I demanded. "What's wrong with you?"

"It wasn't me," Roy said, without asking what I was so angry about. "I still have the stock."

He denied, denied and denied. And I knew he was lying.

"Listen you prick," I said, trying not to get nasty. "I know where every share is. Do me a favor. Buy it back." What he was doing was outright stealing.

Then I hung up, still furious. I called my boyhood friend Danny and told him I had a problem with Roy, who I figured was Mobbed-up.

"He's obviously got connections," I told Danny, "and I don't know what to do with him."

The call to Danny was out of the blue. We hadn't spoken in some time and our lives had gone in different directions. My life would have been very different if I had taken the time to consider the long-term implications of asking him for help. The call caught Danny off guard.

"What do you want me to say?" Danny asked. "You know I know nothing about Wall Street."

Of course, it didn't matter what Danny knew or didn't know about Wall Street. What mattered was what people knew about him, that he was Mob, and that he was my friend. I explained to Danny that Roy had basically flipped the stock, costing me $400,000, and I needed help.

"Okay, we'll go up and talk to him," Danny said, and I set up a meeting.

Roy insisted that the meeting be in his office, so that's where we set it up.

At the same time, there were problems with the Country World deal. Apparently Grady Sanders had not been honest about the land. There were liens on the property for legal reasons never quite clear to me. I turned the matter over to our attorneys and then became suspicious concerning what else we might not have been told. We had an accountant go in and look at the books after the first few million went in, and he gave us bad news.

"This guy is spending seventy-five thousand dollars a month on the corporate American Express card," the accountant told us. "He paid for his daughter's wedding with your money."

It didn't end there. Grady was plundering the checkbook and he either wasn't interested in developing the land or he wanted to do it while milking the business at the same time. We were angry at Grady because the partners in Country World had flown out to see the land, seen what he was allegedly doing, and did not believe in him because there was so little work being done on the land.

But we believed in the future of the project and we were so focused on our personal gain that we didn't let the complications of liens and cash squandering deter us from selling the stock. You could say that was an understatement. We sold three million shares at $6 a share, which represented $18 million divided among the four of us and the brokers handling the work. I had asked Gene to save some stock for the future, and he had answered, "Don't worry, we'll print more." He was right. In effect, we had a printing press because we owned the firm, and we could always get our CEO to issue more stock for more money.

As we looked at it, that meant $3 million to the company, $3 million to $6 million to the brokers, and $12 million to us. I made approximately $3 million on that round—that first deal, ever. I was rich. This was the kind of thing I had wanted to do when I left Whale. This was the way I knew Hickman and Shel did deals, and now I had done one with my own firm. Furthermore, we weren't finished.

We did a Reg S to Beno's offshore companies and brought the money back through a Russian diamond trader from 47th Street named Aleks Paul. Aleks was a shrewd diamond merchant. But we had nicknamed him "Don't Fuck Around" after an incident in Florida when he let the other partners use his credit card to rent a car. As a joke, they hid the car, tore their shirts, then went to him and told him they had been the victims of a car jacking.

"Don't fuck around!" Aleks had said in his Russian accented-voice.

"No, honest," my partners told him. "A car-jacking. You've read about them. They target tourists in rental cars, follow them, and wait for a good time to pull them over and steal their car. Most of the rental car companies have stopped putting advertising on their cars, but not the one we used."

"I said, don't fuck around," he told them.

The nickname stuck. Speaking Russian, Persian, Italian, English and Hebrew, Aleks kept international bank accounts for buying diamonds from South Africa. He could wire money from account to account, and then buy diamonds for resale in the United States, leaving the money in Europe, unseen by the Internal Revenue Service. Then the stones were sold for cash, an arrangement that was handy for money laundering.

Lex and Gene knew Aleks and we set it up so we could wire money from Beno's offshore account to Aleks' offshore account. The money would come in as diamonds and jewels, and our jeweler would sell the stones for us for cash. This was a standard way of moving money by people interested in keeping their cash transactions private. Drug dealers liked to convert money to diamonds to get it out of the country because they could carry diamonds back in a small pouch. No one was looking for something like that at the overworked customs points. It was breaking the law since the diamonds were worth more than the $10,000, but the odds of anyone getting caught were far less than with a suitcase filled with money.

If you've ever seen ten million dollars in a suitcase, you know it's a big, heavy load. But $10 million in stones can fit in the palm of your hand. Diamond dealers always needed cash to buy more stones, and it was a perfect setup for us. No money was coming back to the U.S. in any traceable form. It was the ideal way to break the paper trail. Except for one thing: bringing the money back in the form of diamonds was money laundering. And the federal government was now running Operation Street Cleaner, a top-secret program to eliminate some of the corruption on Wall Street.

CHAPTER TEN

Meanwhile, there was Roy Ageloff to deal with for stiffing me on my Country World deal. Roy was a cocky, arrogant guy who knew his Mob connections would frighten the average person. It didn't concern him that he was not on the books of his firm as a broker and that he was playing an unlicensed role even though he was trading as a partner. It didn't matter. He had the best office in the firm and the office was the ultimate status symbol within a brokerage firm. It was proof of his trading ability and everybody in the business knew it. Roy also didn't care that more than half of his staff were people who had not been able to pass their broker's test. After all, he had failed it six times himself, eventually realizing that he did not need one. Instead, they'd hire a Russian kid to take the test for them at $5000 a head, signing up for it in different states so he wouldn't be noticed taking the same test in the same place. Nevertheless, Roy acted as if he was big time, and in a way, he was.

He had insisted that I come to him at his office on Water Street and meet in a room with the two goons he kept on the payroll. He wasn't expecting to see me come in with someone like Danny. I don't know if his goons knew who Danny was, but they understood his type. He had a cold piercing look to his eyes when he was pissed, and he was pissed by what he saw. The goons understood that. They might not have known his father and uncles were leaders of a major crime family, and that his father had been put away for his part in twelve Mob murders during one of the wars within the family. But they knew he was somebody they needed to respect. That was why, when Danny said, "Leave the room," he didn't have to raise his voice. He didn't have to try to prove he was more powerful than Roy. He just told the goons to leave, and they did.

Roy was suddenly very humble. *He* knew what Danny was, and that what had begun as a business meeting had become a sit-down, a situation used in the world of organized crime to resolve disputes and griegeneces. Each party to a sit-down tells his side of the issue, and then both have to accept the resolution set down by the highest-ranking family member. In this case, that was Danny.

I explained how Roy had taken the stock I had sold him and sold it right back at a huge profit right after promising me not to.

"Wrong," Roy said. "I still own it."

"Prove it to me," I said.

"I don't have to prove it," Roy said. "I still own it. Period."

"If you've got it, show us the proof of it," I said. Roy was getting nervous.

"If it's not there, I'll buy it back," Roy said, pretending to be accommodating and lying through his teeth.

We weren't getting anywhere. I was out four hundred grand and this guy was arguing that he still had the stock. I was enraged, and Danny was listening to these lies.

"If you can't prove it, you better buy it back," Danny said. He didn't follow up the remark with anything. He just let the words sit there, and they had an effect. Then we left.

It looked as if the issue had been resolved. I had seen how easily Danny had intimidated the two thugs and made Roy speak to him with respect. But it turned out that Roy's business was connected to a Mob family closely linked with Danny's. That meant that two crime families were profiting from Roy's actions. Danny may have cared, but the reality was that his position was not strong enough for anyone to worry about my firm going out of business. Actually, in this case, I was looked at as competition and probably as a good heist.

Meanwhile, our license had finally been approved. After eight months of stalling by the NASD, White Rock was able to move into offices at 17 State Street. Walter "Dutch" Durchalter and I were on the ninth floor, with the Russians—Gene and Lex—in a small office on the fourth floor where they could do the investment banking and take care of the offshore bank accounts.

I was in charge of running the firm, and my responsibility included recruiting. In that I was hampered because I couldn't give signing bonuses like the bigger firms. We had already spent between $750,000 and $800,000 of the $1.5 million we had raised. We needed the rest for daily operations. Nevertheless, we wanted aggressive sales people who knew how to manipulate. We knew we would have to take guys who had already blown up their books somewhere. Ones who were still doing well in a firm would want cash we couldn't pay out yet. So to get quality guys that would work in our small firm would be difficult. In addition, they might have big egos that would get in the way. I figured I needed a great car to convince them that I was making a lot of money, so I bought an Acura NSX. Then I followed that with a yellow 348 Ferrari Spider with only 2,000 miles on it that cost me $119,000. I paid cash to avoid putting it on the books.

The car had the effect I wanted on young guys who saw that with only a few years on the Street, I was running my own firm and drove an Acura NSX and a yellow Ferrari. I was particularly looking for young operators who were somewhat like I had been or older guys I had known as a teenager, and that I felt comfortable with. I got two of Whale's top producers—John Sciascia and Radcliff Bent—to come aboard. I also tapped my old relationships with Gruntal and Shearson. Dutch was bringing in connections from various places he had worked.

Though we didn't have money to pay signing bonuses to brokers, we had millions in cash in our deals to make working for us attractive. But cash deals meant that secrecy, and therefore selection of the right broker, was important.

I would take brokers to Scores, the best topless bar in town, buy them drinks after work, and talk to them.

"So how many books have you blown up?" I'd ask.

"Oh, three," a young guy would say, careful not to dampen the cuffs of his $800 Hugo Boss suit on the rail where someone had spilled a drink. He would be watching the girls and his clothes at the same time.

"So how much money did you make on those books?" I'd be watching him with one eye and the girls with the other.

"Oh...I made a half million last year, six-hundred thousand the year before...." Now two luscious girls—a redhead and a blonde—would be shaking their tops off, and they'd be jiggling right in front of us. The music would be heavy disco.

"And what do you have now?"

He might not answer immediately. He'd be watching.

"Huh? Oh, zero right now. I'm starting from scratch."

I'd let him watch for a moment. The girls would be moving down the line to another set of customers and the tension eased. I'd signal the waitress for another round.

"That's the point I'm trying to make to you," I would say. Now I could get it across while I had his full attention. "You're going to lose the old way. Nine out of ten brokers pick losing stocks, so why not pick a stock that pays you? What's the point of blowing up on a dog blue chip that some self-serving analyst recommends? Why blow up the clients until they stop loving you? You pick two or three stocks that are losers, and that's it. You'd be starting all over again. You burn out and it's all over. So why don't you buy my stock? I'll pay you really well. And at least if you blow up, you've got a million, two million in the bank."

"Two million bucks," he'd say. I could see his mind computing figures. "That'd be nice. For a start."

Okay. Those kind were the live ones. They know that what I was saying made sense. We were in the springtime of the coming bull market, before the high-flying Internet stocks that tripled overnight. But we were already seeing scams that made money out of nothing, like a new product called All-Man that Roy had taken public. All-Man was a sports drink intended to compete with Gatorade and it had been written up in both the business and sports sections of the newspapers. The stories predicted that All-Man was going to be a hot product and would take a big market share. People were desperate to get a piece of the action, and the IPO for All-Man raised at least $20 million.

The problem was, believe it or not, that there was no drink. All-Man was nothing more than a former professional athlete with a fax machine, an answering machine, and an understanding of the insanity that was taking place. Don't ask me where the money went. I never knew, and it wasn't just All-Man. There were lots of IPOs making money out of nothing—in 1993 there were 617 IPOs done by brokerage firms and more than 90 percent of them would fail.

I was going out all the time, recruiting. My wife was patient with me. I was never home, just like when I was at Whale still learning the business. Sometimes I would sleep at work when it got too late and I was so tired I couldn't go on any longer. Once we had a full staff, I did the daily pitching in the office myself. I'd stand on top of my desk and pitch out loud so everybody in the office could see me and feed off that. I was hungry, and I did everything I could to make the others hungry. I would have guest speakers like Big Al and other top producers. I used to give inspirational meetings most mornings and I'd start by pointing out the boardroom windows at the Statue of Liberty.

"See out there?" I'd say. "That means freedom to you." I'd be talking to rookie cold callers who were eighteen, nineteen, maybe twenty. Many of our brokers weren't much older and didn't know any better than to start their careers at a place like mine. I urged them all to grow within the firm. Experienced brokers wanted the corner office and the cutest secretary who, ideally, would put out. A young rookie, hungry to learn and to please, wanted to build a career. He'd just be looking for a place to work on the phone. So my meetings would play off of that.

"Look outside," I would say, "And you see the water, and you see the rest of America to the left. There are three-hundred million people who live out there. All you need to do is figure out how to get a dollar from each one. And how much would that be?"

And they'd say, "Three-hundred million dollars."

"Well, obviously, you can't call three hundred million people," I'd respond. "It would take you a lifetime. But you can definitely call a lot of people and ask them all to do a trade with you that would give you more than a dollar. You might get a fifty-dollar or hundred-dollar trade or a million-dollar trade. Whatever it is, you have the opportunity out there to reach everybody, and I'm giving you the opportunity by giving you the phone.

"See the phone? It has a green light and it has a red light. When you pick up the receiver, it goes green. When you put it down, it's red. You always want to be green. Green is the color of money. Now get out there and call everybody that you can. Don't stop until you make money. Don't stop until you get your goals."

I'd change my pitch every meeting, trying to get cheers from them at the end. The point was to get them excited, and then I'd do contests. Just as I'd seen my mentors doing, I'd take a piece of tape and paste a $100 bill smack on the wall.

"The next person who opens an account gets that $100 bill," I'd say. Then I'd do something similar with Knicks tickets. These were ravenous kids, most of them from Brooklyn, Staten Island and places like that. They had friends who were brokers. They saw them driving nice cars and that's why they came to Wall Street, and that's why some came to work for me. They were possibly the next group of "pasta boys," which was my term for brokers who took cash kick-backs on deals. We used slang like that for things that might cause problems if we talked about them on the phone. But the pasta boys would figure prominently in my career as a broker.

Our company was thriving, despite the loss of the $400,000 from the deal with Roy. We were seeing trading profits generated by our new recruits that compensated for that loss, but my partners were pissed at me for having made the deal with him and I still want-ed to recover it. What I didn't know was that Roy's company was in trouble like I hadn't even imagined when Danny and I had gone to see him.

He was under serious attack by short traders, and he didn't have the means to win the battle. He was determined to support the stocks that were under attack, which was completely irrational. He didn't have the money to buy enough to maintain the price. He had twenty-dollar stocks that he was supporting and two or three more that he had just brought public. The shorts were dumping stocks on him and he was trying to absorb it at an incredible rate to protect his positions.

I realized all this when after the sit-down, I went back to Roy's office to get him to make good on my $400,000. He was on the phone, screaming at the top of his lungs. "Twenty thousand shares! Don't talk to me about twenty-fucking thousand shares!" He banged his fist on his desk and looked around as if he wanted to kick something. Or somebody. "You don't have 20,000 shares you prick. I'll buy it! Do you have more? I'll buy that too, you prick! What? You can't talk to me that way! Fuck you."

He slammed the phone down almost hard enough to smash it. His eyes were wild. He was irrational, and it was obvious that I wasn't going to get him to buy back my stock that day. His firm was collapsing. The short traders were reducing the value of his stocks from millions to nothing right in front of my eyes.

And the way he did business was to move transactions from one client to another, duping the clearinghouse, doing it on the cuff until the brokers could generate real buy tickets. That way, he was putting the clearinghouse on the block. There were dozens of millions of dollars at stake and everything was coming down. If it was as bad as it looked, there would be more than his company in rubble at the end of this. His brokers were jumping out of his company like rats from a burning ship. So while I clearly couldn't collect my $400,000, I figured at least I could grab one of his brokers. The man I wanted was Rocco Basile. Rocco wasn't in the office at the moment, but I ran into him on the street a day later. I was cruising in my new Ferrari like a kid with a new toy at Christmas, enjoying the sound of the stainless exhaust system growling through the canyon walls of the buildings. I saw Rocco on the sidewalk of Battery Park City with a box in his hand and the mellow rumble of the Ferrari caught his ear before I pulled up. Ferraris don't sound like anything else and he turned around before I stopped. It was a nice way to arrive, and I let the engine idle for a moment longer than necessary before I switched off the engine. The top was down.

Rocco already knew it was me and came over to the passenger's window.

"So what's new at the asylum?" I asked him. He hadn't seen the car before, and I let him take it in for a moment. It made a much stronger statement than anything I might say. "How's your masochist of a boss?" I asked. I knew Rocco didn't need to put up with Roy. He lived in Battery Park, near me, and he was a big player. He made as much in commissions as Big Al and the two of them had a running competition, comparing notes each month as to who had made the most. And soon both of them would be buying my stocks.

"I just gave my notice. Resigned. O-U-T out."

"You got someplace to go?" I asked him.

He shook his head.

"Well, I'm looking, and you're hired if you want in," I said. "We have some good paper at $6 with a $2 rip, in cash." Cash was the magic word. It was one I couldn't say to just anyone—it had to be someone I could trust.

"I'm with you," Rocco said. "You want me to bring my crew?"

His crew was a gang of Brooklyn kids that he called the Brooklyn Assault Team. They were a hard-charging bunch, and he also would bring his brother Jack Basile, who was a very funny guy and was to prove a buffer between me and the crew. Rocco started the next day and was a pleasure to have around. Despite his background and where he came from, Rocco was not at all flamboyant. He gave the impression of stability and controlled aggressiveness in the business world. I was dumbfounded to discover that his father took his paycheck every month and let him keep $10,000 to piss away. He had skills that made him an asset everywhere. That's the way he seemed, anyway. He also brought some much more serious baggage which was going to cause my partners and me tremendous grief. But I didn't know how tremendous then.

For the moment, things seemed good. Lynn and I were looking forward to enjoying the lush life at our new summerhouse in the Hamptons, away from the hustle and hassles of Wall Street. The summerhouse in the Hamptons meant stability, respectability, and a social life neither of us could have imagined when we first got married. Our children would enjoy private schools and a nanny. We would join the school's parent teacher organization, volunteer to help in the classrooms and bask in a world of estates and gracious living.

The Feds would see this in a different light entirely. To the FBI undercover team and other law enforcement agents working Operation Street Cleaner, my buying a house in the Hamptons would invite a closer look at my company, since the house had been under surveillance when Al owned it. One reason: Mafia boss of bosses John Gotti had been Al's guest. The Feds' interest intensified when my partners and I began flashing money in ways we didn't imagine would be noticed. Some of the partners and new brokers delighted in expensive women, drugs, closets full of custom-tailored clothing, and trips to South Beach and Vegas.

I deluded myself into thinking I was the conservative partner, investing in real estate and luxury cars instead of prostitutes and Versace. But I was being more conspicuous than I thought. Now that I was palling around with Big Al, it wasn't enough to have a Ferrari. I had to have a Porsche 911 too, in addition to the mid-engine, high-performance Acura NSX, that I drove to work every day. To add the cherry, I bought a 25th Anniversary Lamborghini. It was 1993 and I was truly living the Mobster lifestyle, even going to the Super Bowl and sitting in one of the best seats. The money was flowing in and I was doing all the things I had once bragged to my father that I would do. As an adolescent, I had boasted to him that I would be rich one day, and he had said, yeah, sure. I told him I was going to own a Lamborghini.

Now, my father realized that his son was a winner and wasn't talking out of his butt anymore. I think my father was a big catalyst in my success because I always wanted to prove to him that I was worthy, and that I was going to make my dreams real. I was doing it. I drove my new Ferrari to where I had been an apprentice after high school, and where my father was still working as a programmer. He was being phased out by younger programmers after 25 years of loyal service. When I heard this news, I paid off his debts and told him he was officially retired. It was an emotional day for both of us.

Meanwhile, the Mob was making its way onto the Street, and I couldn't help but feel partially responsible. Some of the kids I hired came from families that were connected, and the potential wealth and riches I promised was definitely an attraction that got back home. And I was about to become very aware of what kind of a problem I had created for the firm by hiring Rocco.

The trouble started with a phone call that came a couple of days after Rocco started working for us. It was for me and the caller didn't bother with an introduction. "You got the son of a bitch working up there. He robbed from us so you owe us money."

I knew the voice. Not the person, but the type—very Italian, very gangster. It was like the voices of some of the relatives of one of my oldest and best friends, and they were in jail for murder. It turns out Rocco had been working a scam at his previous firm that was called the "Black and Blue Market." It involved running crooked deals on the books after closing time. It was discovered just about the time he left Roy's firm and as far as I was concerned, his problems had nothing to do with me or White Rock. But Roy's firm, as I already knew, was connected to a powerful family, a family which was now pressing Danny's cousin to have Danny put pressure on me.

The family was now being run by "Allie Boy" Persico, who had just gotten out of prison, and was making a statement about his renewed control by meting out punishments where they were deserved. One of the punishments he ordered was directed at Rocco, and the person given the job of handling it was my friend Danny. As upsetting as the phone call was, I had so much else going on that I didn't focus on it right away, as in retrospect I should have.

My partners and I had netted $12 million on our first small cap deal, and White Rock was already known as a hot operation that people wanted to join. When Roy's firm crashed, I had grabbed not just Rocco but some of the young cold callers and brokers. Now we had people wanting to get in even though there was no room left at our table. We didn't have as many phones or seats as we had cold callers and we literally had kids sitting on milk crates, calling on cell phones. We were at the top of the heap of new small cap firms, and I guess things were just too frantic for me to turn my energies to the situation with Rocco until it hit me between the eyes. But that would come a bit later.

First, a situation arising with Country World needed attention. We had pretty well sold out our position in Country World, but we wanted to support the stock because we had brokers helping us who had taken as much as a million shares each. We didn't want to blow our relationships with these people, so we started putting back some of the money we had made to support the stock. We assigned about $500,000 to the trading account to support Country World. We wanted that stock to be up there so that the next year or the next deal, we would be able to feed off the momentum of what we did. We wanted to be able to go back to our existing syndicate of brokers and say,

"Hey, that Country World stock is still at six bucks. We're doing this deal, so here. Here's a million shares of this you can buy."

Of course, it was a pipedream because what we were asking was impossible unless the stock went liquid. Brokers and their clients always lose stock and eventually you can't support it any more without losing the money you made. But what actually happened was that I began seeing more stock out there than what I had issued. The float had only been three million shares, and from the sheet I was getting every week from my clearing firm, it added up to 3.2-million shares.

The extra 200,000 shares were coming back on the market against us, which meant somebody was shorting us. It's not that I was naïve about short trading. I had encountered it before and I understood it, but this was the first time I had ever personally come up against it. Short players have a number of ways to hone in on a target stock. Sometimes an insider provides a tip that the company is not what the prospectus implied, or there is an abrupt change in management that comes to public attention. Sometimes the short player just believes that the stock is trading at too high a price for the company's real value. Whatever the case, the short player feels he can manipulate the company into a downward spiral for his personal profit.

The Country World deal was a perfect target. Its value to an investor—the people who had bought $18 million worth of stock in it—was the potential it was seen to have as a generator of profit when it was developed. The idea of the raw land being the site of a bustling, profitable casino was what had made the stock worth buying to the investors and kept the value of the stock afloat.

The challenge to Country World came slowly. First there was an offer to sell 2,000 shares of stock from an owner neither my brokers nor I had known before. With a stock issue such as Country World Gaming, we knew where every share was held. That was the control that enabled the brokers to maintain the price of the stock. An unexpected offering like that was not enough to cause concern by itself. Clients sometimes changed brokers, and when they did, they often altered their stock portfolio. The new broker had to prove his worth to clients and to generate personal income through the clients' purchases and sales. But the sales continued, one day after another, at 2000 or 3000 shares a day. After a month, about 200,000 shares had been sold, and I knew our first business deal was being shorted.

The key to the shortsellers' profits is often negative insider information. For example, suppose a man has a brother-in-law who worked for a pharmaceutical company. The company's stock is selling for $100 a share, a price that had been stable for several weeks. Over dinner the brother-in-law mentions that office rumor had it that a new hair-growing product about to be launched later in the week was going to be withdrawn. It seemed to cause an allergic reaction that causes itching and general discomfort. Excited by the insider information, the man might offer to sell 1,000 shares he does not own—odd as it sounds, it's legal—for a total of $100,000. He can't pay the money without mortgaging his house and selling everything he owns, but he is not worried. He's certain that when news of the problem reaches the public, the stock will drop at least five or ten dollars a share. He will be able to place a buy order for the 1,000 shares at perhaps $90 each, and then pass the stock to the buyer who had agreed to take the shares at $100 each. His short-selling profit will be $10,000 and he never actually owned any of the stock.

Sometimes short selling worked for the average investor. Usually it doesn't. The average player might get lucky, but more likely the insider tip is wrong. In the case of the pharmaceutical company, the research staff discovers that the allergic reaction was actually the result of improperly prepared shellfish salad served at the corporate party celebrating the new product launch. The hair grower is as good as hoped and the stock rises to $110 a share the day the short player has to make good on his sale. He will have to spend $110,000 to be able to meet his obligation, taking a loss of $10,000 if he can find a way to get the money.

Professional short players maintain a float of stock they do not have. For example, suppose the short player, operating as Company A sells 2,000 shares at $6 a share. He is obligated to buy 2,000 shares a week later at the market price to cover the stock purchased from him the week before. But instead of going to the market and actually spending the $12,000, he buys the stock from Company B, which he also owns. Company B does not own any of the stock, either, but a week later Company B covers its obligation by buying 2,000 non-existent shares from Company A. After the initial sale, the short player is buying from and selling to himself, delaying a week at a time the date when he actually has to make good to the original buyer. This is called "floating a short." Short players who do not feel comfortable creating the image of multiple buyers will work with a friend or an informal trading group, all engaged in the same type of manipulation.

Short players can also enjoy great leverage for their trading operations. If a short player is a broker/dealer, he can maintain a trading account where he can justify shorting stocks legitimately because he makes himself a market maker in that stock. He is therefore entitled to take a long or short position to make the market. Market makers may also legally leverage their money, putting up a million dollars and getting ten million dollars to trade each day. This is another way he is able to ravage companies.

Once the short player has accumulated a block of 50,000 shares, for example, there are two ways to make money. The most common is to release information, true or false that will drive the stock down.   Very often the short player acts when an IPO stock is grossly overvalued at the time the move is made. For example, the IPO for the new casino development took place at a time when everyone was buying a dream. The land was owned but serious development was just beginning. If the casino and other amenities had been built, the stock would soar in value.

The average stock investor looking for money over a long period of time is willing to wait for construction to take place, for the casino to open, and for favorable publicity to generate strong interest in the stock. Two or three years after the IPO, the stock will rise so that the average return on the original investment will be several times what would have been earned from other financial opportunities. However, when the short player comes in, the project, like Country World Gaming is still more dream than bricks and mortar. Bad publicity can start a selling drive, and as every broker knows, buying begets buying and selling begets selling.

Typically, that $6 stock will drop to $4 or $2 or less. Sellers are willing to take almost anything in order to reduce their potential loss. The brokerage house responsible for the stock cannot maintain the value at the start of the selling spree, though the brokers will try to slow the decline. The short player moves in and buys all he can at the lower price. Then he makes good on his original debt and pockets substantial rewards. He takes $6 a share for the shares he did not have when he made his original sale, pays $2 a share (more or less) for the shares he actually has to buy, and pockets $4 a share difference. At the same time, such a selling frenzy often destroys the company whose future once looked healthy, while the short player makes out.

There are exceptions. Sometimes the owners of a stock believe in it. They see the value going down and refuse to panic because they purchased for the long term. However, it is doubtful that enough stockowners will ride out a short attack to assure the stability of the stock. Usually the handful of owners who make such a decision simply slow the process to an inevitable end.

The other exception is the one to which I would soon be exposed, and that's the extortion maneuver. A short player with a large financial backing goes to the broker and hits him up for a settlement, in a form of the old-fashioned shakedown. Negotiations would be made so that the broker's loss would be limited to perhaps a dollar or two per share for perhaps 100,000 shares.

Before I knew it, I was buying hundreds of thousands of shares of Country World Gaming. Five thousand shares a day, ten thousand shares a day. The numbers were going up and I smelled a rat. At first I thought it was "back-dooring." That's when brokers who are supposed to hold the stock start selling it. I figured it was one of the outside men handling the stock, like Big Al's other buyer Andrew Bressman, who owned his own firm A.R. Baron & Co. Bressman was seeing similar problems with the shorts at A.R. Baron and I figured he was probably dumping mine to save his and I started doing research to find out if I was right. I called them out and demanded that they send me their run sheets.

That means I was asking them, "what is in your house? What does your clearing firm have on file that you own? I don't want your sheet. I want it from them." So they sent me their run. And when I got the paper work, The Brow still had what he should have. Big Al was down 20,000 and Andrew was down a big 150,000. We had bought a lot more than that, and I went to Gene to see if he could explain it.

"Gene, something's seriously wrong. We're buying a lot of stock and we're burning all our profits now. We're putting it back in. What's going on?"

"I don't know," Gene said. "We'll start digging around."

I started reading the prospectus, we all did, and magically, Gene figured out that Abe, the guy who sold us the project, had some secret shares. Not secret in that they were evident with digging, but they were the types of thing I could miss with a quick reading and with too much reliance on Gene, whom I came to think might be in on it with them. I was getting paranoid.

More research showed up a million shares buried in the fine print. They had some convertible preferred stock that had been converted into a million shares of common, and they were hitting us with it. The guys that sold us the shell were pummeling us with the stock when we discovered the million shares of stock; Gene called Abe Salaman and threatened him.

"You son of a bitch," Gene yelled, "You hid a million shares from us."

He then went on to say something that made Abe feel as though he was in physical danger, if not of being killed, certainly of being beaten. I never heard the threat, but there was no question that Gene, in his anger, had gone too far, as he had done before. His threat would come back to us in the form of a worse threat that I would be thrown out of a window. It would lead to a sit-down for Lex with the New Jersey-Philly mob. I went to Danny again, this time to see if he knew anybody from the short side that was connected to this one particular short company—the Bonero Brothers.

Country World Casinos was being subjected to a classic short player maneuver. Trying to support the issue by buying the offers was costing too much money, and the fact was that all the excess stock buying was being generated by the boardroom brokers, who wanted to be paid for their work. I was already in for $4 million because I had to repay the brokers to re-buy it again. For a stock that I paid two dollars on, I had to pay another two dollars for the additional shares.

Otherwise the stock would get too long on my trading desk and I had to repay. The brokers still benefited from the trading. As the stock went down, I still paid thirty percent. The problem with my incentive program was that it was totally illegal. No matter what my motives, the approach to moving the stock and to paying fees to the brokers supporting it fell into the categories of conspiracy and money laundering.

Then the stock kept going down and I decided to let it go. If it tanked, it tanked, and I would let the market dictate where it should be instead of supporting it. I could no longer see a reason to support it, and I resolved to let Country World Casinos trade on its own. I didn't know how serious the repercussions would be from my withdrawing support for the stock. As it turned out, it led to the need for more sit-downs with factions in the Philly-New Jersey Mob that had a strong interest in the stock. By ending my support of the stock, their inside position on it dropped from a holding at $6 a share to pennies on the share. That gave them a lot of reason to be unhappy with us.

Lex had to go meet the mob representatives in hotels and airports to try to resolve all of our differences. There was great anger mixed with disappointment in the deal. No one wanted to spend money out of pocket on a losing deal. Everyone realized that there had been unrealistic expectations, that the mob had been its own worst enemy. Yet no one wanted to take a loss. No one wanted to be responsible.

To make matters more difficult, one of the mob captains was Frank Coppa, Sr., a guy known as Fat Frank. Coppa was a skilled and notorious short player who brought along other short players. We didn't know it, but the Country World situation led to their decision to work against us in every deal we entered. They said nothing and did nothing obvious. But once each new deal began to look like a winner, the scorpions struck, their stings slowly sinking each frog. We did not think about the fact that we had been involved in juggling the mob, insider-selling, and back-dooring stock from the relationship with Al. The volume of problems we thought we were leaving meant the potential for disaster.

Danny met me to tell me he knew somebody that knew Ron Bonero of the Bonero Brothers. His name was Turk Rambo, a friend of the family and the muscle behind Bonero. We set up a meeting in a Brooklyn coffee shop. We showed up with Lex and began telling Philly which stock was under attack, and asked whether he could please tell Bonero to leave our stock alone. But that armistice would be short-lived.

CHAPTER ELEVEN

"To carry out our illegal activities, my partners and I had secret agreements with many people, including other brokerage firms, their principals and brokers, officers of issuing companies and members and associates of Organized Crime Families. The Organized Crime members and associates helped our illegal activities in various ways, including resolving disputes over money and other aspects of our dealings...."

—From the confession of Sal Lauria

When White Rock was finally in operation, we were looking at doing our first in-house deal. The Country World Casinos deal had been, on paper, handled completely away from our firm. The first White Rock deal was a company called Holly Products that manufactured gambling equipment like gaming tables used in casinos throughout the country. It was a good business because the industry was growing internationally. Indian reservation gambling, border gambling casinos in Windsor, Ontario, and Niagara Falls, Canada, and expanding legalization in several states such as Michigan, were all adding to the demand for equipment. Holly Products made its money before a casino opened and did not have to deal with the vagaries of the travel, tourism, and gambling junket industries. Changes in the economy might hurt the casinos in one part of the country or another, but by then Holly Products had already banked its profits.

This was not one we could work ourselves because we did not have the go-ahead from the clearing firm and we needed to build up capital. Instead, we gave the deal to The Brow and his firm, J.W. Barkley, who set up a secret trading agreement where both firms would benefit on the cash side of the transaction. The deal would be handsomely syndicated to our firm, and our new recruits would be able to open accounts on the deal and invite selected brokers to get some of the inside cash. The company was an excellent one for investors, and I was enthusiastic. The deal was for one million shares of stock to be issued at $5 a share. There would be three million warrants at 10 cents each, with a strike price of $5.50. We planned to strip the warrants so we could buy them for $100,000, then pump up the price of the stock since the warrant price would follow. When the warrant price reached $6, we would sell it, making $18,000,000 to divide as we chose.

The problem was that Larry Berman, the Holly chairman, knew what a solid company he had. He made enough money to drive a Rolls Royce. But Larry wanted a little something extra out of this in the form of a ten percent kickback from the sale of the warrants. As an insider, Larry would have stock he could not sell without creating panic. He would only be able to use its value to borrow against. A ten percent kickback—$1.8 million—would make him millions in a way that investors would not know about.

When the deal hit the street it was instantly successful. We owned the float and could do anything we wanted. The stock quickly moved to $10 and the warrants allowed us to sell them at $6. We began working the warrants through some pasta boys. They agreed to move the warrants on a six-for-two arrangement, meaning that for every $6 share sold, they would receive $2 in cash. This would mean that for 200,000 shares—a total of $1.2 million—we would receive a gross profit of $800,000. Four hundred thousand of that would go to the pasta boys, with the $2 per share received under the table representing the equivalent of a gross commission of $8 a share. The money was so great and the crime seemingly so minor that when a deal like this came up, a lot of brokers went for it, and now we had internal pasta boys and the original syndicate from Country World working together.

Even with all the convolutions and kickbacks, Holly Products was solid and the stock remained a good buy. It actually had revenue and earnings. But my pride in the deal was tempered by the news that the Securities and Exchange Commission (SEC) was investigating Country World Casinos. There were too many names that were also involved with the gambling casino in ways that were raising warning flags for the government regulators.

The problem with Country World Casinos was that there was money to be made everywhere, and everyone involved was scheming in every direction. There was big above-the-table money, big below-the-table money. There was big Reg S money, big overseas bank accounts money. There was money for bribes, money for the IRS, money you could report and money you had to hide. The trouble was the amount of scamming going on. I had believed in Country World Casinos because the land was so desirable. Both Donald Trump's real estate people and the owners of the Tropicana wanted that land and I knew that at least two other legitimate casino companies had made an offer on it.

What I didn't know was that the title to the property was in question so there were no real plans for the development for which we raised money. We eventually learned that of the $3 million we raised for the casino, no more than a million was actually used for the land. Grady had this convoluted scam going where he'd take the property, claim to be developing it, and then run it into bankruptcy. He had a different company established that he'd use to buy the bankrupted property, then start the scam all over again. This time it was headed by his girlfriend. I didn't know how he did the others.

The Country World scam had been going on so long it was hard to establish who actually owned what. All that would eventually be certain was that the money was being earned through milking investors in a casino that would not be built, bankrupting the operation, selling it, and starting over again with new money. I didn't realize fully what was going on because I was working my moneymaking ventures from New York City, and was too busy celebrating what I believed was my success.

We were still partying with the brokers in those days. We had the house in the Hamptons, the money was rolling in, despite our combat with the shorts, and I was still doing great things for my top-producing brokers. One summer weekend I had a party and I thought it would be fun to go out on Wave Runners, those things that hold one or two people. You ride them like a motorcycle on the water. They go fast and can easily be maneuvered. I figured they were just what was needed to reward the brokers. I went into a store that had nine Wave Runners on the floor. I asked if there were any more in back, but the clerk said there weren't. I took them all...emptied out the store...and had them dropped in the water near our summer home. I paid for everything. I took everybody out to lunch, and when we came back, we all went riding.

I kept in touch with some of my childhood friends and enjoyed sharing my newfound wealth. Big Al had a 33-foot Sea Ray coastal cruiser with only 27 hours running time on it, and he agreed to sell it to me for half what he had paid for it. I let my good friend Mike use it just for taking care of it. He would take my family out, acting as captain, and meet us while we were wave running—as a kind of oasis in the middle of the ocean.

That's how much money we were making. And in spite of the problems with Country World, we had other deals. As soon as we were a licensed broker-dealer, we were selling other stock. The money was coming in from the legitimate side of the street. It was just the IPOs and all the inside stock that made the big killings in a short period of time.

But there were also juvenile antics to ease the tensions of the office. Rocco's cold callers, his Brooklyn Assault Team, were young and thought like high school kids. Sometimes they got out of control. One day a delivery guy brought a big order of Chinese food and they only gave him a dollar tip. He unwisely complained, saying "Oh, you guys are really cheap." They took the egg rolls and started hitting him in the head with them. Then the rest of the food went into the air, making the outer office look like a giant firecracker had exploded inside the container. Chicken, vegetables, shrimp, and other ingredients began flying in a Chinese food free-for-all. In the midst of the mess was this small Asian man, livid with rage, cursing several laughing employees in a mix of English and Chinese. He also called the cops.

I paid the guy, and gave him a big tip, which may have been the closest I would come to getting control over the chaos that was increasingly dominating my life. The problems in Colorado continued to grow and we knew Grady was a liar. I had three million shares of stock to manage and my two biggest brokers, Al and The Brow had a million shares each. It was the smaller brokers, the ones who could only handle 100,000 or 200,000 shares at a time who were the problem. I had to know where all the shares were held. A computer print-out of every share of stock held within the various stock brokerage firms helped me track what was happening, but this wasn't easy for the smaller brokers whose clients might only buy 1,000 shares that were easy to resell.

I also had problems getting the brokers to buy back the stock when their clients either wanted to buy something else or switched to a broker who was pushing other stocks. What I found was a lot more selling than should have been there. That's when I discovered that the shell wasn't clean. Gene had claimed that the shell was 99 percent clean. That missing one percent should have tipped me off, but it didn't. What Gene didn't catch—or maybe as I mentioned earlier, he was in on the scam. I never did learn which—were those 100,000 shares of preferred stock we didn't know about. Since they were convertible to a million shares, from what I could see, the scumbags at Country World had sold at least 600,000 shares behind our backs. Along with our brokers, The Brow was unloading stock. I called him and told him I would not give him a cash payment if he didn't buy it back.

The Brow and I began arguing, and Dutch got involved. Dutch saw things getting hostile and tried to distance himself by saying that he didn't cut loose any. But I knew better. They were all pulling scams. I told him that the figures showed that The Brow alone was down close to 100,000 shares. The Brow is a big guy, 6'2" to my 5'9"—and he confronted me face-to-face.

"You prick!" he said. "You're going to pay me. I don't care if you need to sell your house to do it."

He was so close I could smell his breath. Dutch tried to break the two of us apart, but it was no use. We had both gone too far.

"You mean, throw my family in the street?" I shouted.

"Yes," he screamed back.

"Fuck you! If the stock goes down because of you, you can kiss my ass before I pay you. If you can show me that you own it all, we don't have a problem."

I knew I was right. The list does not lie. At worst, I was keeping him honest. At best, I would get him to buy the stock back. This was a constant problem with all the pasta boys and the system itself, though it really was a small part of what was wrong. The bigger problem was with the shell masters Abe and their surface million shares.

The SEC investigator in Denver sent us a formal written summons to a hearing in Colorado to answer questions about Country World. The initial questioning had to be done in the region where a possible problem was taking place rather than where the brokerage firm handling the deal was located. Dutch and I made the trip to Colorado with a powerful corporate attorney to help us face the questions. I was somewhat relieved when we got there to testify and found that the man handling the interrogations for the SEC seemed inexperienced. He asked questions about Country World Casinos, about how the deal was structured, who the various owners might be. He asked about the offshore stock and the Reg S information, and we answered. That's not to say we answered honestly even though we were under oath. Our lies might have mattered if the SEC man had known what he was doing. But either he was not as skilled as he thought or his superiors didn't regard the case as being as important as he did. Because a month or two later we read about him suing the SEC for discrimination because they never took his cases seriously. Whatever the reasons, there were no repercussions from the SEC at that time.

I was already angry with Abe Salaman and Grady Sanders for perpetrating the irregularities that had led the SEC to our door. I had called Brady out for what he had done to us with Country World and really ragged on him. I also ragged on Abe.

"Abe, we know that it's you," I said. "You sold a million shares to us. You're a scumbag. You're going to get yours...."

We were all mad. There were calls and yelling going on among my partners and me. Gene called Abe too, and Gene went even farther in menacing him than I did. There was definitely the suggestion in Gene's call that some kind of harm was going to come to Abe. And the next thing you know, I got another telephone call—this time from someone whose tone smacked of the Mob.

"We're from Philadelphia and friends of Abe's. We're coming there and we're going to throw you out a window to prove a point to those Russians who insulted a friend of mine, and there's no way back from this."

I thought the problem was the way I had talked to Abe. If I had known it also involved supporting the Country World stock Abe wanted to sell, I might have done things differently. As it was, I had gotten fed up supporting the stock when the guy who sold us the deal was costing me so much money. So I had let it drop and it went down to like a dollar or two dollars from six.

But this phone call scared me and I told my partners about it. I thought of Danny, of course, but as he was ineffective at the last meeting and the fiasco with Roy, Lex felt we should use somebody else. For some reason, Lex really did not like Danny's family. He never told me why, but he was adamant. Instead he went to his father, a well-known Russian gangster and ally of the Wiseguys. Lex's father was gravely disappointed that his son came to him to use his Mob connections. He had hoped his son was prospering legitimately on Wall Street and he was sorry to hear about Mob players, sit-downs, and other problems. But he was not about to turn his back on his son and he arranged for a "made" man named Ernest Montevecchi, known as Butchie Blue Eyes to represent Lex, the firm, and me.

The guy who had threatened me on the phone, was represented by Frank Coppa, Sr., otherwise known as Fat Frank whom I have mentioned before. He was a captain of the Bonanno family, and Butchie Blue Eyes was a soldier in the Genovese family, but apparently they had already made a deal. When they met, Fat Frank told Butchie the stock was his, not Abe's. He said Abe owed him the money and we had to buy the stock, though we could do it at a lower price so everyone had a good deal. That was the message, anyway.

I think it was some kind of secret arrangement done on the side between Butchie and Frank, and I was beginning to wonder if everybody used the Mob to resolve their problems on Wall Street. It had become worse than the streets of Brooklyn.

What happened in the sit-down and afterward was a typical result of going to the Mob for help. Butchie got Fat Frank to back down in terms of the threat to me. Then Butchie saw there was big money to be made in Wall Street firms, so he made our firm a "white elephant" present of two of the guys who helped him resolve the problems. One was Eugene "Big Gene" Lombardo, a powerful, deep-voiced thug who was named in the upcoming indictment as a Bonanno family associate. The other was Robert DePaolo, a guy who understood Wall Street. Together those two could watch what was going on in our office and report to Butchie. They would make sure the agreements in the sit-downs were followed and that the right people would get paid out of the final sale of the casino stock.

At that same time, I was able to establish that Country World stock coming back was from A.R. Baron & Co. owner Andrew Bressman, who had slowly sold stock back to us instead of to his clients, making a quick $200,000 on us rather than on his accounts. I was furious and I called him on it. He agreed to repay $150,000 in cash and owe us a favor, so I took the offer to cut my losses.

To collect I sent over John Diorio, a friend of Danny's and an ex-cop on medical pension. John had been training in the stock business, acting as a bodyguard and driver. Just a real nice guy, a streetwise person you could trust. John went over to Bressman's office and entered without saying a word, figuring the place was bugged. That was smart, because by this time, it seemed like everyone on the street was watching everyone else. There were Feds, cops, members of the Mob, and the brokerage house owners themselves. Diorio wasn't about to be caught on anyone's wire, so he went in and gestured that he was there for the money. He showed them what he wanted, who he worked for, and when someone tried to get him to talk, he just grunted. He wasn't going to commit himself to anything that could be used against him. So he got the money and left clean. I realized that on Wall Street, there was far less loyalty than there was on the streets of Brooklyn.

Shortly after that, Andrew Bressman was leaving after working late in his office when a stocky, Italian-looking guy walked up to him, accosted him, and demanded, "Are you Andrew?"

"Yes," Bressman answered, nervous because of the way the guy presented himself, but thinking he might be a client.

"I got a great stock deal for you that I want you to buy," the man said. His voice and his manner were intimidating, and he frightened Bressman.

"I don't know what you're talking about," Bressman said. Then the guy slapped him, hard. Bressman's insides froze. He might have pissed his pants. Who knew what would happen next, if a guy with the obvious look of a Wiseguy slaps you?

"I'll be calling you tomorrow," the guy said. "You'll be hearing from me."

Bressman was sick with fear. This was obvious intimidation about stock transactions and he needed help. He called Big Al, his only Italian friend with Mob connections. But Al was connected to the Gotti family that was constantly in the media and help from them might have subjected Andrew's business to very troublesome attention and involvement. Instead, he called me and I decided to help. I figured that using my connections would impress Andrew while also doing him a favor. I also thought I could use Andrew in the future, working directly with him. There was money to be made and all it took was one call to Danny.

The man who threatened Bressman called again the next day. Danny asked me for the man's beeper number, and Bressman passed it on so that Danny could contact him. It turned out that the man doing the threatening was a captain in one of the crime families and a made man. He had a lifetime oath to the family, and both etiquette and respect required that no one talk directly to him unless he was also a high-up made man. Danny explained to him that Bressman was already spoken for, which meant that Bressman was under Mob protection and that required the captain making the threat to back off.

All the same, this called for a sit-down, and we decided we would send Diorio and a street-smart bouncer called Forty. This could technically have been called "Wiseguy fraud," since neither of these guys was directly or indirectly connected with organized crime. They were just friends of Danny's, like me. But they both looked tough and sounded convincing, and it was a scam we thought maybe we could pull off. Why not? There seemed to be no limit to what we could run on Wall Street, so we might as well try this.

Danny and I drove up in one car with Diorio, Lex and Forty in another. When we got to the location where the meeting was going down, we spotted men in position all over the street. From the way they were dressed, they could have been Feds or they could be other Mob guys. They were wearing suits and blended in the neighborhood, but they also sometimes didn't belong. Diorio, especially, spotted what was going down because of his background in police work.

Danny said he had to back out. He hadn't cleared this with his own family and he didn't want to get into the middle of something without approval by higher-ups. Forty and Lex went to talk with the Wiseguy and Diorio and I pretended to be involved with other matters. We didn't want them to think we were there as back-up, though that was why we were there. Lex did the talking and the man agreed to back off, especially after Forty identified himself as a made man, showing appropriate power and thus demanding respect.

Afterwards, Danny came to me and said that he wanted to get paid for handling matters like that and he wanted to go ask Bressman for money. I said no, telling him I would cut him in on the next deal we did with Bressman instead. I said that would bring him far more money than he might get from a shakedown.

By now Danny had decided he wanted his own firm and he got a friend from Brooklyn with a broker's license to be his partner and legitimate front. Gene agreed to help them raise money and then we would work with them on a 60/40 split. Danny would be a secret partner. It was ironic that Danny had to turn to legitimate business to achieve the wealth he sought. Many crime bosses who commanded fear and respect only took in as much as upper mid-level management at a major corporation. The truly big money I was generating for myself, others in my firm, and selected clients, had previously eluded Danny. Now he had opportunities that had previously seemed impossible.

I saw myself helping a friend. I knew that if Danny were a short order cook in a Brooklyn restaurant instead of being part of a major crime family, I would feel the same about helping him. It was friendship that drove me, not a sense of payback. No one else thought that way, perhaps not even Danny. Danny had been doing me business favors. He had arranged sit-downs. He had provided muscle. His friends had been given jobs that would not have existed if they were not used to dealing with both sides of the law. I now faced it: I was Mobbed-up, a fact that was multiplying other problems I would soon be facing with law enforcement.

I didn't like seeing my firm as a Mob operation or a Mob front, but it was a fact that Danny's presence permeated every conflict. If he wasn't there, Butchie Blue Eyes was. Butchie was also being brought into a number of new deals so he could make more money than he had been earning. His birthday was coming up and Big Gene suggested that a sizable gift would be appropriate. After all, he did help with Fat Frank and didn't get anything for it. We leased him a Porsche 911 Cabriolet and since no one but me had good credit, the car was under my name. Big mistake on my part—putting a Wiseguy in a car with tags registered to me!

We wanted to know what was going on with Country World in Colorado. We knew the Country World board of directors had hired some big Las Vegas company to come in and bail them out and sit on the board as well. My partners and I decided that, as a board member of the casino corporation, I should attend the board meeting coming up and I flew to Denver. I walked into the outer office of where the meeting was being held, and the secretary said I was not allowed at the meeting. I told her I was a board member and I should be in there.

"No," the secretary said, "the meeting's already started."

"I just flew in from New York," I told her. "I have to be in this meeting."

"I'm sorry, sir," the secretary said. She was really being difficult and I was getting angry. I stepped outside to use my cell phone and called Lex and Gene. I told them they were not letting me into the meeting and they jumped on it.

"'What do you mean, they're not letting you in?" Lex yelled. "Go in there and tell them where it's at! Tell them that they'll wreck this company, that the funds have been funneled down, and…you know…try to protect us as best you can."

That gave me the incentive to go back and push the secretary aside as she rose to block me. Then I slammed open the boardroom door on the men having the meeting. I paused at the entrance and the secretary rushed up behind to make it clear she had done everything in her power to keep me out. Then I addressed the meeting calmly.

"Guys, I represent all the voting shares that the public owns," I said. "I own every share of this company in its float, and I control all the warrants. I control all the common stock. I think I had better be sitting in this meeting."

Looking more calm and controlled than I felt, I sat down in an empty chair at the boardroom table. Then I continued.

"Right now you know that the stock is decimated," I said. "The company hasn't done anything it's supposed to do, and quite frankly, the lawsuits are going to start hitting."

That had a big effect. Systematically, one by one, every board member put his tail between his legs and resigned. But I wasn't finished.

"I'm going to vote at the current market price—twenty cents a share—a million dollars worth of stock to Holly Products," I said.

I meant what I said, and I used the control I had to push out the former president and management. He was furious and went to his lawyers. But I was in the right and we got the property back, putting it under control of Holly Products.

Then we promised Larry Berman that we would fund the building of the casino. We would float a small secondary to give him enough money to prep it, to get it going, and then go for a state bond issuance to build a casino. The state was willing to float a bond to build a $60 million dollar facility there and our goal was to really build it, to really make the thing work. That's why we merged the two companies, in effect putting a Band-Aid on Country World, and we stopped the lawsuit because the clients were getting shares of Holly Products in lieu of the Country World stock.

It's one thing to lose money on paper. It's another thing to have sold it at a loss. The shareholders who saw the value of their holdings drop really didn't have a complaint when Holly Products came in to bail it out. They had taken a risk, saw it go bad, and then we gave them hope with the new deal. The only problem was for the people who were convinced by some broker to dump the stock entirely, and now they saw it might rally and they no longer had a piece of the action.

The pressure was building for me. Some of it was in response to the myriad side deals that had to be created and overseen as the IPOs were prepared and manipulated. There were pay-offs, kickbacks, and funds being transferred overseas. Lex was working behind the scenes, and Gene was still active as a broker. However, Dutch and I had to be the front men for everything because Gene did not relate well to people, including the other brokers in the same firm.

Gene, savvy as he was, did not have a good aura about him. He didn't have a decent personality. He was effective raising money in person, but he thought that all brokers were alike, that they were all replaceable like widgets and wadgets. He'd call them and they'd try to tell him about their problems. "Hunh," he'd say, "you guys are just like mooks and monkeys. Don't worry about it. I don't wanna hear about it."

He'd say it in his whiny voice, and it didn't have a good effect on the brokers, including me. Gene was a hustler, determined to make any deal he could, anywhere in the world where there might be an opportunity. He was perpetually seeking the next big score, all the time making himself vulnerable to enemies, whether in business or among law enforcement officers who would eventually begin tracking him. He had what I found to be the Russian criminal mentality where, eventually, you always try to get something over on your partner. Worse for me, Gene felt no loyalty towards anyone other than himself, no matter how he might have prospered through their help.

Yet, I had sold him to my brokers as a genius, putting him on a pedestal, the same way Lex had sold him to me. It hadn't worked with Dutch. He hated Gene and they were always at war. That's why we were all happy to have Gene down on the fourth floor with Lex. At White Rock, Lex and Gene were a combination of helpful partners and necessary evils. Outside Wall Street, in Brighton Beach, a community next to Coney Island, they were role models for young Russian teens who aspired to be just like them. That became a serious problem for us.

CHAPTER TWELVE

U.S. Dept. of Justice: Press Release, Mar. 3, 2000 (continued)

In furtherance of their fraudulent schemes, the White Rock and State Street Partners, and others, entered into undisclosed arrangements with members and associates of LCN (La Cosa Nostra) Families. Pursuant to these arrangements, the defendants FRANK COPPA, SR., ERNEST MONTEVECCHI, DANIEL PERSICO, and EUGENE LOMBARDO provided protection for individuals and resolved disputes relating to the fraudulent sale of stock and warrants. These activities included the following:

(b) In or about, and between December 1994 and February 1995, the White Rock Partners learned that the defendant ROCCO BASILE was being extorted by LCN (La Cosa Nostra) associates to repay money purportedly owed to the owners of another brokerage firm. MONTEVECCHI and PERSICO negotiated with other members and associates of LCN families so as to enable the White Rock Partners to retain the defendant ROCCO BASILE and others with whom he worked, including the defendants JACK BASILE and GIUSEPPE TEMPERINO, as White Rock brokers and cold callers.

Our office at 17 State Street was in an area of high-rent, exclusive businesses that represented the top level of power and wealth in corporate America in the 1990s. Headquarters of airlines, banks, other brokerage firms, and communications companies were housed on different floors in our building, and in other aluminum, steel and smoked glass towers on the street. State Street was part of Wall Street, and work dress was fashion-conscious, money-conscious, pinstripes, silk, worsted and wool. It was clothes you saw in ads in *Esquire*, the *New Yorker* or *Vanity Fair.* Black Lexuses stopped at the curb to let brokers out before being parked in nearby parking garages that cost hundreds of dollars per month per space.

State Street was a long way from Bensonhurst, in Brooklyn. It was just as distant from Brighton Beach, the Russian immigrant community where Lex and Gene had come from. The steel and silent elevators and deep pile office carpeting of 17 State Street seemed a world away from Brighton Beach and the street gangs there. But, it turned out, not as far as we thought.

The Brighton Beach street gangs were big and powerful, with young members not unlike the hustlers and car thieves who had worked Brooklyn a few years before. The difference was that the Brighton Beach street gangs did not limit themselves to one ethnic or racial group. Most members were the sons of Russian immigrants, but some were white or Puerto Rican. At the time they noticed that two of their neighborhood guys, Lex and Gene, were tooling around Brighton Beach streets in a Mercedes 500 and a Jaguar convertible. One gang leader, Paulie, a Puerto Rican kid, decided to pay a visit to Lex and Gene's work place.

The fact that Lex had been to jail for a bar fight should have added respect to his reputation, avoiding confrontation. But the young punks could see the level of success he was enjoying, and that was enough for him to be challenged. Paulie had two issues he claimed he needed to settle. The first was with a young Russian immigrant's son named Gabe, a gang member who had been inspired by the same wealth and power on Wall Street as I had seen from Brooklyn. Gabe had started out as a cold caller, just like me, and was now a Pasta Boy, a broker in a world of money, and prestige.

The problem was that gang membership was for life. That meant getting a gang tattoo on the ankle right after initiation so the Brighton Beach gang members could recognize each other until their dying day. Gabe had decided to lose the tattoo once he made it on Wall Street, and had it removed by plastic surgery. The gang found out about this and decided to come and confront Gabe. They also had a larger purpose. That was to shake Lex and Gene down for a $60,000 "investment" in a music video they wanted to make.

This was a transition era in music, when music videos were dominating a number of cable stations and were sometimes played in clubs. Hip-hop was in its early stages, disco was folding for the second time, and break dancing was not yet out of style long enough to be considered retro. But every neighborhood seemed to have a few kids who knew they would become the next big thing if only they could make their video for MTV and the record companies. So why not ask two wealthy guys from the 'hood to help some kids still there, still pursuing a dream?

Of course, in reality it was nothing more than a shakedown and I happened to walk into the middle of it. I had taken the stairs down from the ninth floor to the fourth floor to say hello to talk to Gene and Lex and when I opened the door to our fourth floor office, I saw three guys in the vestibule outside the elevator and a fourth guy standing inside right next to the secretary. They were all wearing bomber coats—those long down coats that hang thick and loose. The way they were standing, it was obvious they were packing handguns and maybe shotguns. You'd never notice it if they were going down the street. The coats would hide it all. But inside our office, where no one was going to see them except somebody who worked there, they wanted us to know they were packing heat.

I was terrified. More so than when I had come close to the dark side of Danny's world. I had been to sit-downs involving armed thugs, but they had left the room when Danny dismissed them. The power was implied, not a physical presence. And Danny was a friend. These were explosive young gang members with guns who probably had a history of violence. They were not anybody's friends. They had no allegiance to anyone in the office, and if they killed everybody who saw them, there would be no one to say they had ever been there. This was potentially a life or death situation.

I could see somebody was talking inside Lex's office so I went to the conference room. Dicky was in there with Gene, who was pale with fear, his bow tie wobbling as he talked. Big Van Lombardo, the gangster who was our in-house watchdog, was also there and I was glad to see him on the phone, calling for backup. Lex rang the conference room phone as I walked in and I answered. I don't know how he managed, but he spoke in a calm, quiet voice.

"Look, can you get some help?" Lex asked. "I need some help in here."

"Sure," I said. "I'll get somebody."

I had some luck with me. As far as the young gang members knew, I was just a guy who happened to walk in on the middle of their shakedown. They didn't know I was Lex and Gene's partner or in any way connected with the company, so they didn't pay much attention to me. I used the phone to call Danny. Then Gene went in with Lex, and I phoned upstairs to get Nick Blasso, a pal and one of my top brokers, who belonged to the Downtown Shooting Club. It is almost impossible to legally carry a handgun in New York City, but many people keep guns in their apartments and Nick was one of them. He liked to shoot for fun and I had gotten into it, too. Some shooting club members kept their guns in the lockers at the shooting club. Nick had two handguns in his apartment around the corner in Battery Park City, next to where I lived.

Nick and I left the building and raced over to his apartment where he got a nine-millimeter for me and a .50-caliber for himself. I don't know what he had in mind with that thing. It was like a .44-magnum or a .45. It fired a gigantic round that probably would have gone through the walls of the next building. We hid the guns under our suits and hurried back to the office.

We were both skilled shots, at least we were against paper targets that didn't shoot back. This might be very different. The gangbangers might force us into a shoot-to-kill situation, and I had never even been in the army. I had never even been in a situation where violence meant anything more than using your fists. The Mob used a face slap as a warning, and the next step was to give someone a beating. These young gangsters looked as if they were ready to use bullets as their first message. While we were getting armed, Danny had sent over John Diorio and Forty, both packing nine-millimeter automatics. They knew how to handle themselves in a street situation.

But the ace came from the guy Big Van Lombardo called over: a gang member who would have far more power than these guys shaking down the Russians. When Nick and I came back, John Diorio and Forty were there, so there were four of us in the conference room with guns. If any shoot-out happened, we thought we could take care of it, but we weren't sure.

I had been in a tense situation once before with Diorio and

Forty, who had worked security at the nightclub the night the midget pulled a gun on me. But this was different. Just carrying a weapon in there was scary, and the idea that anyone might die was terrifying.

So far, the gang was trying to be cool. Paulie, the head guy, let Lex talk with Gene to tell him what was going on. Lex told him Paulie was asking for a $60,000 loan to do a music video. There is no way to know if the guys with guns under their coats were there to scare people to keep things cool, or to shoot people if Paulie felt like he was getting dissed.

Then the elevator opened. The guy who came out of the elevator was the gunsel Big Van had called in. He was a Puerto Rican, and he was dressed like he'd just finished sanding sheet rock dust. Everything was white, powdery. He had beady cold eyes, and three tattooed tears coming from his eye. It was a prison thing. I had seen those tattooed tears in movies, watching *Law and Order* and all those crime shows. Three tears. That meant he'd killed three people.

He didn't say anything. He just walked into the conference room where he saw Big Van. Then Big Van said, "Sal, can we use the other office?"

"No problem," I said.

"This is my guy," Big Van said to me. "He's going to take care of this."

I didn't get this. The guys from the Brighton Beach street gang were heavily armed. There were three of them with guns under their coats and they all looked like they were ready to use them. Van's guy was in work clothes, no trace of a weapon.

"These guys are all packing guns," I told him. "Are you packing?"

He looked at me with those cold eyes and then slowly put his hands up. Nothing in them. Just hands, calloused from work, maybe a little extra bruising on the knuckles.

"All I need is these," he said. Calm. So sure of himself it was scary. And those three teardrops coming from his eye. I knew I was looking at power.

"He's head of the Latin Kings," Big Van told me, as if he was talking about a foreign head of state, or a military commander.

"That's the biggest prison gang in Spanish Harlem."

I knew about the Latin Kings. They had a bad reputation. And the kids in the office with Paulie were from some bullshit punk outfit out of Coney Island.

"I'll go talk to them," the Latin Kings guy said. But he wasn't in a hurry. He let them cool off for a minute. I was blown away with this guy. This was the most tense situation I've ever been in my life. Everybody had guns, and if one guy fired it would be bloody mayhem. This was an elite office building in Manhattan, and here was a for real facedown of gangbangers!

I took Nick downstairs. There were so many goons up there, if shooting started, there'd be a hail of bullets where anybody could get hit. I wanted to be in a better position. In the event these guys did have a shoot-out and anybody makes it downstairs, Nick and I would get them downstairs.

Outside, Nick and I saw the two guys sent over as backup standing with something over their hands to hide their guns. It was scary. I looked at the 50-caliber Desert Eagle Nick was holding. You see them in movies now. They're the big-ass gun with the wide base. They're made for the Israeli army and they shoot through walls. You could put a nine-millimeter bullet inside the 50-caliber bullet. It only holds six shots because the bullets are so big. It's legal. You can buy it in the store. And if you shoot into a crowd, it kills about three people with one bullet.

Nick and I picked spots outside where it looked like we had triangulated the building. I stood by a car, facing the building from one angle. Nick did the same from another. We figured which car was being used by the gang, and wanted to be able to shoot anyone running to it if necessary. But the way the back-ups were positioned in the building, a shoot-out was likely to result in the two brokers and their back-ups shooting each other. It was surreal. First we had Danny and the sit-down, and now this. Fire with fire. Gangsters come, and we find gangsters to defend us. Russian street gangs come; we find a Puerto Rican to protect us.

And then the gang members left, the guy from the Latin Kings left, Paulie left, the gangsters left, and it was over. It seemed over but it was not. The street gang couldn't get any money, but they wanted revenge and told us they'd kill Gabe for having his tattoo removed.

"We still want Gabe and we're going to kill him 'cause he took off that tattoo," Paulie told Lex on the phone later. "That symbolizes that he's dissing us. He's dissin' the crew, man."

Now we had to defend our own, which meant another call for help. This time Big Van enlisted a member of the Bonanno family who knew Paulie and his crew well enough to pay Paulie and his gang a visit at their clubhouse in Coney Island.

"Look, will you guys stop with the shit?" the Bonanno's guy said. "We're going to throw a grenade in your club right now."

Paulie's gang knew who the Bonannos were and they backed down. But it took two visits to calm these guys before the threat to kill Gabe went away. I was glad we were able to help Gabe. He was a fun guy and a really good producer. But Lex, Gene and I knew that we had incurred serious debt. We knew the moment a man requests a favor from the Mob, he owed that person or that family. I had gone to Danny. Others in my firm had approached other families and we were compromised. Worse, although we did not know it, our names were beginning to appear in confidential government reports, and we would soon be investigated in our own right. Our sales approaches, our associates, our trips within the United States and abroad were becoming a part of the records of several different agencies. And the word was out among brokers that we did cash deals.

At this point, my partners and I held a meeting to try to get things under control. First, we had problems with guys back-dooring our stock. Then we had owners of our deals going to the Mob to resolve issues. Now we had permanent Mob guys on the fourth floor, overseeing our business and protecting us. It had become too crazy. We all recognized the fact that our firm could not last much longer. White Rock was definitely not going to become the next Merrill Lynch. We decided to start other firms so we could sell multiple deals among ourselves and completely control floats.

Through all this, I was fighting to make money, to build my business. Jack Hickman and Dicky, back at Whale, weren't going through this, were they? And this was in midst of trying to create a home life for my wife and children that would nourish and enrich them. Lynn and I were an interfaith couple. I'm Catholic and she's Jewish. We each valued the traditions and faith of our families and we each could understand how our two faiths interrelated. We were teaching our children to celebrate Passover, and we were teaching them the Easter story.

I was determined not to bring home the sometimes frightening world of my growing brokerage firm. I avoided mentioning Danny's intervention, the sit-downs, the invasion of the Brighton Beach/Coney Island street gangs. I didn't tell my wife about the near shoot-out and the moral dilemma it had posed for me. I didn't tell her of my fears.

But we had been compromised by our mutual acceptance of the safe full of money. It was as though we both felt that so long as only cash was involved, so long as no one was being physically harmed, the hiding of capital, the money laundering, and the other crimes could be left unexamined. We delighted in our children at home, and I concentrated on my work only after I left the house we so lovingly shared.

The biggest problem was that my firm was a corporation in which it seemed as though each person had a scam of his own, in the midst of a stock market that was insane. When I got involved with the Street in 1990, the Dow was at 2,513 and the Nasdaq at 410. By the time we opened our firm in August, '93, the Dow was 3,681 and Nasdaq was 742. It was the beginning of a bull market that would take the Dow close to 12,000 and the Nasdaq to 7,000.

Gene, especially, had been hustling wherever he could. He had maintained ties with the Russian Mafia, the organized crime underbelly of what had been the Soviet Union. The break-up of the USSR in 1991 meant financial opportunities for rogues. Dishonest military personnel stole weapons and sold them to international terrorists with the Russian Mafia acting as go-betweens. Russian leaders were on the payroll and often brought into investment scams being worked throughout the world.

Ironically, Gene's Russian Mafia contacts were acting in ways they had learned from the Americans following the Vietnam War.

Funds skimmed from the Post Exchange (PX) system, gold obtained illegally, and other items were being brought into the United States by opportunists. Some of the individuals involved had connections with the Nixon White House, and kickbacks may have gone as high as to the President himself.

Allegations were later made that President Gerald Ford was aware of this problem when he pardoned President Richard Nixon after the latter resigned from office. Nixon was not pardoned just for the Watergate scandal that brought his downfall, but for all crimes. The statement did not seem meaningful until members of the Mafia claimed in writing that Nixon had benefited from their actions. In addition, CIA members, presumably connected with rogue criminal activity, were involved in taking stockpiled weapons abandoned in Vietnam, then selling them to various militant and criminal groups in the United States and elsewhere. I had actually met Nixon on a flight to St. Bart's in the Caribbean, and the former President had asked if he could hold my daughter in his arms. I had said, "sure," and pulled out my 35 mm to take some pictures.

Eventually Gene and Lex would become involved with deals that ranged from a Russian leader's effort to buy an American stock brokerage firm to obtaining missiles from the hands of Osama bin Laden. Meanwhile, Gene was working his own scams with various stocks and brokers, both domestically and internationally. He lived the fairy tale of the billionaire lifestyle although he had only a few million in the bank. His involvement with White Rock was just another vehicle for increasing his earnings. Yet Gene was either unknown to Federal authorities or less of a concern than Lex.

Then, Lex's sentencing finally came up for the bar fight on the eve of the day I had passed my broker's exam. The judge refused to listen to all the arguments on Lex's behalf against prison time and sentenced him to serve 18 months. It's likely that he would not have gone to jail if his father wasn't a gangster. Before the trial, he had been offered a deal where he'd get no jail, no probation, but would lose his broker's license. He hadn't thought the charges were bad enough for him to lose his license and that was why he had fought it. That was a mistake.

This was the early days of the Mob being connected with Wall Street and the prosecutor seemed to be trying to send a message. After his conviction, Lex lost his license, and instead of staying free, he got 18 months. The offshore bank accounts and stock positions were his responsibilities and we figured we could use his knowledge while he was in jail by going to see him with any problems.

Lex served approximately a year in jail, and while he was behind bars, I was faced with the immediate problem involving Rocco Basile and the scam he had pulled on his former boss Roy. Danny's cousin, the acting godfather of the family, told Danny there had to be a meeting about Rocco and Roy.

Roy's brokerage firm Hanover-Sterling had fallen apart in a spectacular way, taking out a clearing firm and losing a hundred million dollars of clients' money. The local business writers had learned of his troubles and were covering the blow-up of his firm. Now Roy was looking for money from any direction, and he claimed to his Wiseguy that Rocco had scammed his firm out of $250,000. Rocco admitted having Roy's money, but claimed it was all legitimate, not proceeds from the "black-and-blue" scam.

What Rocco had done was wait till the manager had gone home for the night, then backdated the time stamp clock in the trading room. He would put the stock on the trading desk. There were fake tickets of the firm's stock position that would be on Roy's desk in the morning. Roy would come in and there would be an extra hundred thousand shares sitting there looking like the deal was made the day before.

The approach was simple. Roy would go home. The market was closed. Rocco and others would pay off Roy's trader in cash to accept a ticket from one of Rocco 's clients. Rocco would get paid on that stock whatever he got paid—commission or cash—he wasn't supposed to sell it back to Roy's firm, but he did. The trader made big money—fifty grand, a hundred grand—handling the "wooden tickets," and Roy usually did not catch on. In the morning Roy would call the trading department and say, "How much stock do we have?"

The trader might say that they had two hundred thousand shares to sell, and part of that stock was Rocco's that he had dumped in the trading account that he wasn't supposed to sell. That's why they called that the "black and blue market"—they were giving black and blue bruises to Roy. In the end, Roy figured it out.

As I saw it, this was a problem between Rocco and Roy's firm, not mine. But Danny came over to the office and told me I had to fire Rocco. This was the first time Danny had ever spoken to me like this. What he was doing was giving me a condition, telling me something I had to do, on the authority vested in him as a made member of a powerful family.

"Why do I have to fire Rocco?" I asked him.

"Word came from upstairs," Danny said. I don't think he liked saying what he had to say, but he had to say it. "You have to fire Rocco."

"Rocco's one of my top producers," I told Danny. "He's got some personal issues with another firm where they're saying he stole money. I don't see why what he did in the past should affect me."

Danny didn't take it any farther right there with me. Instead he told the big Wiseguys that I wasn't firing Rocco. They told Danny he had to come up to my office and smack me and then drag Rocco outside and beat the shit out of him. Danny came back and told me that.

"That's what I have to do," Danny said. "I don't have a choice. You fire him, or I smack you."

Danny and I had played stickball together as kids. Now Danny was being told what to do by the organized crime family run by his cousin Alphonse "Allie Boy" Persico. The family was using Danny, because he was my friend, to try to squeeze a quarter-of-a-million dollars out of Rocco.

"You have to fire Rocco," Danny said. "Or I have to smack you, then beat the shit out of Rocco," he repeated.

"I'm not firing Rocco, Danny," I said. "I don't give a shit. I don't want to fire the guy." For all I knew, they wanted Rocco for themselves to make money with. He was worth millions to me in commissions. He was my mushroom!

"Well, then, I gotta do something," Danny said, meaning he had to beat up Rocco.

"Well, do it to him when he's outside," I said. "I don't care if you beat the shit out of him downstairs, but don't do it in my firm. The guy has personal issues. They have nothing to do with me. This guy is going to be buying a shit load of stock from me."

Danny explained that the family thought differently. "If he works here, they're going to want the quarter of a million dollars out of you that they claim that he stole."

"It'll be a cold day in hell before I come up with that, Danny," I said.

Both Danny and I crossed a line from which there was no turning back. I had refused to cooperate with a request from members of a mob family that was becoming increasingly influential on Wall Street. Danny refused to follow a family order issued by his cousin out of respect for our friendship.

Danny and I talked about it later.

"You know, I went against them," he said. "I'm supposed to follow their orders and I didn't. You're my friend and...you know...I can't go against you. I know you didn't do anything wrong."

What Danny left unsaid was that this was going to cost one of us. Maybe both of us. And they would still go after Rocco to get the money.

I let Rocco know I wasn't going to back him up when they came after him, so he went to his neighborhood in Brooklyn and found a gangster to speak for him with help from his father, a well-known Sicilian. There was a big meeting that led to a financial settlement that squashed the whole thing and allowed Rocco to stay with me, leaving Danny's family pissed off with him and putting me solidly on Allie Boy's shit list.

CHAPTER THIRTEEN

U.S. Department of Justice, Mar. 3, 2000

United States of America
- against -
FRANK COPPA, SR.
ERNEST MONTEVECCHI
     Also known as **"Butch"**
DANIEL PERSICO
JACK BASILE
ROCCO BASILE
LARRY BERMAN
JOHN CIOFOLETTI
WALTER DURCHALTER
     Also known as **"Dutch"**
EDWARD GARAFOLA
DANIEL LEV
EUGENE LOMBARDO
EDMOND NAGEL
ALFRED PALAGONIA
ALEKS PAUL
JOSEPH POLITO, SR.
LAWRENCE RAY
ABRAHAM SALAMAN
GIUSEPPE TEMPERINO
     Also known as **"Joseph Temperino"**

It was further part of the conspiracy that, in or about November 1994, White Rock underwrote a secondary offering of Holly Securities (the "November 1994 Offering"). Pursuant to this Offering, Holly sold 350,000 shares of Series D Convertible Preferred Stock (the "Holly Preferred Stock"). As compensation to White Rock for agreeing to underwrite this secondary Offering, the defendant LARRY BERMAN and others caused 4,000,000 Holly warrants to be sold in a private place-

ment to nominees of the White Rock Partners, the defendant JOHN CIO-FOLETTI and others.

It was further part of the conspiracy that, as a part of the November 1994 Offering, the 4,000,000 Holly warrants that were secretly controlled by the White Rock Partners, the defendant JOHN CIOFO-LETTI and others in the name of offshore and other nominees were registered for offer and sale to the public.

It was further part of the conspiracy that the White Rock Partners, the defendants JOHN CIOFOLETTI and others caused these 4,000,000 Holly warrants to be fraudulently sold to the public. The defendants ROCCO BASILE, JACK BASILE, AND GIUSEPPE TEMPERINO, together with others, sold Holly warrants to their customers at White Rock. The defendant JOHN CIOFOLETTI arranged for Holly warrants to be sold to customers at Barclay and the defendant ALFRED PALAGONIA arranged for Holly warrants to be sold to customers of Blair, though many of these sales were executed through accounts at Baron.

It was further part of the conspiracy that defendant LARRY BERMAN and others sold in excess of 1,000,000 shares of Holly common stock to offshore entities that were secret nominees of the White Rock Partners.

My partners and I were running scams to increase our incomes, not to hurt stock buyers. We wanted to take a piece of the bridge financing or private placement in ways that would not be detected. We had been using a series of false companies and individuals—people and businesses who did nothing but receive a percentage of the money made this way at the time of the IPO. The rest of the money went to my partners and me. But we had so many deals going on that anyone studying the paperwork would start seeing the same names over and over again, and there was concern about using the same companies as in the casino deal. Though there were individuals capable of providing money this way, it was rare that they would invest in more than one or two private placement or bridge arrangements. The repetition of their names would alert an investigator to look more closely at what was going on. That's why we needed new names and new companies to act as beards, carrying out the front action in exchange for a piece of the profit.

Aleks was already making six percent on the millions of dollars that needed laundering, and when Gene and Lex offered him another ten percent to become another "beard" for our IPOs, he agreed. In addition to Aleks, we used Danny Velt, an international hustler who could find ways to make money no matter what was happening in Europe and the Middle East. After the Soviet Union collapsed, he bought Russian helicopters and sold them to South Africa. He invested in a Ukranian trucking company. He was legitimately wealthy, and he and Aleks could actually invest their own money, which they chose to do. They would get their 10 percent payback for the entire amount they let us park in their accounts as beards when the deal went public. We would take the rest and divide it among all the insider players, including ourselves.

Another beard was a Russian called Vlad, a professional killer and a heroin addict whose real name was Eugevny Tedesco. On Brighton Beach he was called "Vuolva." I never understood why Gene and Lex wanted to use him, and it was not clear if Vlad used drugs just because he liked them or if he needed the drugs in order to live with himself. Either way, drugs were a definite problem in his life and, as it turned out, ours. The more money he made, the more he could spend on heroin, and under no circumstances would he venture any real distance from his heroin connection. The guy could have all the cops in New York City looking for him and he'd never be far from his dealer in Brighton Beach.

Vlad was a hazard to have around, which shouldn't have taken a genius among us to figure out. He was in the fourth floor office one day with Lex and Gene, when Gene was shouting at two brokers over some deal. They were mad and they were yelling, but it was nothing serious. Just three hotheads who had no intention of hurting anyone. They'd talk. They'd yell. They'd work it out, and then it would be over.

Vlad left during the shouting and came back with some extra-large, heavy-duty trash bags, the type you could use for clearing heavy metal and other junk from a vacant lot without risk of their tearing. He arrived just as the two brokers who had been shouting at Gene were waiting for the elevator to the ninth floor. The argument was over, and there was no trace of hostility in the air. Vlad looked puzzled, and so did Lex who had come out to the elevator for a last word with the two brokers.

"What are the trash bags for?" Lex asked.

"Them," Vlad said, nodding at the two brokers, who were getting onto the elevator. He looked disappointed, even peeved as the elevator door slid shut, the two brokers inside it.

"What do you mean, for them?" Lex asked.

"For the bodies," Vlad said, as if he were explaining something too obvious to need comment. "You stick the bodies in the bag so you can carry them downstairs on the freight elevator. They look just like trash. You can toss them in the dumpster or stick them in your car trunk. Drive them to Jersey or someplace and get rid of them. Nobody looks in these things—too heavy to tear. A good seal will keep them from stinking before they turn into landfill. I've used them a lot with guys who were acting like those two punks."

Lex was aghast. So was Gene, and so was I, when I heard about it.

"We were having a discussion," Lex explained to Vlad. "It got a little loud because that's our nature. You're Russian. Don't you ever have somebody yell at you without killing them?"

Vlad looked at Lex like he was talking hot air, and didn't answer.

"Look, they were mad because they thought we were wrong," Lex said. "I was mad because I thought they were wrong. We yelled. We talked. We got it settled. It was no big deal."

Vlad shrugged. "I'd have killed them," he said.

It occurred to Lex that Vlad probably never left anyone like that alive. This should have been a warning to us. It wasn't. But it was only part of the craziness going on. Like the thing with Danny's cousin Alphonse, whose street nickname was "Little Allie Boy" but whom we called The Philosopher. We called him that because he never gave you a straight answer. Instead he talked in riddles. I never knew if he was trying to protect himself from the cops or if that was just the way he was.

As I mentioned, Alphonse had gone to prison on racketeering charges with his father Carmine (Junior) Persico in 1986, and had been due to get out in 1993. But his release was delayed when the Feds charged him with complicity in a bloody two-year long Colombo family war that left 12 dead and dozens more injured between 1991 and 1993. In 1994, Alphonse was out of prison and took over as the Colombo family's acting boss.

Alphonse was involved with all the rackets, especially the vicious ones like loansharking. It was not clear to me if he was a killer or just ordered hits. I only knew he was cold-blooded. That was enough.

Mob trouble came up with The Philosopher because of a kid I had working for me as a stockbroker who was related to one of the five main crime families. I don't think the kid was really involved in the Mob. He certainly wasn't a made man. The trouble was that he was trying to look important by saying things that weren't true. I don't even think he knew he could get me in trouble. Probably he was just stupid. The kid was out in the Hamptons riding a jet ski, when he met The Philosopher and recognized who he was. I guess he wanted to show his importance so he started talking about how he worked for me and that he knew I was connected, because I had bragged that Danny's family was protecting my brokerage firm.

The Philosopher, as a boss in the Colombo family, was always under heavy, constant Federal scrutiny when he was out of jail. He might have been nuts, but he followed rules, and one rule was that you never talk about your connections. He knew that he and his family weren't actually protecting my brokerage firm. In fact, he already resented the fact that Danny had stood up for me against his orders. Now he was hearing from this nothing broker, a guy with a famous family last name, that had been bragging about my connection.

In The Philosopher's world, there were only three things to do when someone outside the family talked like that. You could have him whacked. You could give him a beating. Or you could shake him down for money. But you could only do any of these if you had been wronged. Even if you hated a guy, like The Philosopher hated me, you still had to be certain you were right. I didn't know anything about all this because the young stockbroker hadn't stayed with me long. When shortly after this incident, Danny came by my office a little before noon and told me we had to go meet with his cousin, I had no idea what it was all about.

Danny drove me to this marina in Brooklyn and stopped behind a warehouse building. It was lunchtime and the area was deserted except for The Philosopher and two goons. My first thought was that he was going to kill me and I didn't even know why. Danny was with me, but he's part of the family and he owes them more than he did me. Plus, he's the one that drove me out there.

We got out of the car and The Philosopher was angry. He told me I'd been using the family name and bragging that my brokerage was protected. I was stunned, totally in the dark, and I told him, with all due respect, that he was wrong. I told him that whoever was telling him this was lying. I said I'd known his family for twenty years. I said Danny and I have always been friends. I know the rules and I'd never say anything like that.

"Right, Danny?"

Danny was standing there, agreeing with me. He doesn't get along with his cousin, but the cousin knows Danny was not going to lie. If I'm doing something against the family, Danny was going to side with the family against me, even with our friendship. His backing me up meant something. That's why he took me. The meeting was no different than a sit-down except I'm not in the Mob and nobody told me about this in advance.

Then I see the kid who started it all driving over to where we were having the meeting. The Philosopher sees him—he obviously asked him to be there—but by now he has decided it was okay. I didn't say anything out of line. Danny and I got back in the car and left. I don't know what happened to the kid who had been bragging so much. I don't even know what was supposed to have happened to me. They could have killed me and dumped me in the water without anyone knowing about it. But maybe that thought was overly dramatic. Probably there would just have been a shakedown—a very big one.

With The Philosopher, it was always hard to tell. As I've said, there was something crazy about him, beyond his habit of talking in riddles. There was so much Federal heat on him that you could see government cars tailing him like a convoy, wherever he went, but he used to travel armed, which he was not allowed to do. He acted like he was in danger and had to protect himself from enemies who wouldn't get near him with all that surveillance.

I only actually saw him one more time at Scores, the topless bar where I used to take brokers after work. The Philosopher saw me and came over to speak to me.

"How you doing?" he asked. "You know who I am, right? How's business?"

"Yes," I said. "I know who you are," as though I'm going to forget a guy I thought was going to kill me at the marina in Brooklyn!

"Business is up and down," I went on. "It's the market. You know." I didn't feel that he was really asking what he wanted to know.

"What happens if your firm goes out of business?" he asked—a strange question.

"I'd just go across the street and open another office," I told him, wondering where this was going.

"What if you physically couldn't do it?"

I didn't know what to say. Was he talking about having me crippled? Breaking my kneecaps? I didn't give him a real answer, but just mumbled some inanity.

He smiled and drifted off, leaving me to wonder whether I had been given a warning, or if he was just trying to establish his power. Maybe it was his way of talking and didn't mean anything. I wasn't happy when the Feds nailed him again and put him away—but, you don't feel too safe with a guy like that disliking you and being on the streets.

I thought it was odd about his leading the family. For someone to be given as much power as he had, he didn't have much business sense about the market. For example, his crime family was officially protecting a rival brokerage firm called Toluca Pacific, which The Philosopher decided to use for his own deals, believing he could make a lot of money with IPOs.

Toluca Pacific had opened directly across the street from us and had begun stealing my brokers and their accounts. They were also shorting my stock whenever they could and I asked Danny about it. Danny told me the man running the firm was Alain Chelem, a guy we called Plug Head. The nickname was because he had one of those really bad hair transplants. Some guys get to thinking their heads are like their front yards, and all they need are a few plugs and they'll spread like sod in the lawn.

The way it worked was that he got hair plugs taken from wherever they do it—the back of the head, the neck—I don't know. Maybe a dozen hairs in a plug, maybe less. Then they surgically implant them and they grow long like any other hair. The idea is to get it so long that when you comb it, the hair covers all the bald spots that surround the plugs. Of course, it never works. Or maybe it does for guys who don't talk about it, but the ones who tell you about it look like a bunch of tiny islands when you're flying over the ocean at 40,000 feet. The guy had spent thousands of dollars to look like a fool, a circus clown, so we called him Plug Head.

Danny's half-brother also worked at Toluca Pacific, so there was a problem when I tried to get them to stop raiding us. Besides, Toluca was under The Philosopher's protection and his only allegiance was to his own wallet. So even if Danny had wanted to help me, he would have been overruled.

Plug Head and I had done a deal years earlier that went sour, and now he was stealing my guys and I couldn't do anything about it. Then The Philosopher went back to prison after the Feds nailed him on loansharking and Plug Head began to double-deal in a bunch of directions, which ended up causing him more trouble than he could have imagined.

In my case, I still didn't consider my business to be Mobbed-up, even though I was often looking to Danny as my Wiseguy contact for help against another branch of his own family. I was doing what seemed possible to make as much as I could as quickly as I could. I wanted the good life, and believe it or not, I thought of myself as principled in my pursuit. Sure, overseas bank accounts, money laundering, and violation of disclosure regulations constituted crimes, but how serious were they? Even if I got caught, I figured three years at the most.

As for Danny, I saw him as a friend, and it was as a friend that I had begun giving him a piece of the action from time to time. I made certain Danny got the early stock for some IPOs, the same way I would for any good friend or preferred client. Danny may not have seen it that way, and I'm sure his family, as represented by The Philosopher, saw favors were being done, and that my firm and I had been compromised. The fact that the Russians had organized crime connections, even though they were Russian and not Italian, reinforced this kind of thinking by The Philosopher and others.

Then there was the matter of the time I might have to serve. On the rare occasions brokers talked about penalties for crimes they might be committing, they usually mentioned a three-year sentence, not based on anything more than rumor and guesswork. They had never talked with criminal attorneys or looked up statutes to see what crimes they could be charged with and what the penalties might be. The three years was Wall Street myth, like a common thief saying, "If I could do a heist, do a year in jail, and have a million dollars when I got out, I'd do it in a heartbeat."

But the people who said those things didn't have a million dollars and didn't know a crime they could commit that would earn it for them. My partners and I had several million dollars each, and the real statutes under which we could be charged for our criminal acts called for twenty-year sentences. Part of the reason that I kept myself from confronting the reality of the consequences was that I didn't want to face what it would do to my family if I got arrested and convicted of a serious crime. Even three years would have shattered me had I been truthful with myself. Twenty years would have seemed like a death sentence, my children growing up fatherless.

The trouble was that neither the Mob nor the Feds saw any part of my life as inviolable. My name, my firm's name, and the names of my associates were appearing in the investigations of everyone from New York City police detectives working gang details, to FBI agents looking into organized crime, to Securities and Exchange Commission investigators. So far as is known, none of the investigators were sharing information with each other. Each agency had its own turf and each wanted credit for an arrest. The only question was who would be first to get enough evidence against me to indict.

Meanwhile, we were using the new beards for the Holly Products secondary since J.W. Barclay was already doing the IPO. That meant that with this deal, everyone we were networking with was going to benefit and have a payday, reassuring our new network of outside brokers, brokerage firms, and internal pasta boys. They would move Holly Products stock and warrants and get paid under the table. The deal went very fast, the stock going from $5 to $15 the first day and the approximately 1.5 million warrants went from 10 cents to 7 dollars, generating $10.5 million to split among the brokers, the partners and the other players involved. The deal went so well that it gave us the image of an up-and-coming Wall Street powerhouse.

Holly Products loved us for the cash infusion they received. Larry Berman, the chairman of Holly Products wanted his usual 10 percent kickback on what we were going to gross on the warrants. The previous casino deal was worthless, but we arranged for Holly Products to absorb the casino, and to repair the damage inflicted by the prior owner, we created a scheme that transferred a million dollars we had raised from the Holly secondary to the casino. Not only had we pulled off a successful offering but we had put a Band-Aid on the casino project and had even sold Larry Berman on taking it over.

The Holly Profits secondary arrangements were fairly simple. One of our beards put $12 million worth of stock through his offshore laundering account and kept $1,200,000 commission. The remaining $10.8 million was divided by me and the others involved. I understood how such actions worked and enjoyed the easy money.

It wasn't so easy with Vlad. We had only put a million dollars through his account and he got to keep $100,000. He had already taken out the first part of his share and then got completely wasted on heroin and decided to just wipe out the entire bank account and disappear. I was outraged. I could never figure out what possessed the Russians to use this lunatic, anyway. It was my money he was taking. I wanted him found and I wanted the money back.

Gene and Lex knew Vlad would stay close to Brighton Beach and his narcotics connection. They sent out feelers through the Russian community and found where he was. Then they picked up two goons in Brooklyn, drove to Brighton Beach in two cars and found Vlad walking near the beach. One car pulled in front of him and the other stopped behind him. They grabbed him, threw him into one of the vehicles, took him to a house and tied him up in the basement. Then they spent three days convincing Vlad of the need to arrange to wire the money. When it was back in the right account, they let him go.

The kidnapping almost certainly was witnessed by some of the neighbors, though no one reported it. The Russian community had a code of ethics to be followed by new immigrants, whether they were straight or involved in criminal enterprises. No one had any respect for Vlad's actions, but they knew that Gene and Lex had given local boys jobs that enabled them to earn big money for themselves and their families.

There would be trouble, though. Vlad was scared, humiliated, and angry. He went directly from the basement to his dealer to buy more heroin. Then he shot up so much junk that he nearly overdosed and began threatening Gene and Lex. He was going to kill them for what they did. He came to the office, not on the 4th floor but on the 9th. His mouth was foaming and you could tell he was wasted. He wanted to talk to the boys. I was really angry and voiced my concerns to Gene and Lex.

Frightened, yet believing Vlad's threats would not be carried out while he was so high, Lex went to Vlad's house to look for weapons. He found several guns that he knew were dangerous beyond their power to kill. They were dirty: unregistered guns that had been used in crimes, and they could put Vlad, or anyone else possessing them, away for life. The guns made anyone with access to them a suspect. Lex didn't think of any of this. He just stuffed the guns in a duffel bag and took them to a self-storage yard, rented a locker and paid the rent six months in advance.

Shortly after coming down from his heroin high, Vlad found out that his dealer had been under surveillance and that his most recent purchase from him had been recorded on videotape. Vlad learned that when he was arrested for possession, and the police quickly pointed out that with the felony convictions he already had on his record, he was a two-time loser and the third time would be life. Vlad would be tried, convicted, and this time he would go away for so many years that he would be an old man when he left prison, if he left at all.

Vlad decided to cooperate as an informant. That was when Operation Street Cleaner became involved and Vlad became one of the first of the inside players on Wall Street to wear a wire, the surveillance broadcast device that would soon become almost as common as a Rolex, especially with some of the pasta boys. As in any deal that involves informing in lieu of a heavy prison sentence, Vlad was expected to deliver dirty players to the Feds. That meant rolling over on his friends and his associates, which he soon seemed to have no trouble doing.

The first man Vlad took down was Aleks "Don't Fuck Around" Paul, our money launderer. Vlad called Aleks and arranged to meet him and another guy at the Marriott in downtown Manhattan for a meal that was under the eyes and ears of federal undercover agents. By this time the Feds had men undercover as bankers, investors, whatever it took. They used Italian-looking tough guys to infiltrate the Italian firms. They used guys of obvious Russian ancestry to go after the Russians. Though they didn't look like Feds, they were so out of place that we usually made them. But Aleks didn't.

Vlad was a regular patron of the Marriott and he was comfortable there. He asked Aleks if he could do some more of his "usual service," which meant money laundering, and that was music to Aleks' ears.

"Sure," Aleks said, downing a glass of Petrus from a $600 bottle of wine. "Sure, I'll do it for you." Aleks was feeling no pain whatsoever, and it seemed like a good time to commemorate his calling and success. He began talking about notable money laundering capers he had done. The Feds were working a wire from a few tables away, feeding the sound to associates monitoring the conversation and recording it in an unmarked van outside. They could hardly believe what they were hearing. It was commonplace for gangsters to talk in coded language, careful not to use a single word that could be directly quoted in an indictment.

But here was our guy Aleks, bragging about some of his favorite money laundering deals, naming names, giving dates, times, places. And even that wasn't enough. He felt so good about himself and his money laundering that he decided they needed to drink to it.

"Here's to the greatest money launderer in the world!" he said, raising his glass for Vlad to clink to, then to the other guy with them.

That was a good night for Operation Street Cleaner and it was the beginning of the end for us. Of course we didn't have a clue about this, because Vlad had already been thoroughly turned and we weren't going to hear anything about this until it came from the Feds. The attention that they were paying me and my company, which was plenty, was based on their belief that I was totally Mobbed-up, because of my relationship with Danny. That made me much more of a target for them than I would have been if I had just run my own brokerage firm.

At this point, they were evaluating my importance in an effort to decide whether I was worth going after to prosecute, or whether it would be better to leave me on the street till later, when they had as much as they needed on Danny and the Mob players they were really after. I had thought of myself as a scorpion. Everyone else saw only a frog.

CHAPTER FOURTEEN

United States of America
- against -
FRANK COPPA, SR.
ERNEST MONTEVECCHI
DANIEL PERSICO
JACK BASILE
ROCCO BASILE
LARRY BERMAN
JOHN CIOFOLETTI
JOHN DOUKAS
WALTER DURCHALTER
EDWARD GARAFOLA
DANIEL LEV
EUGENE LOMBARDO
EDMOND NAGEL
ALFRED PALAGONIA
ALEKS PAUL
JOSEPH POLITO, SR.
LAWRENCE RAY
ABRAHAM SALAMAN
GIUSEPPE TEMPERINO

It was part of the conspiracy that the defendant JOSEPH POLITO, SR. agreed with the White Rock Partners that White Rock would underwrite an IPO of USBNY ("US Bridge of New York") common stock and warrants in exchange for a secret allotment of USBNY warrants, which the White Rock Partners would acquire in the name of nominees and then sell to the public. POLITO and the White Rock Partners also agreed that POLITO would get several hundred thousand dollars that would be derived from the eventual sale of the securities that the White Rock Partners would secretly acquire. It was further part of the conspiracy that the defendant DANIEL LEV agreed to be a nominee for the White Rock Partners. Although the 3,000,000 warrants were in LEV's name, the

*White Rock Partners controlled the warrants and made all decisions
concerning the purchase and sale of the warrants. In return for acting as
a nominee, LEV was promised a substantial profit on the sum he lent to
USBNY in January 1995.*

*It was further part of the conspiracy that, prior to USBNY's IPO,
the defendants JOSEPH POLITO, SR. and EUGENE LOMBARDO and others, took steps to make it appear as if USBNY would use the IPO proceeds to obtain bonding that would enable USBNY to act as a general
contractor on large-scale construction projects. The White Rock Partners
agreed with POLITO, LOMBARDO, the defendant LAWRENCE RAY and
others that RAY would secretly pay $100,000 to an executive of a bond
brokerage firm to facilitate the issuance of bonding after the IPO.*

Playing Robin Hood

From the time I was a kid playing Robin Hood, I had liked to fancy
myself as the master of my destiny. I had my own marijuana business
in high school, my own tile company, and now I was heading a firm
on Wall Street. I had learned the business in ways that seemed to put
me on top of the game. I had my beards, my offshore banks, my primary money launderer. I knew how to structure IPOs so as to provide
adequate kickbacks for everybody. I had learned to pump and dump,
a game that the largest securities firms in the nation were using to
assure high profits for select investors. All I lacked was the where-
withal to fully control a stock deal, and this required creating my own
syndicate.

The concept of the syndicate dated back to the 1920s and has
been credited, at least in part, to Joseph P. Kennedy. The Yellow Cab
Company was his first effort, and Libby-Owens-Ford, described in
Chapter Six, was his last. In Kennedy's case, buyers and sellers of
stock were stationed in different parts of the country so that their
carefully orchestrated manipulations would seem to be happening in
a random pattern. No one realized that Joe and his staff were orches-
trating the buying and selling through telephone calls from their New
York headquarters.

I faced a different situation. The old-style syndicate was not only impractical but, by the end of the twentieth century, surprisingly easy to trace. I decided to create a syndicate of three stock brokerage houses that my partners and I would basically control. The brokers, seemingly acting independently of the other firms, would all work together to control the stock and manipulate the market. Buying and selling would be done among the brokers' clients, giving the illusion of broader interest in our chosen stock than actually existed.

The three-office syndicate violated the rules of both NASDAQ and the New York Stock Exchange. No brokerage house owner could own more than a 10 percent share of another firm without providing full disclosure of that fact. Once the ownership exceeded ten percent, the brokerage firms involved had to handle stock just like a brokerage firm with multiple offices.

My concept for the syndicate involved bringing in two companies run by two of my cousins, but when I broached the idea, neither cousin was enthusiastic. One cousin was my age, the other was younger. Both knew I broke the rules, that I gave guys cash, and that I did offshore stuff that was either blatantly or semi-crooked, depending on how you looked at it. They knew there was potential legal trouble in the way I did business, and at first, neither one of them wanted any part of it. They made their money following the rules and they didn't want to change. At least not until they seriously looked at how much I was making and how much they were making. They could see that I was garnering millions, and my numbers were going up, while their incomes were relatively stagnant. I asked a second time, and the second time they agreed. They didn't want to commit crimes on Wall Street, but they did want the money.

Both cousins quit their "straight" brokerage house jobs with a guarantee of financial support from my partners and me. We would help structure the new businesses, provide the $100,000 it cost to write a business plan, supply the money they needed to build their books, aid them in raising capital and assist them with the cost of legal services, accounting, printing, and related expenses. In exchange, I would have forty percent of each firm.

We also had deals planned with a third brokerage house that

was run by three of Danny's friends, guys who were friends from the street in Brooklyn, but not "soldiers" connected with the organized crime family.

The idea of opening these satellite companies was so that we could do multiple deals within our built-in syndicate group without having outside players back-dooring their stocks to us. We wanted to anticipate success in the partnership by spreading the wealth around, which was why we gave all the new players a piece of Holly Products.

The way it worked, I would sell them fifty thousand of something they wanted, and I would buy fifty thousand of something I wanted. It was great. By NASDAQ rules, whenever you do an underwriting you have to give thirty percent of the deal to a syndicate, leaving yourself exposed to that thirty percent of stock that you may buy back. What better place to put syndicate stock than in your own hands, but under different names? That's why we felt we should open these firms surrounding White Rock, the hub.

My younger cousin and four partners were forming First Richmond, raising the money themselves and using Gene as their agent to help them. Personality aside, Gene had a bearing and a look that made him a good closer. Being so overweight, and always wearing a bow tie, he looked like a banker or an economics professor. His voice was soft and when he wasn't sounding whiny, he could command respect because of what he knew. What mattered to my cousins was that he was very smooth in his pitch and delivery when seeking money. That made him an attractive partner.

Gene began going on the road with the partners for the firms we were going to be working with. Each firm was set up the same way: Four partners, each one responsible for raising at least a half-million dollars. Gene was the closer, the guy who could explain it in ways that got investors to commit. He'd go wherever the big clients were that he thought he could raise money from. He went to Kalamazoo, Michigan, and raised five hundred thousand from one guy, then to a different city for another two hundred thousand.

The problem was that Gene was only loyal to Gene. One of his trips was to Tuxedo Park, New York, the community where the tuxedo was invented. Gene had been there to see an Oriental guy named Charley Sue, who represented a lot of Chinese and Hong Kong money and was a long-time investor with my cousins. As I understood it, Sue originally had no intention of investing in the new firm but Gene wouldn't let him alone. Gene knew the guy was rich, and he could legally act as a stockbroker, so he made a deal with Sue to invest a few hundred thousand dollars. Then Gene diverted the money away from my cousin's company, First Richmond.

My cousin, the one forming First Richmond, was being betrayed right from the start, though none of us knew about it at first. Eventually, it would come back to haunt us because that cousin and his partners wanted nothing more to do with us. That's what they said, anyway. I think they were looking for any excuse possible to ditch the relationship with us right after we helped them get their money. They were cocky guys from Staten Island and when Gene, scumbag that he is, stole a client from them, they used that as an excuse to welsh on the deal. Since it was a handshake deal, it was easy for them to walk away.

Then Charley Sue started buying Holly Products, which at this point my brokers and I were abandoning, because it was being fully controlled by the Mob guys downstairs, and it dropped until it was trading at a dollar a share. Gene kept after Sue until he started coming around to our firm to invest in our company. We didn't actually tell him to buy Holly Products, but he bought it anyway. He wanted to bottom-fish it. But the whole venture with him was a failure for Gene, who traded away a firm useful to us for a handful of commissions. I can see why my cousin was so mad. Charley Sue gave us about a half-a-million bucks to trade and play around with.

We had done things with First Richmond before this and they had bought a bunch of warrants from us as part of the ownership deal we were putting together. After Gene took Charley Sue away from them, they used it as an excuse to break the deal, keep the money and sell the warrants. We were going to take forty percent of the inside paper. Since we were going to keep the offshore accounts, we were going to control the checkbook anyway, but when they broke the deal to be part of the syndicate, we lost the forty percent plus the six hundred grand we had given them. Eventually they gave us back $150,000, but I remained pissed to this day because I still thought my cousin owed me $450,000 when he broke up with us.

I guess it was inevitable that we would get looked into by NAS-DAQ. There was a red flag for them because Gene was listed on our books as chairman, with me as vice-chairman. Gene was not popular with NASDAQ, and to make things worse, when the examiner came in and Gene saw that it was a woman, he thought she was an assistant and excused her from the room. Big mistake. Then, when he realized he was wrong, he sent her, I think it was, a $150 rose bouquet.

That made her really mad. First, he had insulted her, then he had made her think he was trying to bribe her. NASDAQ cranked up a full audit of our operations. They could have saved their energy and the taxpayer's money, because it was totally fruitless. They tore everything apart and couldn't find anything wrong because all our trades were legal. We were very careful about that. The illegal part of what we were doing was selling inside positions, which was difficult to prove.

The inside position was in retaining stock that was undisclosed to the public. But even that would have been legal if I had disclosed my ownership, then waited thirteen months before I did anything with it. What we did was illegal because we brought the money back in cash, failed to disclose the ownership, and we didn't wait the thirteen months.

Okay. Yes, I was a crook because I did that. But how bad of a crook was I? There are crooks out there at every major, respected brokerage house in the country that do almost what I did every day. They just do it legally. They wait their thirteen months, then get a good PR campaign going and get a favorable report from some analyst. The stock goes up five points that day because of the report and they begin selling their positions.

It was still pump and dump. I don't care if you wait thirteen months or two years, or if you get rid of it early as we did. You're still pumping up the stock to make the market rise. You're still taking advantage of the chance to sell your holdings at the best price you can get. You're still fleecing the public in the same way that pump and dump has been used in business for the last two centuries. And even if you're careful how you sell your shares, you're still likely to drive the price down. Who is there to police you?

So you make forty, fifty million dollars. We made the same kind of money but we made it the Gene way, which, in the eyes of the authorities, was the wrong way.

My older cousin had a different background and a different attitude. He had worked for Cooney Base, Gruntal and Company, and at Shearson Lehman. All big firms, and though he always made a decent living—a couple hundred grand a year—he was never really a big producer. He lived okay because even though he had an appetite for champagne and women, he never went crazy. He was a blonde-haired, blue-eyed Sicilian, a very good-looking guy who enjoyed himself. Then he got married and began thinking about the future. He looked at my house, my cars, and the things I could do for my wife and kids, and realized he was nowhere near my league and he had been a broker four years longer than I had. He wanted something more and he didn't think he could ever get it his way, so finally he came to talk to us.

"I want to do this," he said. "I want to do what you guys are doing. I want to get involved."

I set up his firm the same way I had done my younger cousin's. Again Gene helped, but this time there were no problems. The partners wanted everything to be straight. They wanted to earn their money the right way. They might be bending rules, especially with the hidden percentage from me, but otherwise, they maintained their integrity.

The third group, the one involving Danny's legitimate friends, had no investment connection with me. I advised them as a friend, and eventually they bought out my cousin's business. That group was never accused of criminal action and they stayed in business until recently when they closed down.

There was no question but that the deals we made were good ones. My partners and I were working to move into IPOs for companies we believed in and could get our brokers to believe in, issuing stock that would hopefully go liquid on the street. We now had a syndicate and our deals had a reputation of going up, the types of deals that legitimate small cap underwriting companies delight in handling.

As I mentioned earlier, one was US Bridge of New York, a firm making good money repairing bridges and other critical public facilities that were deteriorating with age. Throughout the United States, and especially in the East and Midwest, bridges had been built to last with little more than routine maintenance for 25 years, 50 years, or longer. But by the 1990s, even some well-made structures needed massive repair work and/or upgrading.

US Bridge specialized in that kind of work, and both its business volume and profits were growing steadily. The deal was brought in by Al Nagel who was increasingly hanging around the firm. We were growing fast and needed someone like him to bring in business and evaluate deals the rest of us were already considering. He seemed like the guru who could help us hone in on money to be made. The only salary Al wanted for his advice was a subway token, a sandwich, and a small piece of the deal if he liked it. The company also had an accountant to explain the deal, one who also represented other companies we would be looking at in the future.

US Bridge showed $1 million on $10 million in sales. If Joe Polito, the US Bridge chairman, was willing to play the game we wanted, we would get another three million, plus fees and commissions. I was thrilled. This deal would bring our biggest payday and it would make many of our brokers into millionaires, especially the dozen pasta boys who made up approximately one fourth of our employees. Space was at a premium now, and we had to ask William Brock, one of the players in our casino deal, to vacate the area he was subletting. We would be having an influx of new brokers of our own, and could give 30 percent of the deal to our syndicate, making the deal really tight for us.

The IPO broke at five dollars and traded to six to get all the flippers out. Then we gunned the arrangement to ten warrants. This meant that our profit would be in excess of $18 million and it seemed like a perfect formula. And to sweeten the deal, I had the fantasy that the Mob involvement we had been forced to utilize was in the past, behind us.

Our fourth partner, Walter Durchalter, had left in resentment over the fact that we cut Lex in on our deals during the first six months of business even though Lex was in prison. Dutch objected so much to that that he quit and we bought him out. Then he joined forces with Chris Kingsley, our manager at Shearson, to start a new firm. They asked me to join them but the money that we would make on the next coup was too great to leave behind. Besides that, the majority of the pasta boys were my friends, and I didn't want to abandon them.

We replaced Dutch with John "The Duke" Doukas, the glass-eyed, prosthesis-wearing guy who gave me my first job on Wall Street at Gruntal. The Duke brought a different viewpoint to the place. He didn't share Gene and Lex's penchant for shady dealing. He was determined to build a legitimate, fully independent business that would make us major players. Duke had contacts with the big firms, and we were getting new deals that would enable us to grow to a few hundred brokers. That would put us in the big time. We wouldn't have to lavish cash incentives on the brokers anymore. We could just do it like the big firms, and keep it all for ourselves.

By this time, we needed additional office space and we changed our image by switching our name to State Street Capital. We moved to the World Trade Center, which was one of the most impressive structures in Manhattan. The rent was reasonable and the building had great security after its first bombing in 1993. Visitors were required to show ID at the front desk, and that discouraged most of the Mob guys from stopping by, which was a relief. We had a full 40th-floor office and we had successfully taken US Bridge public. The trading in its IPO was stable and as it was our only major deal for the moment, it was easy to track and trade. It only took a few months to sell 2.5 million warrants.

That left 500,000 shares of US Bridge warrants to move, and Duke hired a team out of Gruntal with two big producers as team leaders. In addition, there were 20 others with solid track records, a group we called the AGL Division, and 50 cold callers. I decided to motivate the teams by promising a year's lease on a Ferrari to any team leaders who bought the block of US Bridge warrants. At that time the monthly lease on a Ferrari was just over $4,500, and the cars were so fast that many insurance companies charged their high premiums on the assumption that the driver would be speeding. They had one fee for low mileage, and then charged additional fees for each mile driven beyond that figure. Two team leaders bought the warrants and I spent $108,000 to lease them a Ferrari for a year. That was beyond the legal incentive. But our profit? Three million dollars in one week's time.

Renting Ferraris for two staff members whetted my exotic car appetite and I decided to buy a Porsche to add to my personal stable of cars. I thought a Carrera Four, which retailed for about $72,000, would be right, and found one with the help of a salesman named George, a young guy who was extremely knowledgeable, helpful, and aggressive. His understanding of the product he was selling impressed me because knowing your product is the key to selling anything. I constantly stressed to my brokers and others who worked for us that you should be able to sound enthusiastic answering any question. Here was a guy who was doing it with cars, and being a car lover since I was a kid, there was no way he could bullshit me.

I told George he was wasting time selling cars. With the same effort, he could make ten times the money with just one telephone call. Later that month, I stopped in a Brooklyn gas station and there was George, the Porsche salesman. I asked what he was doing there and he said he owned the station along with his dad and his brothers. This time, I was in my yellow Ferrari, and George was impressed enough to ask me more about my business.

"You come work for me and get your broker's license," I told him from the leather interior of my Ferrari Spider, "and you'll be a millionaire within a year."

The fact that George had sold me a $72,000 Porsche and was now seeing me in a Ferrari worth twice that made my words sound real. I wasn't some silver-haired corporate CEO who had spent 30 years climbing the rungs. I was only a couple of years older than George, and I was at the top of the ladder now.

"Don't take time thinking about it," I told George. "What have you got to lose?" The answer to that question was obvious: what he had to lose was his position in a Brooklyn gas station. What he stood to gain was a position like mine, owning both a Porsche and Ferrari, and who knew what else?

"I've got one of the best guys in the brokerage business to train you," I said, starting the Ferrari engine, then handing him a business card. I was talking about John Sciascia, who I was already mentally lining up to train George. "He'll teach you everything you need to know. And then it'll be up to you. And I know you can do it."

George called, joined up, did his cold calling under John Sciascia's coaching, and became one of my biggest sellers. Then he trained his own high-pressure commando team. I gave him and John the biggest office in the new space, where they had room for a dozen cold callers who would become my biggest pasta boys, or so we all thought. They put together enough buying power that they could do their own IPOs the way I had done at Whale years earlier.

I was trying to meld a great group by using John Sciascia as my right-hand man. Unfortunately, the instant wealth from the US Bridge warrants was too much for John. His appetite for partying, fueled by unlimited cash resources to throw at whatever he wanted, caught up with and devoured him. John turned a trip to South Beach into a binge on cocaine, booze and Ecstasy that strung him out so badly that his wife divorced him and we knew we could no longer use him.

John's flameout was not untypical of the high casualty rate of success on the Street in the 1990s. It was like the tales you heard about in Hollywood with people who suddenly reached the heights of success and then crashed and burned with drugs and alcohol, destroying their careers and lives. The same pattern of instant wealth, unlimited opportunity and freedom from having to follow society's rules led more than one talented stockbroker to complete personal destruction. Usually, the tale began with a cocaine binge like the one that put John out of business.

George may have been lucky to have another example to follow after Sciascia's self-destruction, in the prominent role The Duke played in our company. The Duke had a substantially different background from Gene and Lex, as he had come up on Wall Street as a

manager of a mid-size firm. He had more experience managing brokers than any of us. And, interestingly, with all his disabilities, The
Duke was an amazing ladies' man.

When The Duke replaced Dutch, the firm became divided
between his AGL boys, who had no idea about cash under the table,
and were happy to vie for commissions and company cars and the
pasta boys. The latter only wanted cash, and they began threatening
to walk out, which would have been certain doom for the US Bridge
deal. It was really immaterial to The Duke what happened with US
Bridge because he had made a couple of million instantly after taking
over from Dutch. We had sold the last block of stock and he felt thoroughly confident with his new recruits.

CHAPTER FIFTEEN

District Court, EDNY

It was part of the conspiracy that, in or about and between November 1995 and June 1996, the State Street Partners agree with "John Doe #1" a director of Cable, whose identity is known to the grand jury, that State Street would underwrite Cable's IPO on the condition that the State Street Partners would receive a secret allotment of Cable securities which would be held in the name of an off-shore nominee and then sold to the public in aftermarket trading.

It was further part of the conspiracy that, on or about January 26, Cable entered into a bogus consulting agreement with an off-shore entity, U.K. Hyde Park Consultants Ltd. under which Hyde Park would receive 400,000 shares of Cable stock and warrants to purchase an additional 450,000 shares of Cable stock. Hyde Park, which was actually a nominee controlled by the State Street Partners, subsequently transferred these shares of stock and warrants to U.K. Midland Group Ltd., another off-shore entity controlled by the State Street Partners. The Cable stock and warrants held in the name of Midland are sometimes referred to herein as the "Midland Securities."

It was further part of the conspiracy that, on or about June 5, 1996, State Street, together with First City Securities, Inc., a brokerage firm in which Gene Klotsman, Salvatore Lauria and Lex Tersa had an undisclosed interest, underwrote the Cable IPO prospectus, registered and offered for sale shares of Cable common stock and warrants.

Part of the high-wattage work environment was finding ways to blow off the stress outside the office, and one means of doing that was what we called "Wild, Wild West parties." We staged them at irregular intervals, usually when there was something to celebrate. There were no spouses present because none of the men wanted to be reminded of words like trust or fidelity, and everybody wanted to be able to lie about participating if the truth ever got out. Everybody played like fraternity brothers, only we rented a luxury Manhattan hotel suite, stock it with an unlimited booze supply and a crew of absolutely beautiful, willing young women who were there to party and only to party.

We held a Wild Wild West party in honor of the members of our brokerage syndicate that we had successfully put together, and also in celebration of Danny's birthday, as a way of thanking Danny for his help. I was still fooling myself with the notion that our business was not really connected with organized crime, and I thought that by rewarding Danny with a show of respect and pleasure like this, rather than making him a partner, I was keeping the business clean.

I regarded the girls we hired to entertain the guests at the Wild, Wild West parties in the same self-delusional light. I was a family man. I doted on my wife and daughters and made it a practice to avoid going into the city on a Saturday unless it was to bring something nice home to my family. In my mind, the Wild, Wild West parties didn't really involve cheating on wives or jeopardizing the family. I didn't even know the names of the girls who would be showing up, nor would I remember them after the night was over. They were not affairs. They were not mistresses. The parties were a part of doing business, like taking a client to Scores and paying for a lap dance.

My sister had worked for my brokerage for a while, and she, along with the other women who worked in the office, had visited Scores a few times. They had been amused by the "look but don't touch" frustrations created for brokers and customers when I treated them to lap dances. The law let the women do anything they desired short of intercourse so long as the man did not touch them with their hands.

For Danny's birthday party, we rented the penthouse of a Manhattan hotel and Gene and Lex had expensive Russian madams book every girl available, to stay as long as any of the men wanted. One Russian madam sent five girls and two other madams sent ten girls each. The bill for the women was $15,000, which was about half the budget for the one-night party.

When it was over, when the men had returned home to bachelor pads or families to whom lying had become second nature, the man who mattered was Danny, the guest of honor. We had spent lavishly to make him feel appreciated, to feel loved as a friend who had been helpful in critical ways to our enterprise. We meant to reward him in a way that honored him without acknowledging him as an organized crime link to our brokerage business.

But whether we recognized it or not, by this time Danny's continued presence was no longer a secret to law enforcement. Regardless of what Mob thinking was, the Feds saw us as running a corrupt money laundering operation protected by, influenced by, and beholden to several members of organized crime families. There may never have been a formal arrangement, but the actions were as good as a confession, and the Wild, Wild West parties were as much a part of documenting a conspiracy as the overseas bank accounts. I was clearly in full denial.

Meanwhile, the high living and the fast money were taking out another of our brokers. The next one to spiral out after John Sciascia was Big Al, who was squandering the millions he had earned with the US Bridge stock. He had become a builder-owner of ultra-luxury homes. The first one cost him $3 million and I thought this was his dream place, the type of home you create once in a lifetime and live in until you die. Instead, there were three others. The first one he sold to me; the next two he rented for big money; and the fourth one he called home until he built something else.

Al threw monster house parties in the Hamptons and at one of them, he and a friend binged for three days on drugs and booze. The next thing I knew, Al was at the gates of my house in his new Ferrari 512, babbling incoherently on the intercom about drugs and paranoia involving his girlfriend, who was eight months pregnant and having an affair with John. Al was hallucinating and needed a place to crash so I let him stay in the basement.

My basement had a well-stocked bar and game room, a bathroom, and plenty of room for someone to live the good life. Al locked himself in there and helped himself to all my expensive champagne and went through the heavy stash of coke he had brought with him. He was a complete mess. I tried to find help to get him out of my basement, but none of his friends wanted anything to do with him. Finally Lex came over, amused by the absurdity of a man getting as totally wasted as Al had. Then Lex decided, since Al was incapacitated, to borrow his Ferrari to drive to a party in the Hamptons.

Two days later, I found some people who were willing to come and carry Al out. The place was trashed and I started cleaning immediately, frightened that my kids and their friends would go down there and get into something awful. It was obvious that Al was not somebody I could do business with again, and a number of friendships based around him started to cool. Al eventually went into rehab. All the people he introduced me to had their own agenda, and it didn't involve getting rich as they helped my firm grow. Fortunately, we had enough brokers by then so we could have the outside pasta boys stop buying from us and we could still control the float.

The client list kept growing as I learned to seduce big money players by offering them whatever it took to please them. One of these was a Norwegian named Eric who came to New York occasionally. I knew he had enough resources to drop a million or two on stocks and not care if it went up or down in value. But I had to do something to set me apart from the other brokers going after his business.

The answer was the secret practice that luxury hotels have of keeping preference files on their wealthy repeat guests. Some hotels maintain a small file box filled with cards. They feel this is more secure in this day of computer theft and hacking. Other hotels use their computers, the information protected by secure passwords or disks that are accessible only to a few.

Eric was known to like women, and that information was in his file along with the type of food he had ordered in the restaurant in the past, room service requests, and anything else that could be learned about him. For the hotel, the service began before Eric arrived. A room was prepared with the type of liquor, fruit, and snack food he was known to favor. Clothing in the appropriate size for use in the workout room was placed carefully in one of the dresser drawers. The radio was reset to the station the maid noted he listened to and condoms were discretely placed in the drawer of a nightstand, since women were known to visit the room.

I made a dinner date with Eric and then took him to Scores, the city's most popular topless bar. Eric loved Scores. Finally, I took him to his hotel and he suggested that we go somewhere else, but I encouraged him to return to his room, telling him he'd enjoy the rest of the evening more in his room. Eric went to his suite and when he opened the door, he was greeted by two beautiful Russian women who made it clear that they were there to do whatever he wanted, as long as he wanted. Gene had arranged to send him two $500-a-night girls, who were tipped handsomely on top of that. The hotel concierge had also been tipped well. It was against hotel policy to let prostitutes work the rooms, but Gene prevailed on the night management to make an exception, and they did.

Eric called the next morning and said he had never had so enjoyable an evening. He told me that whatever he had wanted to do with the women seemed to please them as much as it did him. He actually convinced himself that he had driven them wild through the night, that he was a sexual Superman who left them spent, wanting more. Then he dropped the casual news that he wanted to invest in two of my latest deals, giving me $800,000 for one and $700,000 for the other. Eric was not overly concerned with the sales pitch or the risk factor. I had given him so much pleasure that the least he could do in return was buy some stock—for $1.5 million.

Then we did a flurry of private placements (PPMs) including some in technology for friends of Gene's that I was sure were frauds he was setting up for himself. One was a dinner stadium in Orlando that featured the American Gladiators live every night, which is a story in itself. An accountant for US Bridge brought us the deal with the original creator of the concept, which involved an Elvis impersonator who actually thought he was Elvis. We raised close to $5 million in a private placement, and within months realized that Elvis was nuts. There were limousines, private helicopters, a big office, all the bad qualities of a new CEO trying to jump-start a new business, and we threw him out.

The US Bridge accountant took over and then he went nuts, too. We caught him embezzling a million dollars. We cut our clients and our losses and did a PPM for the manufacturer of a roller-blade that sported a new angled wheel layout. We gave them $400,000, and then within months we found out that they didn't own the patent. They were a straight-out fraud, and we got our money back.

We did do a private placement for one company that made computer peripherals while home PC's were in their infancy. The CEO found a way to take our money and screw us out of the deal with slick legal moves and stock manipulation, and outfoxed us. It was 1995 and there were deals all over the Street. Everybody who owned a firm wanted in and they were taking any deal, just to take something public. We had a joke among ourselves when we saw a shit deal: "They just took a stop sign public and it's up 300 percent!" The NAS-DAQ was still only at 1,000 and the Dow was at 4,500. There were 548 IPOs that year, and the next year, the most profitable for all investment banks, the number of IPOs topped at 768.

In this frenzy of initial public slaughter we had found a deal that looked like it was almost too good to be true. As is always the case with deals that appear too good to be true, it was.

The second IPO I planned for my company after US Bridge was for Cable Shoes, a company that made costly men's shoes. The shoe business was a profitable niche market and Cable, though never pretentious, was a leader in the field with forty million dollars in sales. This was another deal that could have been a legitimate winner if we had handled the IPO straight. But we didn't. Doing it by the book, the money wouldn't come fast enough from an IPO and there wasn't enough of it. In the long run, my impatience and greed cost me a lot more than I gained.

"SAL LAURIA did (a) employ devices, schemes and artifices to defraud; (b) make untrue statements of material facts and omit to state material facts necessary in order to make the statements made, in light of the circumstances under which they were made, not misleading; and (c) engage in acts, practices and courses of business which would and did operate as a fraud and deceit upon members of the investing public, in connection with purchases and sales of securities of US Bridge of NY, Inc. ("US Bridge"), and by use of means and instrumentalities of

interstate commerce and the mails, in violation of Title 15, United States Code, Sections 78j(b) and 78ff.

"It was part of the scheme that the defendant SAL LAURIA, together with others, acquired ownership and control of a substantial number of US Bridge common stock shares and warrants, which ownership and control were not disclosed to the public.

"It was further part of the scheme that the defendant SAL LAURIA, together with others, paid substantial undisclosed compensation to brokers to induce them to recommend and sell US Bridge stock and warrants to investors.

"It was further part of the scheme that the defendant SAL LAURIA and others sold US Bridge shares and warrants that they secretly controlled at artificially inflated prices, thereby generating substantial profits." Similar criminal charges were stated for their handling of the shoe company.

The more boldly we entered the world of money laundering, pump and dump, and other frauds, the more brazenly we advertised our presence on the Street. By the time we moved our offices to the World Trade Center, Gene and Lex had taken the penthouse floor of the new Donald Trump Building at 40 Wall Street. The Duke had made some of the decisions in appointing our main offices in the WTC, and he liked nothing but the best. The office walls were mahogany, the entryway was granite and the two corner offices had built-in bars. The furniture was among the finest available for offices. By the time all the furniture was installed, The Duke had spent approximately $700,000.

US Bridge had been the last deal in the old offices. The shoe company was the first deal in the new ones. And to signal the change, I alerted the pasta boys that there would be no cash under the table for selling the shoe company IPO. This was no casual decision. It was a necessity to accommodate my old boss, The Duke, who was my new partner, and had brought with him enough money and brokers so he could make demands. Since only eight or ten of the brokers were receiving cash, he was not concerned with their quitting. I was.

"I'm going to have a mutiny," I told The Duke. "These guys are not going to stand for it. They are going to sell back all their US Bridge stock, which will hurt the momentum in the new deal. They've been getting paid cash in everything we've done so far and now I'm going to tell them, this is a good deal and you're not getting any cash?"

The Duke argued with me face-to-face. I could have argued back, but it was my firm and I wasn't going to fight myself. So I told Duke if he could pull it off and the guys don't resign, go ahead, tell them there's no cash in it. We called the pasta boys into my office and broke the news. They were upset, but we had so many rookies, so many young brokers already at the firm, that we didn't really need the pasta boys. We had enough buyers to put the deal over without them if they chose to bail out, especially with George now ready to devour the whole deal by himself.

Gene and Lex had arranged for our firm to take over the shoe company IPO for a $300,000 payout to Fat Frank Coppa, Sr., the notorious short player who controlled a brokerage firm that had signed the deal for the Cable Shoes IPO. We believed we had an agreement. Then Frank called to speak to me, at first congratulating me on getting the shoe deal. Then he told me he wanted 75,000 shares of the stock to help some brokers who had their own firm and needed some start-up stock. I told him politely I couldn't do that, that the shoe deal was oversold, and I needed the shares I had. I was figuring I could slip him a few thousand shares, but 75,000 was out of the question.

Then he told me he was sending his son, Frank Jr., over to our office to pitch a deal for us to handle a chicken franchise he wanted to do. Frank Jr. owned a couple of chicken restaurants and wanted to do a franchise, and his father Fat Frank wanted us to finance it. The chicken deal was typical of the way a number of business owners were thinking in the 1990s. Franchises were popular just before stocks in the electronics industry and Internet businesses took off.

The idea was that someone with a viable business could get rich leasing the idea to others using the original business's name, sharing the advertising expense and getting the right to utilize whatever made the business unique. This might mean anything from a niche market-staffing agency to a restaurant. The problem was that most customers did not care about the franchise. The success of Kentucky Fried Chicken (later KFC) and Popeye's Chicken and Biscuits led many restaurants to try to duplicate their success, and most of them failed.

We weren't interested in Frank, Jr.'s chicken restaurant franchise deal, and when he came over to the office, I told him that. The Internet was starting to fire up and we were looking more at tech companies than at chicken. Besides, there was a chicken hustle that went public through Whale not too long before that and it really bombed out.

Then Frank Coppa, Sr. called and said he wanted to see me, and we needed to meet at a downtown hotel. He also mentioned how much my business was making, in a way that made me realize he was suggesting I was vulnerable to short traders. I had thought of my company as a strong one, figuring that I had traded US Bridge really brilliantly, even hurting the shorts a little bit when they came at me, getting some revenge, because I had muscle and I could move markets. I had buying power. When you have a lot of brokers you can put in fifty thousand to buy and move the stock up two points. I had the muscle and the firm was making money. I had built a million dollar trading account up to about five million in cash, just trading other stocks, getting involved in other people's IPOs, actively trading my own stocks and others. I had never been a trader by profession, but I started getting the hang of it.

Because I knew Frank was a serious Mob player, I called Danny to establish how I was supposed to act with him. I also knew that Frank was a short player, and I told Danny I didn't know how to handle the situation. Danny told me to tell the guy you're not interested.

"Don't back down with the guy," Danny said. "Just tell him how you feel and don't do anything you don't want to."

That sounded good to me, and I went to meet Frank Sr. at the hotel. I had heard he was fat, but he was a lot fatter than I had imagined. He had a cigar in his hand and he weighed about four hundred pounds. He looked like the actor Danny DeVito blown up to maybe six times his size.

His son Frank Jr. was with him and I said hello to his son first, since I already knew him. Then I said hello to Frank Coppa, Sr. He didn't say hello back. He just looked at me. Then he said:

"Hey, kid, you know what I do?"

"Yeah," I said. "You're a short player."

"So why you telling my son you don't want to do his deal?"

"So why should I?" I asked him. "What are you gonna do, short me?"

"You're a good target," he said, puffing his cigar. "You've got five million dollars in capital."

All of a sudden my feelings changed. This guy had information about me that he had no legitimate access to. He had gotten inside information before the meeting, the kind of information the stock market investigators were not likely to have.

"Five million dollars in capital," Coppa said again. "I could take you out tomorrow. I could short you down till you're zero."

I wasn't going to show that I was scared. I knew I could start a business again if this one went down, and I understood there would be times when a broker's book or the whole house could blow up. But I didn't want my new business destroyed because a guy wanted to boost his son's income.

"I don't want to do a chicken franchise," I said. "It doesn't look like a good deal to me."

That's when he gave me a look, the kind of look I had seen in the eyes of mobsters who had absolute power, and knew they had the absolute ability to wield it. His son knew it, too, and you could see the smug confidence on the son's face.

"Here's what," Coppa told me. "Not only are you going to do the chicken deal, but you're also going to give me seventy-five thousand shares of your shoe deal."

This was the classic way Mob muscle is wielded. A bad deal is offered to someone who doesn't really have much choice but to take it. Out of a sense of self-respect, he turns the deal down, thinking he has the free will and right to do so. Then the man he's dealing with shows his power, and makes the man another offer—a much worse one. If he's smart, the man takes the second offer, because the next one will be even worse.

The chicken deal was bad enough for me. But giving this guy 75,000 shares of stock in the shoe deal was a disaster. To do that, I would have to take the stock away from somebody—a good client or a good broker.

"I can't give you seventy-five thousand shares," I said.

"I didn't ask you if you were interested," Frank Sr. said, getting up, the meeting over. "I told you that's the deal." Then he and his son left.

We had already paid Coppa $300,000 to turn over the shoe deal and this was a shakedown. We both knew that the shoe stock was going to go from five to fifteen. That would mean giving him $750,000, on top of the $300,000 we had already given him. I was furious about this and so was Lex. The threat had been clear: if we didn't give him $750,000 worth of stock in the shoe company IPO, he would destroy us by shorting.

Lex and I talked it over and it was clear that I was in a corner. If I didn't give in to Frank's deal, he could crush US Bridge, which was the only stock I cared about. I really didn't want to hurt the people involved.

Lex was angrier than I was, and being a more volatile guy than I am, he set up another meeting with Frank, and threatened him right back. He wasn't talking idly, either. He had his father, and he also had Butchie Blue Eyes, behind him.

"Listen, you fat fuck," Lex told him, right away. "Don't ever threaten my partner again, or you'll find yourself going out a window." Frank knew Lex was someone to be reckoned with.

"Calm down, kid," he told Lex. "We'll work something out."

Lex was out for blood. That was when I realized once again that I was trying to hold up the last deal for the benefit of the next deal. If US Bridge went down under a short attack, I would have had a hard time selling the shoe deal. I told Lex that the chicken deal was out of the question, but I'd look at the shoe stock and see what I could come up with to satisfy Frank and keep him off us. My company was going too well to jeopardize everything for a matter of principle and 75,000 shares of stock. We were a full-blown operation with about 150 brokers, a huge payroll, big trading, and a lot of power. We actually had some of the short traders scared of us at this point.

What bothered me was what Frank Coppa, Sr. knew about our finances. He knew too much even for a source, in terms of somebody that he had giving him information on us. I figured maybe we were bugged, and I contracted for a professional sweeper to come up and check, a procedure that I would do periodically till the end of my career. We had to make monthly reports to NASDAQ to show how much capital we had, and it was possible he was getting those reports. At least that's what I thought at first. The sweep turned up a bug in my office in my trading operations phone where all the money and the transactions happen. That was the phone I used to give the go ahead to buy or sell, near where we reconciled our stock positions with the clearing firm every morning.

I didn't know if Fat Frank got hold of my NASDAQ report or if he was the one getting information from the bugs, but however he had it, we were in trouble. We knew the government was looking into all this as well, so we had it checked to see if the electronics were government issue. There are two types of bugs. There is one type they use routinely, that every branch agency can use, and this was definitely not that. Then there was one that was sold for professionals outside the government. That was the type we had, and though the government might have picked some up to throw us off the scent, I doubted it. But there was no way to trace the signal back to the snoops. We just knew that since the bug was in my telephone receiver, someone had to have been in our place at night to plant it.

The bug was more than a listening device for my telephone calls. It turned the mouthpiece into an open microphone. The telephone worked like it always did. You hang it up and the line was no longer in use. But this little eavesdropper continued to broadcast all the conversations in the room. Nothing that went on in the office was missed by the recorder spinning away in some nearby van or office.

Not that I was a stranger to surveillance equipment. I installed miniature cameras in my office. These were cameras that were extremely sensitive, picking up images even in the low light of night. The lenses were the size of a shirt button and could be hidden almost anywhere. They provided a multiple channel monitor so I could watch from my private office what was taking place in every part of my suite of offices. The monitor served both as security and entertainment.

We had a broker who was dating a woman in the office and he was certain she was so taken with him that she'd never look at another man. One of the guys bet him $1,000 that he could get her to have oral sex with him and the broker took the bet. We all went into my office and watched the monitor when the guy approached her with the offer. She couldn't get his zipper down fast enough. We were standing there, watching the screen, cheering her on while her broker-boyfriend didn't know what to do.

The discovery of the bugs and the threat from the short players was nothing to laugh about. Then I opened the newspaper to discover that the FBI had been upstairs on the 47th floor of the World Trade Center doing a cash sting from a dummy firm it had set up to catch promoters and dirty stock brokers. The fake office was staffed entirely by FBI agents playing stockbrokers to lure in promoters. Promoters went around pitching stock to different brokerage firms to get them interested in buying it. And for that service, they got paid in stock. Sometimes the promoter paid the brokers in cash for pushing their stock, and that was what the FBI was looking for.

The stock that these promoters played with was called S-8 and it was free-trading stock. The promoter got his shares from the company as payment for pushing the stock. But he could use a portion of this to pay someone in a brokerage firm to sell it to clients. The company using the promoter knew exactly what he was doing. They just gave him the stock and told him to get results.

Pitching stocks to brokers is a tough business, and when he finished his pitch about the stock, and why it was such a great deal, the broker might ask: "What's in it for me?"

That's where the promoter had to make an offer. He had a heavy incentive to move the stock because his pay was determined in part by how much the stock went up. He got shares based on where the stock started, and he made his money on how much it went up, which was a factor of how much of it he had moved. That's why he would offer a cash incentive—a bribe—to a broker as an inducement to buy it. And that was what the FBI sting operation on the 47th floor was set up to catch.

While that was in full operation upstairs, we were trying to figure out how to deal with the Frank Coppa situation. The guy was a major problem and if we couldn't figure out how to appease him, he was going to crush us. Lex had warned Coppa not to threaten our partners, but Coppa had not backed down. He had said we should do the right thing anyway, that we should give him something. This was the classic Mob business approach—favor for favor. But I had already done him the favor of giving him three hundred grand for the shoe deal. I paid. I couldn't help it if he got buyer's remorse or seller's remorse or whatever you want to call it.

We were all agreed that we didn't want to do his son's chicken deal. We also had planned to go to France for the month of August. We had already rented a villa. We figured we could appease him with 30,000 shares instead of 75,000. We decided to tell him that was all we could give him and hope he would understand. Then Nick Blasso, one of our pasta boys, decided that the chicken deal could be his big break. He knew Frank Junior, and believed that if he did the private placement, he would get a million shares for himself and probably Mob recognition. We told him we wanted nothing to do with the deal, but that we'd let him raise the money in our brokerage. We were just not going to take it public ourselves and we would not put our name on it. He could do the deal privately if he wanted to, but I made it clear that there was no way any other broker in this firm would be involved. I wasn't going to burn their liquidity or a client's money on a deal I had no interest in.

Nick decided to raise the million dollars, take a good chunk, give us some of it (which we declined), and then find an underwriter for it. It would be his own underwriter, not ours. I figured that when the Coppas, Sr. and Jr., heard this, they would assume that we would be going to go all the way. Blasso would be going to the Ranger games with Junior.

It may be that we stopped a major short player from attacking us for the time being, but we made a big mistake with Frank. His firm closed down and his two partners wanted to work with us. They had been big producers before they had joined him so we figured they were out for whatever they could earn with our up-and-coming brokerage. We did think about their relationship with Frank and it did occur to us that they might be joining us to spy for him. And we were very careful around them. At the same time we were looking at doing an IPO for a company called Fun Tyme that was like an indoor amusement area for kids, a variation of Discovery Zone, which was big right then. It involved taking a large space in a strip mall or covered mall, then filling it with things to climb, places to jump, video arcade games, and other activities.

It seemed like a no-brainer. Kids would love it. Parents could give them money for tokens and let them play while they went shopping. Teenagers could hang out there for dates. But Discovery Zone just got cracked from forty dollars a share down to six bucks/share when Fun Tyme was being put together as an offering. I wondered why Fun Tyme would do well against Discovery Zone, when Discovery Zone was doing poorly. Still, we had invested $600,000 of our own money and needed to get the deal done.

Oppenheimer, our clearing firm, recognized the gloomy prospects, and told us they would not underwrite the offer, so if we went ahead with it, we had to find another company. The clearing firm was critical because the brokerage doing the IPO only puts up about a third of the money to get the underwriting done. The clearing firm puts up the rest, just in case the clients don't pay. Since the clearing firm is taking a risk with the brokerage house, they have a degree of influence.

Oppenheimer liked the shoe deal and were ready to underwrite it. But they would not do Fun Tyme. We wanted to find a new underwriter at the same time we were supporting US Bridge against attacks by short players. I soon learned that because the stock was above $5 for US Bridge, it was legally marginable under the National Market System. The brokerage house could make a judgment call on going marginal, and a decision was reached to five-hundred-thousand shares on margin to a company going short and clearing with Bear Sterns and Dick Harrington, Gene's former friend.

However, the head of clearing did not like Gene. Everything was legal that was taking place, though I know it was because John, The Brow, got greedy and needed to buy other cash deals and put our stock on margin while Dick Harrington of the clearing firm wanted to destroy us. He'd had a long feud with Gene, and this was a way to hurt us without violating any of the rules. It was a battle, a financial struggle for the life and well-being of our firm, and I was up for it. I had built this company and I was going to keep it alive and healthy. I began scheduling morning meetings that were like a football team's locker room at half time. I'd call everyone into the boardroom and begin talking to them. I'd preach. I'd pace, using my hands. I climbed on the desks. Whatever I had to do to get their attention.

"Everybody has to buy a thousand shares of US Bridge," I told them. "We got some shorts jerking us around, but we're not going to let them hurt us. A little pressure will make us stronger, make us do better. Look, I got a pair of top seats for the Yankees game. The guy who buys the most in the next 24 hours gets them. We're going to keep the shorts from knowing they can hurt us."

I gave them other incentives. I pinned a hundred-dollar bill to the wall for the first guy who bought a thousand shares. Some of the guys were still cold callers and some were rookie brokers. But they were still all street hustlers, and a pair of tickets to the Yankees or the Mets, or a hundred-dollar bill—these things still mattered to them. It was the street hustler mentality. A hundred bucks won in a bet, a scam, or a hustle tasted sweeter than twice that much earned straight. The bigger brokers would get different incentives, such as a higher payout on a particular trade.

It worked. They knocked our position from the desk from 300,000 shares—a dangerous exposure to 100,000. Then somebody suggested the clearinghouse Straker-Wort. I went there to see Garry Salomon and he okayed the underwriting of Fun Tyme for no more than the standard capital required on Wall Street. I said we had five million in cash, along with some in stocks, and some here and some there.

Salomon said he didn't care so long as we had the assets so we did the transition work to switch over to them. The accounting was a nightmare, but we transferred over to Straker-Wort and the first thing coming out was the shoe company. It was the hottest deal we had done and we needed the brokers all psyched up. At this point the pasta boys were unhappy and threatening to quit. For one thing, they hated The Duke and for another, they weren't participating heavily on the shoe deal and weren't getting paid their cash chops.

But the rest of the firm was enthusiastic. They could smell the money and see how they could jump-start their own books. George, the former Porsche salesman and gas station owner, wanted to build a name for himself. All of the new guys The Duke brought in wanted to stake their own territory, and they would be doing most of the work.

But our activities were not going unmonitored at this point. We were getting attention from law enforcement and regulatory agencies that looked at our activities in a cold, cruel light. According to NASD investigators, The Duke was running a policy that completely violated NASD regulations. The government action didn't come for five years, but in March, 2000, a NASD complaint would charge that Doukas, "The Duke," had "put in place or enforced a 'policy' that prevented some customers from selling specific securities from their accounts." This included a "no net sell" policy at the firm: brokers were not allowed to sell certain securities unless another customer could be found to buy them.

The complaint further alleged that as a result of this policy, customers in certain instances had their sales delayed or could not sell securities from their accounts. In addition, eleven of the brokers improved their business by:

- Trading without customer authorization
- Failing to execute customer orders
- Failing to execute orders promptly
- Making improper price and performance predictions

This was all going on in spite of the fact that the shoe company was our first straight-up deal with tons of inside position—a very legitimate company. It looked good; it looked hot. The Duke said he had exercised due diligence on the deal and I saw no reason to double-check a man with his background. He believed in the project so much that we were willing to cooperate with mobsters like Frank Coppa, Sr. to get it done. Then I got a call from the head of clearing at Straker saying he needed more cash.

"Wait a minute," I said. "It's only a seven million-dollar deal. All I really need is three million bucks to cover the third I need for the syndicate."

That was the standard. That's what Oppenheimer used to require me to have in cash: a third of the money based on the value of the IPO. That way, if the deal busted, the clearinghouse was only on the hook for two-thirds. But he told me that I needed one-to-one with them. That was unheard of, and I was short a million bucks.

He said: "Yeah, well I can't take it public unless you have a million dollars that you could put into the account for at least a week."

One million dollars for one week!

I called around. I tried to see if I could borrow a million from A.R. Baron, but they were having problems. Everybody was having problems. NASDAQ investigators were raiding firms. The shorts were attacking heavily. There was trouble all around, so I called back to my guy at Straker and he said to call a friend at a brokerage firm he cleared for.

"Call him up," he said. "Tell him who you are. Tell him that I said to call you, and see if he'll give you a loan because I know he's got some liquid assets."

Once again it was a scam that I felt I had to go along with. The firm he recommended had a history of causing me problems. One of the partners had created a mirror stock for American US Bridge, which was essentially a scam to dupe investors into buying the wrong stock by listing it with a deceptive name. The way the stock listings worked, you could have two companies with the same name trading under different listings. US Bridge might be listed on the market as USBR and the mirror stock might be listed as USBA. The first company was aggressively seeking new business and working to handle existing accounts with quality work at a fair price. The second company existed solely to gain investors by fooling them by using the same name.

I was no longer troubling myself by worrying about dealing with unethical players. Money and profit had to come first, and I stood to make millions of dollars for my firm and a few select clients when we took these companies public. I called the firm my Straker man had recommended and found that they would loan me the money—$900,000—but for a ten percent fee. For a loan that would be repaid in a week, that came to $90,000 and 30,000 shares of the shoe company. That put the total interest I would be paying at $390,000 for seven days. But I felt I had no choice but to give in to this monstrous usury.

I agreed to the loan, knowing the clearing firm did not even need the money. I was convinced it was a scam. I knew I had been set up. I also knew there was so much money to be made from the IPO that it was worth the loss to get the deal completed. It went public and took off immediately, going from five to fifteen dollars a share. My brokers were going crazy. They had signs on the door, "Sell your shares here," because they had so many orders for it in the after-market. There were only buyers and no sellers. The deal looked like a home run.

The joy of finally representing a company whose stock had genuine value because of the quality of the product was short-lived. The stock stayed strong, but I was already encountering major questions. The day the stock went public, even as the price steadily advanced, I was faced with a couple hundred thousand shares being sold back. This puzzled me. If I owned the whole float, where the hell would I buy a couple hundred thousand shares? The answer seemed to be my new partner. The Duke had held back on me when he structured the second-round financing, and had arranged for millions of dollars worth of stock to be shared with some of his former Gruntal brokers. Gruntal had handled the initial financing of the private placement, then had lost all of its sales force. The shares essentially became free agents that were picked up somehow by Frank Coppa, Sr., who then sold them to me.

This made me thoroughly angry with The Duke. I was supposed to be his partner. If he had told me the truth, it would have been okay. But it was not okay to have lied to me. And it was a mistake to let me try to guess who was back-dooring me because I was handling trading and I saw every share that came in. I watched the cash register. In the midst of the frustration and the euphoria, the men who had loaned me the $900,000 showed up at my office. The shoe company stock was trading, the brokers were going crazy, we were handling the deal, and in walked these two guys who shook me down for $90,000. Still, Cable Shoe was a big success. Then three weeks later, when we were getting ready to do the Fun Tyme deal, I got the same type of phone call.

"You don't have enough money. You need another loan."

It was just like before. The committee at the clearinghouse wanted one-to-one security for the loan. The deal was for $6.5 million and I was a million short. There would be another loan, another ten percent payment for a week's use of the funds. It was obviously a shakedown. I didn't need the money, but I was playing along because it was the price I had to pay to get the deal done. We had $600,000 of our own money in Fun Tyme that we had bridged the company with, so it was important for us to take it public.

That was why we went back to the same guy for a new loan, this time for $1.1 million, requiring us to pay $110,000 plus shares in Fun Tyme. Whatever we would do, whatever we were underwriting, he wanted a piece of it for his brokerage firm to put out and open new accounts on. We paid the toll because we had to play the game. The stock went from five to eleven. Another home run.

I finally felt I was reaching the top of the game. I had a big broker sales force, and I could bring deals in higher, as high as I wanted. For a few days I basked in my success. I took the private placement stock I had gained for handling the $600,000 in bridge financing and provided options to the pasta boys as a reward for their going along with the changes. They paid $1.50 for shares that were now worth $11, making them instantly wealthy.

And then it was over.

My partners and I decided to go on a vacation, certain in our own minds that everything was well in hand. The Duke would go to the villa, along with me, Danny, Gene, my older cousin Sal, and the new beard that was my first cash deal partner on Candies Shoes. He was living in London and fronting for the next two deals. Lex would stay behind, running the firm despite the fact that his conviction meant he was not allowed in the office. I said to Lex before I left:

"Look, Lex, stay up here and keep a very low profile. Just watch the trading account. Make sure nobody's dumping stock. Make sure there's no black-and-blue going on. Just watch the cash register. That's all you have to do."

I knew my in-house trader would watch and alert him to any stock problem.

"You have to decide whether to buy it or drop the bid," I said. "If you see ten thousand shares, obviously drop the stock. If you see a thousand shares, just buy it."

Then we went on vacation. I was relaxed, even knowing I was traveling with a Mafia family member whose brother, father and cousins were under constant Federal surveillance. I was comfortable even though the man I had left to oversee daily activities was committing a crime every time he set foot in any brokerage firm's office, much less one in which he had an intense financial interest. I even ignored the implications of an FBI sting being conducted in my building while I was making my deals, even though I read about the bureau's operation daily.

However I fancied myself, I was a frog and the scorpions were circling in preparation for an attack.

CHAPTER SIXTEEN

In the end, it was the money. In 1996, when I was going to work with my cousin's firm, the market had doubled to 5,500 and the NASDAQ had tripled to 1,200. A family of four could live decently in urban America for $35,000 a year. Or less in some regions where housing was older. I considered it a bad month if all I earned was what the average American needed to support his family for a year. There were weeks when I earned more money than the highest paid entertainers and sports stars. I weighed jail time, not in terms of personal or family disgrace, not in terms of years away from my growing daughters, but in how much I would lose per year and how much I would keep. Three years of jail time—a lifetime for my children—and a fine of a few million dollars—the gross annual income for some of the small businesses whose services I occasionally used.

It was the drug addict's reasoning all over again. It was as though I was on the street, looking to get high, and found that the best dope available was being offered by a man I knew was an undercover narc. "I might get busted," I would reason. "I might go to jail. But it's such good looking shit that if he'll only let me get high before putting on the cuffs, it will be worth the time off the streets."

I had become an addict, and this time the drug of choice was money. I could look in the mirror and see a seemingly healthy man in a $2,000 suit, a $150 necktie, and $500 shoes. I was viewed with respect on the street, and I had moved far beyond my immigrant roots and my one-time status as a Brooklyn street hustler. I was someone who might have been a senior diplomat at the United Nations Building or a corporate CEO. I was Sal Lauria, a man of distinction, worthy of respect.

Yet to too many others, I was Sal Lauria, the frog, boxed into a corner, with the scorpion ready for the kill. My pump-and-dump schemes, my money laundering, my behind-the-scenes manipulation of IPOs were, to others, little different than what street corner hustlers did when they set up a table for three-card monte or a gutter craps sharpie with loaded dice.

The Federal authorities were increasingly a presence on Wall Street. Numerous brokers were being indicted and others were wearing broadcast equipment to help the FBI and others build cases against still more firms. In that climate, Gene and Lex decided to go to Russia. Things were hot in the former Soviet Union. The privatization of all the industry over there meant lots of opportunity to make money.

I didn't want to go there. Lex and Gene knew Russia. Gene's father was a well-known businessman with connections to both the Communists and the new business leaders. Lex's family was big in organized crime. They could go anywhere, do anything. It was a good situation, but it wasn't something I knew. I understood Italy. That was my first home. I spoke the language, but they kept telling me that there was no opportunity in Italy, and they were right. So when my cousin called to tell me that Aleks Paul, our money-laundering jeweler, had been arrested, I agreed we had to get out.

Aleks had just made bail to get out of jail and that evening I went to a diner near my house to meet him and his two Russian partners, Erik and Alex, whom I would also see on the run in Russia. They were investors in The Duke's new firm, having taken over where we left off. Aleks told me about the arrest and what had happened. He said they came to the house and asked questions about my partners and me. I was just trying to make sure that I knew where I stood. I knew I had to leave.

At this point I didn't want to talk with him anymore because I suspected he was wired. A week before I left, Aleks came to visit me at home. I was in the front yard of my house overlooking the cliff looking over the water and we walked over to the bluff near the house. He took off his shirt to show me that he was not wired. He wanted to know if Lex and Gene were going to stay abroad. He asked me if I thought he should cooperate. Vlad had already rolled, which is how Aleks had been busted, but apparently Aleks had not yet made any decision about cooperating. He was scared and I was sure he was definitely going to roll. He was too damned nervous.

Lex and Gene and I decided to have a shredding party with our corporate documents to avoid leaving a paper trail that could get us indicted. Pump and dump schemes were difficult to prove at best. We had committed serious infractions, stolen millions and our clients were victimized, but that was the least on my mind. We had carefully recorded our offshore activities and those records had to be destroyed.

Lynn and I emptied all the safes and moved jewelry to more secure locations. I gave an old high school friend $500,000 to hold for me. Lex shared his partners' concerns, but he was also worried about losing records concerning the European bank accounts. Since the type of money holding and manipulations being done overseas were legal, Lex saw no reason not to save some documents from the shredder. He did not think about the fact that if they were found in the United States, they were still proof of U.S. laws being broken.

Lex took the documents he wanted to the storage box where he had stashed the guns he had taken from Vlad's house. He didn't give a thought to the weapons. The incident was over and the guns were in a bag, unavailable to anyone who might wish to use them. Lex didn't tell the rest of us what he had done.

If he had, we would have stopped him. There was no reason why critical details such as account numbers couldn't have been written separately, perhaps in code, and placed where they couldn't come back to create problems. By saving the paperwork, he was preserving evidence of criminal actions. A storage box lease is over when the time expires. Then the lock may legally be broken, the box opened, and the contents confiscated for sale. Lex had leased the box for six months and he didn't stop to think that the trip to Russia he was planning was going to last longer than that.

Meanwhile, I helped out at my cousin's firm, First City, advising them on how to do the dance that would enable them to accomplish their first two deals. I wanted their premises also swept weekly, and we found that even our own employees were spying on us. A baby monitor above my cousin's desk was transmitting to us and we found that a group of brokers who had come in with us on the Israeli technology deal were taking advantage of us. We fired them immediately. A second deal was loaded with goodies. We got stocks and warrants. It was beautiful, in my eyes, and it worked in part because the place was filled with the old pasta boys who had followed me to my new business. I knew we had spies in the firm and we tried to be as careful as possible.

Odd things were happening around me. The first was the reappearance of two pasta boys who had not worked for some time. Joseph Burco had gone with Dutch, and called me out of the blue to ask for a job. What was strange is that he wanted to talk outside in the open in Battery Park, and that he wanted to make sure that there was still cash in our deals. He must have mentioned the word cash ten times while trying to make me say it.

The second encounter was with Gabe, the same guy we had saved from the clutches of the street gang. Gabe called out of nowhere and asked to come and hang out for the day. The Feds were trying hard to catch me and I knew it. I went home one evening set on convincing my wife we should move to Monte Carlo. To my surprise, she agreed. We started to prepare all our documents when I realized that if I left I would probably never see the money I made on the last deal, so I decided to stay long enough to cash in—just like an alcoholic having one more for the road before he calls it quits.

The deal was with a technology company that went from $6 to $16 a week later. But before I could congratulate myself, the short players moved in. The place had changed, the game was the same. Stock One brought a comfort level. Stock Two, and by extension me, was the bull's eye in the sights of the short players' rifle scopes. I was angry. This was not going to continue. I called Danny, never thinking I was getting us deeper in with the Mob. I wanted results and I wanted them now. I wanted a meeting that would change things once and for all. I didn't want to have to keep looking over my shoulder. I didn't want to have to make deals, then hold my breath, not only while I saw if the stock price would rise, but also whether and when the shorts would move in to destroy what I had created.

By now, Danny knew the problems better than I did. He knew which Wall Street firms and players were connected to which Mob families, and he also knew when rival firms might be protected by different members of the same crime family. By now it seemed doubtful to me that there was any brokerage house on Wall Street that was completely clean. Whether they knew it or not, the largest, most respected firms still had individual brokers who were linked with organized crime. There is just too much money in the short playing, in the pump and dump schemes, in the secret world of bridge financing, to keep them away.

Danny made his calls, and then told me someone very close to him could possibly set up a meeting with the key short players.

"Who?" I asked.

"Plug Head," he told me.

I agreed to a meeting without hesitation.

"Okay," I told him. "He doesn't like me, but he's out of the business and trading as a short."

Plug Head agreed to meet me at the Plaza Hotel, one of New York's stateliest old buildings, just off Central Park. Security was everywhere; the staff looking like the Secret Service in their dark suits with two-way radio bugs in their ears. Professional musicians played discretely in the background, and the service was impeccable. No one would bother us.

Plug Head was familiar with the stock in play, and he knew many of the groups that wanted to crush it for their own profit. What he didn't know was how fast and intense the short action had become. I told him that Ron Bonero of the Bonero Brothers, my major short-playing adversaries, had initiated the short action. They were ready to knock the stock down and had gotten off a sizable position. All the other leech traders would follow their lead, so if we could make a truce with Bonero, it would help chase the smaller players away. The question was how many shares Bonero was short, and where would he like us to cover him in his position. The stock was down to $11 a share by then, having dropped $5 from its peak.

We agreed to a second meeting at the Plaza, and this time Plug Head brought news from the Bonero Brothers. He explained that Ron Bonero himself was not personally shorting us, nor was Bonero Brothers shorting us directly. Instead, they were working under the orders of Jordan Belfour, who was new to trading short. Belfour was legendary in the business of selling. He had started out working for a meat wholesaler, going door to door offering homeowners meat to stock their freezers—sides of beef and massive quantities of hot dogs. Belfour used his selling skills to become a stockbroker operating what was allegedly the biggest boiler room in the country, Stratton Oakmont. It was also one of the first to be closed down by the Feds.

I didn't believe Belfour was our problem but I went along with the story. Plug Head explained that Belfour would need to have me cover the stock at $9, which would assure him a $100,000 profit. Then Plug Head said the arrangement would assure that they would back off the one stock. But there was no guarantee that they wouldn't short a different stock of mine in the future, which meant I was being set up for ongoing blackmail. What didn't feel right about all this, beyond the refusal to back off in the future, was that the timing of the short play was too perfect. They had to have inside information from somewhere. I knew something was wrong the week before we decided to do a lot of buying in the stock in anticipation of a block of stock being cleared for sale by NASD for one of the beard accounts.

After leaving the Plaza, I asked my cousin, the chairman and lead partner of our firm, to check into this and to sweep his whole place for bugs. But I also wanted to know who was handling the legal stuff on the paperwork. Other than the main players, the only people who knew about a big block of stock coming on the market were the lawyers. My cousin told me the name of the lawyer who handled the paperwork on the stock that was shorted. Suddenly I knew the leak. I had been at this guy's daughter's bat mitzvah, along with Plug Head, before he became a short, and the Bonero Brothers. Our lawyer was also their lawyer for some things, which meant he was the leak. He was the guy who gave them the information so they knew which stock to watch for shorting.

We immediately stopped using the lawyer and his firm. Changing counsel meant that it would take about six weeks to clear the block of stock. We thought it would be a good idea for the Bonero Brothers to remain short. We felt it might be good for them to go short even more, and we would cover them with the block when it cleared. Plug Head and I met again to discuss the trading strategy and he told me the Brothers agreed to the arrangement. We would keep buying from him indirectly so the other shorts would not know what we were up to. The fee would be a minimum two points or twenty percent on all the shares he had short.

The price for stopping the never-ending short action was a bargain for me. At least we were in bed with the one person who had really been badly hurting me throughout my career. After the arrangements were agreed on, Plug Head and I would spend a lot of time together to make sure that the trading would go smoothly. Bonero did not want to deal with me directly and did not want to meet with me even though I had met their Wiseguy once when I was with Danny and we were trying to deal with our first shorting problems.

Turk Rambo was no longer an issue because he had gone to jail for tax evasion, though he left behind Big Louie, his brother-in-law. Pony was known as a savvy market player like Frank Coppa, Sr. He had also told me when he met with Lex and me that we would be okay, that the Bonero Brothers would not hurt us. I assume he had that power, but I think Pony forgot to tell Bonero before he was locked up.

For the next six weeks, Plug Head and I commuted from the Hamptons together and every day I motivated the pasta boys to start buying with the usual inside commission. At the same time, Plug Head explained to me how they had all traded against me in the US Bridge deal, and he laid out the details of how the Bonero Brothers did what they did. He also identified the organized crime family protecting them. He mapped out a network among the short players that was amazing. It was painful to see because I was looking at my own past, and I could see the mistakes I had made, and how my work was manipulated.

Plug Head then invited me to go fishing in Florida on his yacht in Fort Lauderdale, which is where Ron Bonero happened to be. Plug Head planned to surprise Bonero by introducing me without telling him I was coming down. At this time we were close to the six-week mark and we had been shorted close to 400,000 shares. We got to Florida, and the next day we went to breakfast before heading out to sea. Bonero was at the restaurant, apparently having eaten and gotten back into his truck when we arrived. Plug Head hurried over to him while I went inside. Ten minutes later, Plug Head came in and told me that the guy did not want to talk. Except for the fishing, the trip was a waste of time. Obviously, we were still in trouble from Bonero Brothers and there was still tension.

We finally had to cover the short position, but by then there were other forces in play. Someone had alerted the NASD that there was something wrong with this deal. The registration for the stock was held up, and the brothers were carrying a $4 million short position, blocking the money for other trading. They wanted out or Bonero was going to crush the stock.

That put us in a bad spot. First City did not have the capital to hold such a large position and Plug Head did not want to wait for the stock to clear in order to get his 20 percent profit. He wanted out immediately at 10 percent profit. This was a disaster. We paid the brokers to buy the stock, and now we needed someone to hold a big short position. We could only hold 150,000 shares, which left 250,000 outstanding. This was a problem, so we told our brokers to sell us back the stock they had just bought. They would owe us, buying more later on, creating an accounting nightmare. They would also get to keep the cash because there was nothing else we could do.

The Mob involvement kept escalating. We had finally stopped the raiding of our stock by firing the law firm that had been representing us. But once again, we were faced with Mob shakedowns. Once again it was cheaper to pay than to argue. We had solved the raiding solution except there was another problem. The Wiseguy left in charge of protecting the Bonero Brothers in Pony's absence, his brother-in-law Big Gus, told Plug Head that they wanted $75,000 in cash. We paid up.

As it turned out, Plug Head was stealing—burning our candle at both ends. Lex and I were infuriated at him because he had all the information about what everyone was doing and who was trading against us. Lex flipped out and I was surprised he didn't hurt or kill Plug Head. There was no violence, but we obviously stood to lose even more than we already had. We slowly sold most of our stock position and settled back to lick our wounds.

I was a market man and there wasn't any more fight left in me at this point. I had asked Plug Head why they had to short the deal.

First he said that it was because it was at $16. Then he laughed, and told me the truth. Finally, I was learning the real story. The shorts had come after my deals simply because they were my deals, he said. The targets had not been the deals; the targets had been me. The short attack was personal! The scorpion had to sting the frog. It was his nature.

Lex was also having problems. Butchie Blue Eyes had supposedly guaranteed the US Bridge bonding and the $100,000 fee that was never returned. Now the Mob wanted it back, and the guy collecting for Joe Polito was Al Garafola, his Wiseguy partner, the brother-in-law of Sammy "the Bull" Gravano. Sammy the Bull was the confessed murderer who was given a new life in Arizona as a result of testimony that sent John Gotti, then head of the Gambino organized crime family, to jail for life. Al Garafola told Butchie that if Lex didn't pay, he'd be chopped into little pieces and I'd still have to come up with the cash. This was a threat to be taken very, very seriously. Once again there was a sit-down. The two guys who took the money were on the lam so it was a very tense time. As it turned out, the matter was never resolved and the money was never returned.

I resigned from First City before it closed down. Then I went to our 40 Wall Street office to evaluate what to do next. I knew I wasn't going to handle another IPO. There were too many people waiting to take advantage of me. It was time to change the formulas we were using. One thought was Reg D, which was like a Reg S. There were also investment schemes that Gene and Lex were conjuring up. But nothing was effective. There was too much heat from all sides and we could no longer focus. We all needed to get away.

I met Big Van in the elevator one day and he told me they were still making money with Holly Products and that he was going to open his own firm. He said they had issued a zillion shares and were always looking for buyers for the stock which had reached full penny stock status. Later that day, almost like magic, I got a call from an old friend from Gruntal looking for a big block of Holly. I knew this had to be a set up, and I played along to see who the rats were. Irv Fryberg and Jonathan Lyons arranged a meeting to buy the block and when I get there, the first thing I noticed was a third guy, a big, tall, Italian who could pass for a gangster until he spoke.

"So how much cash is in this stock?" he asked. That told me I was talking to a Fed. It was a setup, all right. I answered without hesitating.

"If that's all you're interested in, you could be paid in gold bullion, or wire, or check, as long as its legal and kosher."

That put a premature end to the meeting, which went through an awkward ten minutes of word-shuffling before I climbed into my 850 BMW and watched them stare at me with a look that was amazing. The two brokers were evidently nervous and relieved, and the Fed disgusted.

I went home knowing that the walls were caving in and it was only a matter of time. We all began preparing to leave the United States and none of us thought about the storage box as we planned our trip. We were envisioning deals in Russia, where Gene had established a business base on a trip to see Russian President Boris Yeltsin, supposedly a friend of Gene's family. Yeltsin had risen to power as part of the democracy movement encouraged by Mikhail Görbachev, then the leader of the former USSR.

Gene's planned get-together in Russia was a strictly capitalistic meeting to discuss the possible acquisition of Shearson Lehman, which was up for sale. There was no set price, though Gene had learned that an offer of $780 million would likely be accepted. He felt he could raise the money with the help of Yeltsin and a man they called the Russian Godfather, who was put in jail weeks after Gene had wined and dined him. There were plenty of very wealthy Russians, some of them from the old Communist system where stealing had been a way of life for the privileged, and some of them new millionaires becoming rich under the democracy movement. Yeltsin knew them all or could find people to help, and Gene planned to cut him in for a piece of the action.

Gene had flown to Moscow and gotten a room in a hotel next to the parliament building known as the Russian "White House." He went to bed unaware that a take-over plot had begun. Then members of the State Committee called a press conference. The plot's leaders came across as drunk and incompetent.

Next came equally ineffectual aggression during which the plotters and their dwindling supporters tried to take control of the White House. However, normal precautions to neutralize the enemy were ignored. Foreign television crews were unrestricted in their movements. Satellite TV, which could be used by everyone from foreign powers to the pro-democracy followers, was never jammed. No one thought to take control of the telephone system. And when tanks were sent into the streets, passers-by walked over to the young tank crewmen asking why they would even consider using weapons on their fellow citizens. The soldiers listened to them and most decided to not fight.

To do it right, the plotters should have arrested Yeltsin, but again the State Committee had no sense of how to seize control. Then the conspirators delegated Pavel Grachev, Commander of Soviet Airborne-General Forces, to run military operations in Moscow, never realizing that he did not support them. With no one to stop him, Yeltsin drove to the White House, entered, rallied his associates, and went out to lead a crowd of tens of thousands of citizens gathered outside. Then the loyalists began constructing makeshift barriers of old trucks, rubble, and anything else they could find to protect the White House, and the fledgling Democracy it represented, from attack.

At one o'clock in the afternoon, Yeltsin walked from the White House and climbed onto a tank stationed at the side of the road and denounced the State Committee members. The State Committee went ahead with their attack on the White House, using tanks run by soldiers willing to obey orders. When gunfire erupted outside his hotel room, Gene rolled to the floor, grabbing his cell phone and sliding under his bed. He called me just as the citizens loyal to the democracy movement were urged by Yeltsin to fight against the plotters.

"I'm under the bed right now!" Gene told us, and we could hear gunfire in the background. Then Gene told us he was going out to join the battle and help. "I'm going out there to defend Democracy," Gene told us. "I have to go now." Then he hung up. He told us later that he had gone downstairs in the hotel and found everyone on emergency footing, and since he wanted to help defend the Russian government, he was given an automatic rifle. He went out to back the loyalists before he discovered that the assault rifle was empty. He had a gun with no bullets in it, but he joined the defense line around the White House anyway.

He told us that the tanks moved around Moscow's Garden Ring Road and thousands of loyalists, including Gene with his empty assault rifle, held fast against the tanks. Three of the resisters were accidentally killed by confused tank drivers who no longer were certain what to do.

Gene and the others, including many children, formed a human chain around the White House. The men supporting the Communist coup either faltered, decided to help the pro-democracy movement, or refused to cooperate further and the revolution was over in a matter of hours. Gene surprised everyone with his bravery, yet he was never able to consummate his business deal. Shearson Lehman was later sold to American Express for approximately $1 billion. However, the pro-democracy forces remembered the courage of the Russian-American, living in the United States, who had left his hotel to join them in the streets. It was a reputation that mattered when he went back much later with Lex, and I joined them as our business collapsed.

There was another advantage to having Gene and Lex in Russia, aside from the business deals they could do. They could be the scapegoats for any problems my cousin might have with the authorities. I told my cousin to protect us, to claim ignorance and say that the two Russians did it all. That would buy time without hurting either of them. I was gradually realizing that the FBI and other investigators involved with Operation Street Cleaner had penetrated all my business operations to one degree or another. Every crime I had committed in order to increase my income was known or soon would be. My connections with Danny had branded my businesses as Mob-owned or Mob-controlled. The only good thing was that, as I said earlier, I was not an American citizen. I lived in the United States and I was married to an American. I was raising my daughters as Americans, but I had never taken out the paperwork necessary to become a citizen. So I could leave the country more readily than if I were a citizen. At the same time, I could also be deported and my rights were almost non-existent.

I decided that I could probably fight the charges coming down more effectively from abroad. I saw little recourse if I was arrested in the United States. However, I reasoned that if the arrest warrant was issued when I was out of the country, I could have my lawyer arrange a deal for my voluntary return.

I finally accepted the reality that my life was out of my control. I had to leave my wife and daughters, my home and my life. But there was no time to feel sorry for myself. Gus, a partner in First City married to the daughter of an organized crime family, discovered that he had been doing business with a FBI sting operation. Gus's father-in-law had heard about a Staten Island jeweler with good international connections. Many in the Mob were using the man to move money and Gus had started doing the same thing. The sting had gone on for months. The jeweler worked from a building filled with audio and video equipment. Everyone who came inside was filmed and recorded. Every transaction, every deal, every request for an illegal operation became part of a permanent record that would be used as evidence to bring the criminals to trial.

More firms were closing down. A.R. Baron & Co. was one of them and its owner Andrew Bressman had gone down with it, and we knew he would turn us in.

I had already gone to the Russian embassy to get my visa so I could travel back and forth to Moscow for the coming year and I knew it was time to bail. Gene, Lex and I had already prepared our escape plan if we had to stay abroad. There were no indictments as yet, so there was nothing to stop me. I booked my flight for just after Christmas and spent what I thought might be my last holiday with my family in the United States.

My parents flew up from Florida and I let them know that I had to leave the country for a while. It was probably one of the worst holidays I've ever had at home. Very somber. When we were alone, my wife was very upset that all these things were happening. She never was a part of the business. She knew I was doing things that were illegal when I first started bringing home cash for our safe. We talked about income tax evasion, something that didn't seem to be much of a crime. But she either didn't think about other possibilities or didn't want to talk about them. She had the house, the kids, and the ability to do anything she wanted. Now it was coming down on her.

"I have to go away," I told her. I had gone many times, but this was different and we both knew it. We should have left and gone to Monte Carlo a year earlier. But I had to stay for one more deal that turned out to be a nightmare.

"For how long?" she asked.

"I don't know. Maybe indefinitely." That was when she started to cry. I had never seen her cry before. We had been through some crazy times. We had had problems. But I never saw her tears. "Who knows," I said. "If things get really crazy over here, I'll call you and you'll come meet me in Europe and we'll live there."

My wife's a pretty strong woman, so her tears hurt me. I didn't know what was going to happen, but I had to stay ahead of the indictment so the lawyers could handle things back here. My fear and sadness didn't change my attitude towards money. I decided I would be productive. After all, if for the moment I couldn't increase my wealth in the United States, the least I could do was to make a bundle in Russia. So I took a plane to Moscow, where Gene and Lex had established the cover story that we were New York bankers coming to do financing for banks in Russia.

We also made connections with pharmacists who could supply us with large quantities of Viagra. The Russian wealthy knew about the drug for men who had trouble getting or sustaining an erection. Even Senator and Presidential candidate Bob Dole had discussed the sexual dysfunction that had hurt his pride and marital pleasure. He told how he had started taking Viagra and redeveloped the sexual abilities he had when much younger. He even did a TV commercial on it. This had led many men, including the Russian generals, to try Viagra, convinced they would be super studs in bed. But Viagra was not readily available in Moscow.

We found a pharmacy connection, and even before I left for Moscow I had been sending "care packages" of Viagra to Gene and Lex. When I went over, I packed as many containers of Viagra as I could. We gave them to the generals and other dignitaries who wanted them. They were selling for $60 a pill over there so they were considered quite valuable. That was why, when the Russians were getting into new areas of business, they were willing to consider using us to do bond offerings for some of their banks.

Gene's father was well known as a major businessman with extensive agricultural holdings through which he subsidized farmers. And, as I've said, Lex's father was a notorious, politically connected gangster who was high up on the food chain. Thanks to these parents and to connections they had made on their own, Gene and Lex were able to set up meetings with the chairmen of top banks at a time when certain Russian banks were floating bonds in the U.S. and London.

I didn't realize the full extent of Gene and Lex's connections until I arrived. I got off the plane, recovered my luggage, and found an official car waiting for me. It was the style you see rolling Manhattan streets on the way to the United Nations—a black Mercedes-Benz with flags on the hood, as if I were a head of state or a diplomat. Moscow was like the Wild West to me. You saw gangsters in their fleets of Mercedes cars and trucks. You saw the business elite and top government officials in luxury limousines. Then you saw everybody else, who basically had nothing.

Our hotel was costing us a fortune so we moved to an American-style apartment near the Kremlin and made the apartment our home base. I hired a secretary who was also a translator, paying her about fifty dollars a week to be available twenty-four hours a day, seven days a week. She translated for me, cooked, and did whatever we needed. We were doing business with banks, particularly with Most Bank, which was one of the largest, and owned by a man who owned the majority of the media in Russia. We even considered a deal to buy the Russian version of ABC-TV, which was available for something like $1.7 million, but decided against it because it had a very heavy payroll.

For the first couple of months things were hopping. We were meeting great people, trying to get deals going, talking with the banks about floating a $100 million bond deal in the U.K. We adopted the customs of the people we were dealing with, sitting in Russian bathhouses, sweating with Russian bank chairmen. We got to meet prime Russian singers and other stars and on New Year's Eve I had a seat in the front row of the big New Year's television show. It was pretty exciting. We were dealing with ex-KGB generals and with the elite of Russian society, and when Lex felt confident with one of these officials, he would tell them he had a problem in the U.S., and ask for help.

Then I began to feel sick. I was exhausted and spent a week in bed suffering pain in the area of my liver unlike anything I had experienced before. I knew I should call a doctor, but I didn't trust Russian medical practitioners. I figured I'd ride it out, and after a week's rest, the pain went away. However, I was physically drained and starting to miss my family intensely.

To escape the loneliness and wanting to make up for lost time, I began working harder during the day, then relaxing at night in a club called Night Flight, the hottest bar in Russia. It was a place where women went to get picked up and hopefully make a little money. It was a pretty jazzy place.

Casinos were legal in Moscow and I went clubbing with Gene's cousin, a small guy with big ears whom we called "Alex the Ears." He was a really nice guy, a music promoter who had brought the Rolling Stones to the stadium in Moscow. He was promoting a lot of western music and it was cool to see the capitol through the eyes of the young, not through those of the KGB or the old timers. We got a good take on the kids growing up in this new free market society. The young people I met were children of the elite and the powerful, either children of rich gangsters, or rich tobacco exporters, or of a guy like Alex the Ears. They had their own private discos in huge houses that didn't look like much from the outside, but were unbelievably fitted out inside. The kids all smoked pot, hash and Ecstasy. It was all either new to them or just more accessible with the government changes. They smoked cigarettes called popparossa, which are made by emptying Russian cigarettes of tobacco and putting in hashish and American tobacco.

I was carefully protected during the three months of my first Moscow visit. There were daily assassinations or kidnappings of rich businessmen reported in the news every day. The bankers were all friends of the KGB or the former KGB. Whenever I wanted to know someone's background, one of the partners would look at me and make a gesture. Tapping the shoulder meant the guy in question had stripes, meaning he had been KGB. Touching the nose told you he was a gangster. It was one and the same to me. KGB and gangsters were identical, I thought. I mean, what's the difference between an FBI agent and a Wiseguy? Very little, if you ask me.

There was more than banking taking place. I discovered how big a factor oil was in Russia. The concern over Chechnya, an area where there was constant fighting, was due in large part to the pipeline that feeds Russian crude oil to the ports where the ships come. They were working on doing a pipeline through Afghanistan as well. The Chechnya war was affected by oil and how to deliver it to the ships in warm water harbors. All of their ports in the north were frozen solid in winter. So I got to thinking about doing something with oil and Russia when I got back to the States. And I also wanted to get back because I was very lonely for New York. I told Lex and Gene I felt like a fish out of water.

"Listen guys," I told them. "I can't live here. I can't participate in the meetings because everything's in Russian. I can't do what I do, which is help make deals. Why am I here? I'm paying a third of the bills and I'll keep paying a third of the bills. But I need to go back."

I returned to New York, not indicted yet, but restless as ever. Missing my wife and daughters had been painful and it had influenced my plans, but it had failed to really make a dent in my value system. I was still trying to find the next source of big money, the next deal, and the next chance to be an operator. I knew I didn't want to go back into a Wall Street brokerage, but I remembered a wealthy former client whose brother was an oil trader.

The client was a wealthy doctor and philanthropist who went to Brooklyn to give medical care to the poor. He didn't charge much, and if they couldn't pay, he treated them for free. He owned farms in Venezuela, along with other real estate. The whole family was wealthy. One brother controlled all the Toyota dealerships in Venezuela. It was the brother who was an oil trader—and who had married into one of the wealthy Arab families—that I wanted to see. His name was Leonardo and he had an office just off Fifth Avenue at Rockefeller Center. I visited him there with a proposition, drawing on my recent Russian experience.

"Look, I've just been to Russia." I told him. "There's a lot of oil there, a lot of oil projects that I could look at. Are you interested in me getting something going for you? Would you like to get involved in an oil field there?"

Leonardo was one of these controlled people who got excited but didn't show it. He offered me a job. "You seem like a pretty aggressive guy," he said. "You understand Wall Street. I see a lot of deals every day. Why don't you work here for a while and look at some of the deals that I do? I'll give you a piece of each deal if you stay."

That was intriguing. I liked having a Fifth Avenue address. It seemed a good place for me to hunker down and see what happened on Wall Street. One of the firms I had invested in was still operating, but I had no part of it. Another was shut down and the stocks were in the toilet. Some of the people I worked with had been arrested. The Duke, with the two Russians and with Aleks, were able to help the firm rebound. They had the skills, but their reputation endangered The Duke.

Leonardo seemed the perfect opportunity for me. I suggested he back me for a hundred grand to go back to Russia and look for projects for him. He agreed and we set up a joint company, each putting in $100,000.

"With a hundred grand from each of us," I told him, "If I find something, at least I'll have some money to manipulate…to put a deposit…bribe…do the things I have to do in Russia to grease the wheels to get things rolling."

I flew back to Russia, settled into the apartment and began talking with Gene and Lex. For the first time I learned that Lex had a scheme that might be able to get us out of trouble with the FBI.

CHAPTER SEVENTEEN

Lex was always hustling and scheming, and his contacts in Russia were the same kind of contacts he had in the United States. The people he knew to approach about deals were crooks. The difference was that in Russia, his crooked contacts were links between Russian organized crime, the Russian military, the KGB, and operatives who played both ways, or sometimes three ways in that shady, dangerous domain. Russian gangsters dealt in oil, currency, drugs and goods, which is not unlike gangsters in other nations. But Russian gangsters in Russia also had war materiel to peddle. Not just guns, like arms dealers in other parts of the world. The Russian military structure had all but collapsed with the fall of the Communist government, and not only weapons but also entire weapons systems were available on the black market.

Tanks, fighter planes, and missiles were all for sale, and so were missile guidance control and other radar systems. And not obsolete systems junked by some former Soviet "republic" or satellite regime that had never been able to maintain them. This equipment was state-of-the-art. There were even nuclear devices to be had for the right amount of money, or so it was rumored.

This was the rich hunting ground where Lex was gunning for deals, a Russian black-market weaponry expanse unlike any that had ever existed before. In this he saw opportunities not just for making profits, but for building a hand that the three of us might be able to play against the American authorities in the cases coming down against us. Lex believed he could find something on the weapons black market that would help the U.S. security position, and perhaps help us with our legal problems at the same time. He made an initial contact with someone connected to the Central Intelligence Agency. He sounded out the possibility of selling them sophisticated Russian weaponry he might be able to come up with. Lex even had a precedent—he had seen Danny Velt, one of our beards, make about $12 million selling Russian helicopters to South Africa.

Lex's unofficial contact in the CIA came to meet him. The CIA wanted a radar tracking system that the Russians developed before the fall of the Soviet Union. It had never been deployed, and the CIA wanted it. Our timing was good. The fall of the Soviet Union had left large caches of sophisticated weapons in former Soviet republics. The CIA was worried the weapons would be sold to our enemies. Buying the most sophisticated radar tracking could provide defense against the threat of weapons in the hands of a rogue state. It seemed a small price to pay to assure long-term military stability.

We looked around through Lex's contacts and found we could definitely get the radar system. For once, this was a deal we were doing with no interest in the money. We were doing it to enhance our own position regarding the legal charges, and also as something that might benefit the country. Money or profit was not an issue. We just wanted the credit for doing it. With a direct line to the radar system, we contacted our lawyer in New York, who went to Washington, D.C. to talk to the CIA, telling them we could be very instrumental buying weapons from Russians to keep them out of enemy hands.

At the same time, Lex was also working a deal to bring both AT&T bulk long distance service and pre-paid phone charge cards to Russia. He figured that with the democracy movement and an improved economy, people would be calling America a lot, and communication was the business to be in. So he was working both the arms and telephone angles while Gene approached the banks to see if he could float a bond for them. We were all busy and we loved it.

I met with a bunch of company executives, talking to the presidents, thanks to Gene's connections. The oil company chiefs liked me because I was both American and Sicilian. For some reason, they loved the Mob. They found it romantic. They told me to introduce myself as a Siciliano, and not a Milano, even though Milan was where I grew up. "They'll appreciate a Sicilian," they told me, and they were right. I would say "I'm Siciliano," and the Russians would say, "Oooh, Sicilian! Cosa Nostra!" When I said I was American, they would say: "Chicago. Bang Bang!" They loved everything they had seen in movies or TV about gangsters in America.

As the days went by, Gene, Lex, and I became ever more involved with the arms deals. The CIA was interested in what we were finding, and the three of us inadvertently penetrated some of the great secrets of the Soviet Union.

Under Communism in Russia, several hidden arms factories were considered so critical to the survival of the nation that many of the top leaders didn't know where they were located. The men in charge of each factory did not have to report to the president, so not even Boris Yeltsin knew the extent of what was in operation. The secrecy was considered crucial during the Cold War because it would be impossible for any one man, no matter how knowledgeable, to be able to pinpoint the locations of all the arsenals. In the event of a U.S. attack on the Soviet Union, something Kremlin leaders expected, ammunition caches under the control of top ranking generals would survive to be used for retaliation and defense.

When Communism crumbled and the Soviet Union fell apart, the men who had run many of the factories were allowed to keep them, just as though they had purchased them in a free enterprise market. Men who had made comparative peanuts suddenly had the means to amass great wealth even by western standards. They began contacting various countries and rogue organizations interested in buying everything from missiles to assault rifles to millions of rounds of ammunition. They also would make munitions and missiles to order—the factories were now, in practical terms, operating as for-profit ventures rather than working for the government.

We ran into guys selling shiploads of arms to Arabs and other Muslims—Libya, Iraq—countries that were hostile to the United States. I was less interested in the radar tracking and other arms deals. I knew that these deals might save us from legal prosecution, but I was doing what I considered myself best at—making money. And on this trip, the source for our new income was perhaps the least exotic of all opportunities—fish.

My New York venture partner and employer Leonardo had a friend who ran a large fish company in Norway. The Russians were major importers of fish, and I was asked to see if I could work out some deals for the Norwegian company. We started a fish trading business in Moscow and took in a few hundred tons of fish deliveries. Things were going pretty well, and we were getting paid on the side from the gangsters that controlled the fish market. We were making some money there, so we were subsidizing some of the costs of being in Russia. Unfortunately, this would be the only thing in Russia that would make us real money.

I was also working on oil deals, but to complete my work I needed to return to New York to confer with Leonardo. At JFK, something happened that was a harsh reminder of the legal trouble in store for me. I was asked to go to a private room by the Immigration and Naturalization Service (INS) for a baggage search. As one man went through my luggage, another officer was on the telephone talking with a FBI agent. It was very quiet and the door was open. I could hear everything, and what I heard indicated how much they knew about my activities.

"Yeah, so you want me to check for money?" said the INS agent. "What? Money laundry? What?"

I was hearing all this, but the guy going through my bags seemed really lame. Maybe he wasn't hearing it or maybe he didn't think it meant anything. I could have had a million dollars in one of the suitcases, but he didn't even look into them all. He sort of opened them, glanced at what was on top, and closed them up. He checked me to see if I was carrying anything, but that was it. He let me go home.

Still, I knew things were closing in on me, and I was desperate to get away from everyone who I thought was wearing a wire or talking to the government. I didn't know what to do next. One day, I was hanging out in my backyard when a neighbor stopped by. I lived in a very affluent area. My neighbor on one side was the former head of Goldman Sachs, and lived in a mansion that had previously been a wedding gift to the Mott Apple Juice family. A neighbor across the street was the ex-CEO of Rolex and another was a man named Steven who stopped by and said he understood that I owned a firm.

I said I owned many firms. Steven told me he had a problem. "I'm in the medical business," he said, "and I own a very big medical management billing company. I just bought a brokerage firm because I'm sick of always giving away all the stock after I do all the work on this company. I've taken many companies public and I need some advice. Something has happened in my firm. I just lost $1.2 million dollars on a trade and I think there was hanky-panky going on."

He invited me into his house to look over some of his documents. In about thirty seconds I knew what happened. "You got rolled," I told him. "The broker is in cahoots with somebody and they just bagged your trading account."

He didn't understand what I was saying. He had opened a brokerage firm with no knowledge of brokerage firms and he was excited to see that I knew so much about them. He knew stocks. He knew how to take things public. But that's a whole different animal than running a firm. He asked if I would come to his office and help him.

I went to the office and I could see the improprieties right away. His brokerage company president was hiring people and paying brokers who were supposed to be on commission. She was actually hiring them on salary, so obviously she had a problem recruiting. Plus, she had given a $250,000 Candies deal to her boyfriend as a signing bonus. I made Steven a proposal.

"Look, give me ten percent of the company and I will White Knight this place," I said. "I'll clean it up for you. I will fire everybody. I will put a good president in place. I will do it right for you, and I have the experience to do it."

He agreed. That gave me a new place to work, one on Wall Street, where I knew I shouldn't be then. But it was an alternative to going back to Moscow, which I didn't want to do. I was working on Steven's firm, helping build it up again, when I got approached by a broker from the past who had heard what I was doing at this company.

"Sal, I need your help," he said. "I'm doing some business where I have some money offshore I need to bring in."

I was wary. I knew this guy was good friends with Danny. Maybe he's working with the man, maybe not, I thought. I decided to test him out and see what was up, so I told him I'd help him out.

If I had trusted my best instincts, I wouldn't have done this for several good reasons. First, the guy who wanted to bring in offshore money owned a very small bucket shop, a totally illegal operation. But the firm that I was working with needed some cash infusion, and, I thought, maybe we could work something out.

"Listen," I said. "I got a firm I'm trying to rehabilitate. Maybe if you have some clients you could raise some money from, we could do something. I could work out for you to get a piece in this firm."

I put the guy in place in the company I was white knighting. But he couldn't do his job. He started doing private placement on the side for himself, using the firm's good name for credibility so I had to throw him out. I knew from all the indictments going down on Wall Street that it was just a matter of time for me, so I decided to distance myself from Steven.

Next, I looked at a currency conversion deal for Leonardo which in this country would be considered money laundering. However, the deal was to take place in Lugano, Switzerland, where such a conversion was allowed. The arrangements should have been simple. Some friends of Leonardo held Italian lire that would soon lose their value because of currency changes. Several countries were going to the Euro and holders wanted to convert their lire into either dollars or Swiss francs, then put it where their governments couldn't tax it.

I flew to Geneva for Leonardo and then went from there to Lugano, where I was met by a chauffeured Algerian diplomat who took me to people who were going to make what was supposed to be a very secretive trade for the equivalent of $30 million. The fee for handling it would be 15 percent and I would report back to Leonardo when I had confirmed that the cash existed. The men took me to a bank and showed me a large trunk of money in a special vault area. It was more money than I had ever seen at one time, and I was certain that the deal was okay.

I went back to Geneva for the weekend and set up the transfer for the trade. Then Leonardo told me he was not doing the deal personally. A friend of his in Zurich was doing it, a former Russian general with $80 million in the bank. For reasons I wasn't told, the general had been asked to remove his money from the Swiss bank accounts and needed the currency converted. I didn't care because I was supposed to make two or three percent of the final deal, which was plenty.

The following week the various operators met, and this time nothing went smoothly. There was obviously bad chemistry between the Russians and the Italians. The cost of conversion was no longer agreeable, and the deal just didn't happen. I went back to New York, and a week later the diplomat called and told me they were desperate. They were willing to give me the full 15 percent, so I got back on a flight to Geneva. The next day I drove to Lugano and told everyone to let me try a small amount first. If all went well with the conversion, we would handle the rest of the Russian's money.

The Russian wasn't interested anymore so I made the first trade myself. I gave 200,000 Swiss francs of my own for the lire. We went to one of the biggest banks in Lugano where the client and a person who appeared to be the manager took me in a high-security elevator to a counting room in an area with safe deposit boxes and a security guard. A second man there, who also seemed to be a bank employee, had a single safe deposit box in front of him and asked me to hand him the Swiss francs for counting.

He took the francs and said he would run them through the counting machine. Then he would come back and run the lire through the same machine. Everything seemed in order for the first five minutes while the man I thought worked for the bank talked with me. Then, when the counter didn't return, I realized I had been ripped off. I also was certain that the Algerian diplomat had something to do with it.

I told the diplomat he was responsible for the money I provided. He agreed that it was a rip-off but assured me that he had nothing to do with it. I should go to the police and tell them what happened. I got sort of lucky. The money exchange with which I was involved was legal in Switzerland. The scam was not, and the police knew the men who set me up. They quickly took the two of them in custody, but they recovered only 20,000 of the 200,000 francs. The rest was gone. I had never seen the scam coming. I was again a fish out of water, pursuing the money while completely out of my element. Just a stupid frog.

In the midst of the stress of the new business, the renewed money laundering, and being ripped off, I developed the same symptoms I had experienced in Moscow. This time I forced myself to get out of bed and go to a doctor. A series of blood tests showed that I had hepatitis C, a blood disease that was attacking and destroying my liver. If they couldn't stop it, I'd either die or need a liver transplant. Either way I was going to have problems for a long time to come.

Exhausted, I had to tell my neighbor back home that I couldn't keep working for him. I had set him on the right path and I got him get in touch with my NASDAQ lawyer so he could go after his former president. The $1.2 million she had helped take him for was definitely fraud. I also thought he had a good infrastructure to recover all the other money his president had paid out in sweetheart deals. As it turned out, he got most of his money back, the lawyer liked the firm's operations, and he got some of his friends to invest in it. They were doing really well for a while but they crossed the line with the new partners and recently were indicted.

I went back to Leonardo, the investor who hadn't really done anything except lose me money. He made a lot of deals, but seemed more inclined to just look at them. He loved only the hunt, so he hadn't committed to anything in Moscow, which had proved smart. The ruble collapsed and so the money would have been worthless anyway. His Norwegian friend stopped shipping fish, so the only thing that still seemed to be going strong were the arms deals. The CIA had sent a man to Russia, and Lex had located the missile guidance system they wanted.

My friends and I thought we had finally found our bargaining chip. The missile guidance system was considered an important asset in planning American defense in the event of war. Our lawyer explained to the CIA that we, the men who had been so helpful, were having trouble with the FBI.

"They're Wall Street guys," he told them. "They have some small crimes that they did on Wall Street, and we would love to work with you CIA people to help clear up their situation."

We were hoping for a free ride or a "Get Out Of Jail Free" card for our crimes on Wall Street. We all figured it was more important for us to be in Russia locating weapons for the CIA than it was for the government to convict us of some small Wall Street scams. So we forged ahead after returning to the U.S. while the others were in Moscow.

What my attorney and I did not understand was the long history of enmity between the FBI and the CIA.

Despite the fact that both agencies were involved in law enforcement, neither was very willing to do a favor for the other. The FBI flipped out when the CIA called to try and get us off the hook in exchange for what we were doing for them in Russia.

"No deal," the FBI told the CIA. "These guys are wanted fugitives. You can't make a deal with a wanted fugitive."

The CIA backed off and didn't want to give us any credit. The situation was even more confusing because no indictments had been handed down against Lex, Gene, and me yet. Or so we believed. We knew that major firms were being shut down. We knew that people we had worked with in the past were being arrested. We knew our own arrests were inevitable, but we couldn't tell what the importance of our arrests might be compared with the others who had already been booked.

At this point I had resigned myself. I figured, "screw it!" When they come, they come. I really wasn't worried about getting arrested anymore. Somehow it seemed like being away from my family was worse than being on the run. I was set to stay in the States, but someone—I think it was my mother or my wife—remembered all our discussions about the advantage in dealing with the indictment from abroad. As things got heavy, as the newspapers kept reporting on firms that were collapsing all around, my wife said:

"What are you still doing here? Get out!"

My interest had been to stay for my family, and their interest was in my doing whatever was necessary to protect myself from a long prison term. I finally saw the light. That very night I had my father drive me up to Canada. I made it through the Canadian border and caught a SwissAir flight into Geneva where I could pick up money. I had put myself in self-exile again. Then I stopped in San Remo and rented an apartment a block from the beach, next to the only gambling casino in the area. The apartment was directly behind a Russian Orthodox Church and I could see the ocean and the dome of the church, and watch them both change colors as the sun rose and set each day.

Lex and Gene and I had agreed to meet in San Remo in about two weeks. But first we were going to Dubai to swap cash for emeralds, which would be easier to travel with than cash in the event that one of our money launderers had given the Feds information on our Swiss bank accounts. Since we didn't know how any of it would turn out, we were going to start out with a minor currency-to-emeralds swap—$1 million. We wanted to see how the trade worked before we converted more. To protect ourselves we had brought in Aleks Paul, who was free on bail and able to leave the country. He wanted to talk to Lex and Gene to see if they were going to stay on the lam, and to evaluate his position with them.

In Dubai, Aleks looked at the stones we were offered as emeralds and said they were junk. The deal was a scam, so we spent a few days hanging around in Dubai and then left, glad we had not lost money. Gene said he had to go back to Kiev to finish some deals. I called New York and found that more people had been arrested, and from their names, I knew that my partners and I had to have been included in the indictments. That meant our names would probably be listed with Interpol, the international police cooperative.

I called a family member who was a retired Italian airport police captain and asked him to check to see if Gene, Lex, and I were in the Interpol computer. He did, and Gene and Lex were both flagged on the computer. I was not. None of us knew how serious the information that led to their being flagged would prove to be. Then we learned it had come because of the storage box Lex had rented for six months. We were out of the country when the renewal notice went out. Nothing was forwarded, no telephone calls came. We had left so many businesses and addresses behind that there was no place to which any mail might be forwarded.

After waiting the legally required time, the storage facility manager had the lock cut and opened the box. The papers meant nothing, and he probably assumed they were worthless. But the cache of weapons was another thing. The manager called the police who had no idea what they were looking at when they examined the documents stored with the guns. But they felt that there might be an interstate or international crime connected with the weapons and called the FBI. When the bureau turned over the papers to men and women connected with Operation Street Cleaner, Lex and Gene's names were sent on to Interpol.

Lex had left the kind of paperwork a prosecutor loves. It had names, dates, account numbers, and enough other details to prove money laundering. It was adequate to get indictments and generate subpoenas. It was adequate to get search warrants if they were necessary. And all because Lex did not pay a storage locker bill.

I tried to reach my partners, but they were working on different projects. Gene was in Kiev and Lex was in Moscow where he had arranged the acquisition of the radar system, then been approached about a dozen Stinger missiles. The missiles had become available through the ending of the Cold War, which had given way to numerous regional wars, terrorist sponsored guerrilla activities, and other forms of violence. The United States and Russia were supplying weapons to whichever leader was fighting one of their enemies.

The Stinger missile was a hand-held weapon that allowed a single soldier to bring down a bomber or other aircraft. In the past such weapons had to be either permanently in place or transported by special truck or railroad car. Often an entire crew was needed to successfully shoot down an enemy aircraft. Now a man walking alone with a weapon that could be strapped on a backpack could do just as much harm. The carrier was able to move quickly and hide in thick foliage from overhead spotters.

The first Stinger missiles would destroy anything they struck, whether a fighter plane or a commercial airliner. This meant that passenger aircraft flying near war zones were vulnerable to being either accidentally struck or deliberately destroyed. Also, a terrorist possessing such a weapon could go to an airport and shoot planes at random.

The United States had supplied the original Stinger missile to Afghanistan when its guerillas were fighting Russia. The missiles gave the Afghanistan fighters an edge, and because Americans were usually not flying in commercial passenger planes in the area, no one worried about what would happen if civilians were occasionally targeted.

With the collapse of the Soviet Union and the end of the war against Afghanistan, at least twelve Stinger missiles were obtained by Osama bin Laden who was, of course, busy during this period aiding and financing any terrorist who would hurt or destroy his enemies. At the same time, a new Stinger missile had been developed with a special computer chip. The new design was capable of detecting any commercial passenger plane in its flight path. The moment it did, the missile would be programmed to instantly change its course and miss the plane.

The CIA was desperate to retrieve the Afghan War Stingers. Bin Laden had already financed the bombing of the overseas embassies and killed hundreds of civilians. He was perceived as someone who would not hesitate to shoot down passenger planes. At the same time, it was known that bin Laden fighters were primarily poor people, and would always make a deal.

Lex was careful about documenting the Stingers. He could not buy them directly from bin Laden fighters in order to return them to the United States. Instead, he used his contact with a KGB general who claimed he had strong ties with Ahmad Shah Massoud, leader of the Northern Alliance. The Alliance were archenemies of the Taliban. They had old ties with soldiers inside bin Laden's camp who would buy the missiles for money.

Lex had a photograph of the Stinger missiles and he had obtained the serial numbers of three of them to verify their authenticity. Our attorney supplied all of this to the CIA, and the agency was fairly well satisfied that we and our contacts could deliver what we promised. The deal was a simple one. The CIA would pay Lex, Gene and me $300,000 for each missile. The Russians would buy the missiles under false pretenses, then immediately turn them over to us and, through us, to the American government. There would be no profit built into the deal. This was not to be a scam. This, as I said, was to buy our freedom from our Wall Street misdeeds. Or so I thought.

Outwardly, there was no problem. The Russians would go to Afghanistan to handle this because that was where the missiles were. They would do whatever was necessary to procure them without tipping off bin Laden that the Stingers were going to the CIA.

We told the CIA we weren't making any money on this deal but did want our immunity. That might have worked, even over the objections of the FBI's New York office. The CIA is not without power at the top level of the American political system, and the Stingers might have cinched the deal we wanted.

But there was a factor working against us: Gene's inherent drive to make out for himself on every deal he did and cut down what everybody else would get. On this one, Gene cut everybody down to nothing, including himself. Gene had the lawyers', our intermediaries', phone numbers, and could not restrain himself from trying to handle the deal with the CIA by himself. What he did instead of pitching the deal we had all worked out, was to tell the CIA we wanted $3 million instead of $300,000, ten times more than we needed. He wanted to make $2.7 million profit on each Stinger.

Naturally the CIA was furious, the agents totally pissed off. They said: "No deal. We'll figure out another way to get those things."

Now we had the CIA saying "no way" to $3 million or $300,000 for the Stingers. The FBI told the CIA again that they would not do business with us because we were fugitives. At that point, we were definitely wanted for arrest. There were subpoenas out for us. Even the CIA was backing off, though we had bought them the radar system and we definitely wanted credit for that. We wanted it to be used for the sentencing and hoped our lawyers would leverage it into acknowledgment that we did help the government acquire something it needed. Lex had all the paperwork and we had a lot of audiotapes. We'd been taping the arms dealers since we started working with them.

There were also oil deals. I was working on Saddam Hussein of Iraq who had large oil holdings he was only allowed to sell for food. We were looking at buying the oil wholesale, then selling it retail. Then we'd use the money to buy food at wholesale and sell it to Hussein at retail. The deals were exciting but impossible to complete then, and travel was restricted. Arrest warrants for all three partners prevented us from traveling outside San Remo while our lawyers negotiated with the CIA and the Federal law enforcement people.

Then Lex and I learned Gene had gone to London. We didn't know how. He should have been picked up entering the country, but he wasn't. We wondered where he was and what was going on. Finally we tracked Gene to the U.S. He claimed he was able to get to Canada, and then sneak across the border, but it sounded fishy to us. We reminded him that if they found him, he was going right to jail. He claimed he just had to see his family, but we knew that he hated his family. Trying to see his family, instead of flying then to a safe haven made no sense. Gene knew he would get arrested if the Feds discovered he had returned. They'd be watching for him at the airport. They'd be watching his family. The only reason for him to go back we were sure, was to cooperate with the Feds. Lex and I worked out a story to tell Gene.

"Whatever you do, Gene, don't get caught," we said. "We're very close to making a deal with the Feds on the Stinger Missiles." Even though the Stinger deal was dead, that got his attention. Whatever deal he made on his own wouldn't have the impact of being able to hand them what they so desperately wanted. I think that's when he decided to turn against whatever arrangement he had made in hopes of a better deal. Then he surprised me by saying he was going to Cuba.

"'I'm on my way," Gene said, like it had been his plan all along. Gene was whining. "I'm going to Cuba. If I go to Cuba, I'll be okay." Then he turned to his obsession with paid sex, and threw in another tidbit: "I heard you can get a mother and daughter for a skinny chicken there."

I was angry. "Okay," I said. "Go to Cuba or back to your FBI friend, you rat!" Lex and I knew that Russians were allowed in Cuba.

Things were getting hairy and Lex and I weren't sure what to do. We thought me might have to be fugitives the rest of our lives if we didn't go back, but we didn't know if we could face prison time. We wondered if we should call our families and have them join us.

Later Lex and I would find that Gene had only made it as far as North Carolina, where the FBI had found him and arrested him. He not only didn't make it to Cuba, he agreed to wear a wire on my friend Leonardo. He apparently had fed the information to them that I, when working with Leonardo, had been in Switzerland looking at a lire-to-dollar deal designed to keep the money free of taxes. But it was a deal that had not only failed but had cost me $150,000. Neither Gene nor the FBI knew these details, but the story was current enough and potentially large enough for them to cut him a deal. But it was not enough of a deal, so Gene decided to go to Cuba and have Lex and me meet him there. Instead, the FBI took him to jail in Manhattan as a flight risk.

Gene created more problems than ever from jail. The Feds isolated informants on one floor, then mixed them with people they wanted to turn into informants. The idea was the non-cooperators would be likely to talk if they thought others had cooperated. You could have two members of organized crime, neither of whom had spoken, suddenly turn against each other, each cooperating individually because of the mistaken belief that the other had broken silence. Gene understood this and was afraid to admit he had helped the Feds. Instead he claimed he was in jail because Lex, I and the others had talked, and he made that claim to people connected with Danny's family. It was an action that needlessly endangered my family.

Gene was kept in the Manhattan holding facility for approximately four months while Lex and I were abroad. I had gone to San Remo, to the three-bedroom apartment that we had rented for $1,000 a month as our European base. Before Lex arrived, I had spent time sitting on the beach, in shorts and sandals, listening to the Rolling Stones, and making notes for a memoir. I was convinced that my life of the previous four years was more dramatic than anything I had seen on TV or movies. I had $5.8 million in the corporate checkbook, a staff of 150 brokers, and many millions of dollars. The firm was at the top of the food chain when it came to small cap operations. I was a success beyond anything I had even imagined, and suddenly here I was, a fugitive sitting in San Remo, Italy, with access to perhaps a million dollars. Sure, it was enough to start life fresh where I was. But it was nowhere near the money I had tied up in assets and accounts back in the United States.

From San Remo, Lex and I took a trip to St. Tropez, where I felt comfortable, and we ran into Dicky from Whale, who was there with his wife and the chairman of a deal I had turned down. Dicky said something really peculiar.

"Hey, Sal, you have a lawyer who is sizing you up and he's working with the Feds."

I knew who he meant. It was the same law firm who sold us down the river to the shorts.

Lex and I called our wives and arranged for our families to come to San Remo to talk about staying abroad. Our loneliness was greater than we had expected. It was one thing to be apart for a few weeks or months at a time, as we had been for the last year. It was quite another to continue without wives and children.

Perhaps if our crimes had been minor or less complex, or if we had a few hundred million like Marc Rich, the financier Clinton pardoned, we might have stayed abroad. Most of our actions considered criminal in the United States did not violate the laws of one or more European countries. The conversion of money for profit was legal. And money laundering, for example, was not even a crime in Switzerland. The conversion of currency for a profit was legal and the police would not arrest someone living in Switzerland who was just wanted for money laundering in the United States. However, there were other crimes we had committed. Because the American authorities had indicted us for a variety of them, at least one was sure to be an extraditable offense in every country to which we might flee.

That meant we'd have to live life as fugitives. Already I had changed my hair color to blond to be less like my photographs. I had rented a car on a corporate credit card that could not be traced to me. I flew into Nice, and then drove over the border in the car. I would need phony credentials for my wife, the girls, and myself. I would show up in computers and I would always have to worry about even a traffic offense. That meant I was limited in how and where I could travel.

As I talked with my wife, I realized she was definitely not ready for all this. There were too many things back home—the school, friends, all the property. She couldn't just disappear without taking care of the assets. She couldn't cause problems for our children. She would have to go back and sell everything, to make proper arrangements. And even then, what? Did we want to spend the rest of our lives looking over our shoulders?

Soon I learned that more people had been arrested. The Feds

had come for them at six A.M. or so. They knocked on the door and rushed in, scaring everyone, handcuffing their target and taking him away. Dawn was a time when they thought there would be little or no resistance, but it must have been terrifying and embarrassing for the families. I didn't want to go through that. We lived in a very expensive neighborhood. Our neighbors were successful people, respected, and they thought we deserved the same kind of respect. It would have been terrible to be arrested like that. I did not want to have my family humiliated that way.

In truth, the idea of an arrest like that was so haunting that I often just lay in bed, awake, all through the night. I was listening for the cars, listening for the pounding on the door, listening for the sounds of men who were going to rush in, terrify my family, put me in handcuffs, and...I didn't know. San Remo was safe for now. By day, I looked at my wife. I looked at the kids. I took Lex aside and talked with him, and he started crying on my shoulder. He couldn't handle the separation, either. He also didn't want to live the life of a fugitive.

We had to go back. While the decision was being made in San Remo, New York's small cap brokerage houses were being taken down in busts and their records cleaned out by federal prosecutors who took furniture and equipment impounded for sale to pay fines, instantly vacating thousands of square feet of office space.

I had to face the fact that I had stayed in the game too long. I had refused to see that my fight for profit had only fueled the ambitions of the short players, of the Mob, of the federal prosecutors looking at corruption on Wall Street. I had been in an ever more profitable downhill spiral, and only in San Remo, looking at my family, holding my devastated partner, did I finally face reality. It was time to surrender.

Lex and I sent our wives back and put everything at home up for sale. Not knowing what we faced, we decided to go on a road trip to see parts of the country we might not see again. We were wanted by Interpol and probably in computers almost everywhere. We traveled with a friend of Lex's who was our Russian arms contact and a Grand Prix motorcycle racer with a clean passport. At the same time, our lawyers back in the United States were negotiating surrender arrangements.

This was a sentimental time for me. We drove down the Italian countryside to the area in Sicily where I was born. We spent a few days in Taormina, and then went on to Agrigento and the Valley of the Temples. I didn't stop to visit any family members. I just wanted to keep traveling, to experience the land and the people I had not seen in so many years.

We caught a ship out of Palermo, an area I had forgotten was a real shit hole. In the center of the city is a rusted monument that is dedicated to those cops and other city officials who had been killed by what Americans call the Mafia. We landed in Genoa, and then went back to San Remo.

The deal was cut so that Lex would go back first. The Feds had reservations about me. In their minds I had waited too long. Gene and Lex had given them what they felt was the most important information. They figured that I probably didn't matter. They wanted more time to review my case and consider what I could add to the prosecution of people they felt were most important to their cases.

I drove to Amsterdam by way of Paris, enjoying what I considered my Last Hurrah. I stayed approximately two weeks, keeping in contact with the lawyers and my family. The time was actually a little too long, especially since I was alone in that amazing city. Instead of enjoying the beauty and the nightlife, I worried that I had waited too long to take responsibility for my actions. I worried that I no longer mattered. That they would throw the book at me, charging me with everything they could and sending me away for twenty years. Thank God for that amazing Amsterdam weed!

It is simplistic to say that the federal investigators only wanted to clean up Wall Street. True, some of the men and women involved with programs such as Operation Street Cleaner were idealists. They wanted to ferret out crime wherever it was found. They were as happy to arrest small-scale players in a boiler room pump and dump operation as they were to arrest the heads of major firms operating the same scam on a more sophisticated scale. They were not seeking headlines or glory. They were fine people who never wanted to see one person illegally take advantage of another. They were also in the minority.

Law enforcement on a federal level is a political action, at least in part. Headline arrests and convictions build careers and enhance reputations. If the FBI director can bring down the heads of organized crime families, the headlines will look good for the Bureau. It will assure financial support from members of Congress who will use their pro-FBI legislation to win re-election. The U.S. Attorney General will look good because he or she is the boss of the FBI director. And the President of the United States will be seen as a person tough on crime, trying to keep America's streets safe. Come election time, the President, if running for re-election, or the Vice-President, if moving to succeed the President, will take photo opportunity walks through the inner cities of America's high crime areas to show how much the candidate cares. The captions for these photos will add the part about the Candidate's record on Wall Street convictions to show his intent to be tough on crime.

Then there is the money. Every two or three years, the business pages of newspapers and magazines mention an arrangement in which one or more of the major brokerage firms agrees to pay a fine of several hundred million dollars. They are accused of what amounts to a pump and dump scheme. They admit to no wrongdoing but pay the fine and get on with their business. No one is threatened with jail. No one person is likely to make headlines. On Wall Street, greed, as I said before, is the engine that drives success. Greed built the railroads. Greed builds the medical establishments; it was greed that fueled it all. But greed has a price and claims many victims.

Among them are the investing public around the world, victims of the systematic fleecing by banker, brokers, and analysts in what has turned out to be the longest and biggest scam in the history of the world, especially the technology stock boom of the 1990s. Wall Street is a quagmire of smoke and mirrors, a place where the investor faces worse odds than in a casino, a market that only gives advantage to the chosen and well connected.

As far as the Wall Street criminal is concerned, if he can reach the financial heights achieved by someone like Marc Rich, he can live in Switzerland awaiting a presidential pardon. Or if like Michael

Milken, he can pay a $500 million fine, and spend a few months in Club Fed, with a $40 million-a-year consulting job waiting when he gets out. I'm curious to see whether the boys at Enron, WorldCom, and Xerox will skate when the dust settles.

My bet is that the top executives at big firms will continue to get away with no personal punishment. The directors of the top Wall Street companies are often men and women of influence, both from political action and from carefully placed contributions. The names are old line—individuals whose pedigree has been clean at least a generation or two. To go after bluebloods like them as seriously as the agents go after the small cap businesses can wreck a law enforcement career or sidetrack a promotion and get an agent dumped into minor assignments. And for every agent who really does care about the little guy, who takes pride in harpooning the biggest fish in the sea just for the accomplishment of protecting the public, many more will let them go for the headlines garnered with small cap firm arrests.

As I prepared to surrender, the names of people being arrested were exciting for the news media. Major crime families were being discussed. Transcripts of wiretaps were being released. Stories of thugs making hundreds of thousands of dollars on the Street were titillating, especially when there was some head banging, arm breaking, and other violence to enhance the story.

In the case of my firm, Gene was the key player both for making the case and for making the headlines. His family connections in Russia, his knowledge, and his brilliance in setting up the money laundering operation were critical to the prosecution. Gene guaranteed headlines, documentation, and everything else that was needed to garner both news stories and convictions.

Lex turned himself in next, corroborating what Gene was saying. As for me, I almost held back too long. Once the government had one person giving testimony critical for conviction, and one or two others willing to confirm what was said, there was no need to make further deals. Anyone else indicted would face the full penalty of the law. Only those quick to cooperate, or those who were capable of bringing down a major name, would have a deal that could drastically reduce prison time or other aspects of their sentence. I was a question mark, though my lawyer finally convinced the Federal officers to let me give testimony, hopefully in exchange for favorable treatment.

We had always talked about doing time for the money laundering. We knew it could all blow up in our faces. We had seen what the government had done to others. There were sentences of maybe three years, maybe more. There were fines of millions of dollars. But usually the person was out in 18 months and allowed to keep enough of the money to make it worthwhile. We figured 18 months in jail and maybe we'd be able to keep up to $10 million.

When I landed in Kennedy Airport, I was facing twenty years in jail. I was taking medicine for my liver costing $700 a month, and there was no guarantee it was going to stop the slow deterioration. There was a strong chance I would need a liver transplant. This wasn't a few months away from my family. This was serious in ways I had never imagined.

I was in the line for Immigration when two uniformed officers came and asked me to step out of line and go with them into a waiting room. They were polite. I was expecting them. And I was embarrassed. When you travel abroad, every few times you go through Immigration you see someone asked to step out of line. Sometimes they're scared. Sometimes they're smiling. Sometimes they're confused. But everybody seeing this knows they've done something wrong. Maybe they're smuggling. Maybe they're wanted criminals. Maybe they're traveling with expired papers. Or false papers. Or almost anything, but everyone sees them as a bad guy.

This time it was me, and it was embarrassing to imagine that other people in line were thinking that about me. In the waiting room, the Immigration officer called the FBI agent who was either listed in the computer as the contact or maybe the person they normally call. I didn't know. I just know it took them a couple of hours before they reached him. Then they did a cursory check of one or two of the bags, and told me to go home.

First I went to Brooklyn to see Danny Persico. I wanted him to know that the shit had hit the fan. "'Don't Fuck Around' is cooperating," I told Danny. "Gene is cooperating. You didn't do anything but they're going to try and get you because of your family."

"So where am I going to go?" Danny asked. "You know, it's funny. I didn't do anything but I'm probably going to do as much jail time as you, Sal."

It was true. He had helped us a little when I asked him, and he had made a little money when I cut him in on deals. But he had set up nothing, owned nothing, never been a part of what we did, and never really had the opportunity.

"I'll never hurt you," I told him. I meant he could count on me, the way I had always been able to count on him, that our friendship was intact and so was the trust that was its foundation.

Then, exhausted, I went home. I got out of the taxi and saw how much my wife and kids had missed me. At least that was wonderful. I knew it was the right decision, and for the first time in months, I slept well. My giving myself up had stopped any sort of home arrest.

A week later I was called to One Pierpont Plaza in Brooklyn, across from the Federal Building. My wife came with me and we were quietly brought in and out of an area where we would not be seen. I was fingerprinted, photographed, and all the pertinent data was taken. Then we were taken upstairs to a brief meeting before a judge who set bail at a half-million dollars. There was more than enough money in collateral in our house to cover it, so my wife signed over the property as the release bond. There were no reporters, no cameras, and no actions that could be humiliating.

Next came the debriefing in a conference room filled with the men and women who were handling the case. They came from several different agencies and jurisdictions, and it was the only time I felt that there was a mild set-up taking place. There was no tape recorder, no video camera. There was no stenographer taking everything down as I spoke. Just people sitting around with notebooks, asking questions, and making notes of the answers they wanted to hear.

They wanted Danny. He was the big Mob name connected with me. They wanted to know if I ever gave him money. They wanted to know if I ever gave him stock. Of course I did, but not the way they were asking. Danny wasn't underwriting us the way some of the

Mob was putting up the capital for other firms on the Street. I explained about cutting him in on deals the way I did other friends from time to time. It was a way of thanking him for his help, not a Mob pay-off. He wasn't a secret partner in the business.

But I noticed that anything I said that might have made Danny look as innocent as he really was they refused to believe, or didn't take down. It was more like they'd ask if I ever gave Danny money, I'd go into the circumstances and all the details, and they'd just take brief notes. The only record of the answers I was giving would be those notes, and I did not know what they were. It was not right, but there was nothing I could do about it. There was nothing I could do about any of it any more. They just reminded me that once again I was nothing more to anyone than a frog.

I've thought a lot about the price someone pays to betray his or her values. I know that we all have a price, and often the first time we sell out, it's for something that seems foolish later. That $300,000 in cash I brought home sealed my fate. If only I had waited 13 months for that same amount of money. If only I hadn't learned from Gene and been seduced by my thinking how easy it all was. Playing it straight, I'd still be out there selling this stock or that. I'd still be fleecing the public. But I'd be like the pasta boys who are still brokers today, probably because they cooperated and never were so in-your-face flamboyant as I was.

CHAPTER NINETEEN

Of course, it didn't end with that first de-briefing with the FBI and the other law enforcement agencies after my surrender. They kept after me, and what they kept after was more about crooked stuff involving Danny. Which I couldn't give them because there wasn't any to give.

"Sure, I gave him IPO stock," I told one of the two FBI agents assigned to me. "Danny's my best friend. Obviously, you know that. He wasn't my 'protection.' I would go to him for advice."

That was enough to trigger a leading question.

"Why would you go to him?"

As if there was any question there. Why would I go to him? Because Danny was part of a family referred to as "organized crime," because he was a good person to ask about dealing with critical issues that came up involving persons in organized crime. But I didn't say that.

"Just because he was my friend." I tried to make it clear that I wasn't the one in the company that dealt with the sticky issues of conflicts with Mob-related problems. That was Lex's department.

"I was running the firm, guys," I told the agents. "I was wearing a suit, every day. I'd be going in and building up the firm. Lex was the negotiator. When it came to dealing with organized crime, he was the one to do it."

They didn't like that, but that was all they were going to get out of me, and they finally accepted that, and sent me home. Danny, I hoped, was safe.

"We'll call you back," they said.

I considered it very gracious that they faxed the indictment to me, rather than serve it with a team that would take me out of my house in handcuffs, which they could have done. That had been my nightmare—that I'd be rousted by a pre-dawn bang on the door and get hauled away in front of my wife and daughters.

But because of my cooperation, they gave me the courtesy of bringing myself in, in response to the indictment. The indictment was sealed because they didn't want the extent (or lack of) my cooperation to be revealed to the lawyers for the other defendants. It was part of the strategy when they were busting a whole group to make each guy believe that the other guys have ratted him out. They didn't want you to know what anyone else was doing in terms of cooperation.

As far as the real facts of the case went, they already had what they needed. They got that from Gene, who knew everything, and had apparently told everything. They had Vlad, they had Andrew Bressman. All these owners and dealers were already cooperating, so there wasn't anything important they needed from me except Danny.

I had already done well for myself and my family by getting the Feds to allow me to come back and cut a deal, one where I would agree to cooperate in exchange for less than the maximum sentence. The extent of the cooperation, of course, was a matter of interpretation. But the bottom line was I was going to plead guilty, rather than go through a trial that would be costly to the government.

The charges against me were heavy: money laundering, wire fraud, mail fraud, and more. Offenses with a potential 20-year sentence. The FBI agents had said they would seize all my assets, except my primary residence. That meant goodbye to the summerhouse, goodbye to all the cars, all the jewelry. I had two houses, one worth $1.5 million, and the other worth $1.2 million. They told me to sell the summer home, which was the more valuable one, and we could live in the other one. They knew I had money stashed, and when they asked me, I told them. I said I had a few hundred thousand stashed in Europe, and told them where it was. If I hadn't, they just would have been tougher on me.

I managed to hold on to about $140,000, which was living expenses until I could figure out where my life was going to go now—a huge question. Wall Street, and the trading that I had learned to enjoy, was over. Forever. I had already agreed to plead guilty to offenses that barred me for life from trading on the U.S. market again. What I didn't know was what kind of sentence I was going to get on my guilty plea, and that was difficult to live with.

Then, in March 2000, they indicted the whole group, nineteen people, in what was billed as one of the biggest Mob-related indictments ever done on Wall Street. I wasn't part of that indictment, of course, because I had already agreed to plead. That made the FBI guys worry about my safety. The ones who were indicted included some heavy Mob figures, and the fact that I already had made a deal was a problem.

"You should leave your house," the Feds told me. "It's not safe for you to stay here. Your buddy Danny is furious. And if he's what we think he is (meaning a Mob guy), you're in danger."

I wasn't worried about Danny, although I was unhappy to hear that he was furious. I was concerned about some of the other guys, particularly Sammy the Bull's brother-in-law. He was definitely known to be violent. And there were others. But I wasn't about to be pushed out of my house with my family, and I told them I would stay.

It didn't make sense that a hit would be taken out on me. There were so many informants working with the FBI. What was the Mob going to do, hit all of us?

But then another issue came up, which was that it didn't sit okay with the authorities—the FBI, the Justice Department, the whole prosecution team—that I was living in a $2 million house. Forget the agreement that I would be able to keep my primary home. Some of these civil servants were men and women who lived in developments, and it didn't go down for them to see me living where I was. So I had to sell the house, and move into a rental house.

This was the time when I began trying to focus on what I would do with the rest of my life. But it was difficult not knowing how much time I would be able to spend with my family. It was a completely open question what kind of sentence I would get. But I knew that I would put my energies and thoughts more in the direction of my family than I had before. I had lost all the wealth that I had amassed, but I still had them and I was very grateful. My family life had not been a smooth road through all this, and there were times when it came close to ending, but it didn't.

Overall, I felt as if I was going through a kind of repeat of the rehab I had done so many years earlier, trying to change my life after wasting so much with drugs and alcohol. In their place, greed and money had become my drug and it was time to cure myself of that addiction.

It was bizarre watching the run-up of tech stocks on the market and seeing the vast amounts of money being made in what I saw as the biggest pump and dump in history and knowing there was no way I could participate. But I vowed that when my sentencing and the repayment of my debt to society was over, I would do things that would benefit other people, my family first.

One day, I got a disturbing anonymous phone call. It was a threat against my youngest daughter, and that was a terrible experience. Then I learned that Danny's lawyer had hired a private investigator to find me. I knew that because the PI showed up when I was out, and spoke to Lynn, who was walking the dog. She told him that I was out, and asked for his number, which gave him the confirmation that I lived there. That made me uneasy. But not really frightened, because what was there for him to take action against me for? If he read the case, which would show what my voluntary testimony had been, he would see that I had not said anything against him. He already knew that I was cooperating, but I was telling the truth. So there was nothing I could say that would hurt him.

It was true that Danny had helped Andrew Bressman, and had collected a payoff for doing it, which I didn't know until the Feds told me. That was what got Danny into the indictment: the fact that after going with me and John Diorio and Forty to face the Mob guys who were threatening Andrew, Danny had gone back to Andrew and hit him up for money. I had told Danny not to do it, that I would give him stock that would be worth more than any money he would get out of Andrew. But he had gone anyway, and I think he got $25,000 out of him. When Andrew was pulled in, he gave them that information and it went down as extortion against Danny, and that's why he was indicted with everybody else.

Still, I considered it my fault that Danny got in trouble over that, because I brought him into the situation with Andrew. But even before that incident, I had discouraged Danny from coming around to my company, because of the way I knew it appeared. It looked like we were connected, which was not good for either of us.

"It will hurt me," I had told Danny, "It will hurt you."

When Danny did get indicted, he pleaded guilty, and pulled a one-year suspended sentence on work release. There were other arrests. On June 17, Turk Rambo was indicted in Tampa for pump and dump manipulations in micro-cap stocks. In October, Alphonse Persico was convicted on a gun charge, and then pleaded guilty to racketeering charges that would put him back in prison until 2011.

In the last week of October, a grim discovery was made in a white brick mansion in an exclusive area of Colt's Neck, New Jersey. The house belonged to Albert Chalem, the man we called Plug Head, and Chalem's bullet-riddled body was found on the floor of his living room next to the body of a man named Maier Lehman, 39, also in the trading business. Lehman may have been killed just because of the unfortunate coincidence of being there when the killer or killers came to take care of Chalem.

Chalem had been at Toluca Pacific when I had spent the time with him that led to my having a sit-down over the shorting of our stock at White Rock. The investigating officers told me what wasn't in the first press reports of the murder: that Chalem had been shot in the mouth, in both ears and both eyes. There was a message in that, and it was not an encouraging one.

"You'd better go into Witness Protection," an FBI agent told me after giving me the news about the double murder. He knew about the time I had spent with Chalem, the way I had worked out an arrangement to work with the short players instead of against them, on the last deal for my syndicate.

I said no to Witness Protection.

"I saw *Goodfellas*," I said, making a joke out of it. "No Witness Protection program for me. I don't want to live in Cornpone, Iowa with a new name, in some little shack, looking over my shoulder the rest of my life."

They didn't ask me why I thought Chalem had gotten whacked, but I think it was because he was very close to the Mob, swearing loyalty to them; but actually blabbing everything to the Feds. It was easy for him to be suspected of being that kind of informant. There had been an indictment against him, and then suddenly there was no indictment. So that made it look like he cut a very serious deal.

I was concerned, but I didn't want to tear my family out of our house. I hadn't come back from being abroad on the run to go on the run at home. I truly believed that if a hit was going to be made on me, it would just be me, and not on my family.

"There wasn't one star witness," I told the agents who warned me. "There were 20 more informants," including Gene, who had already given them what they needed. I knew how many of our secrets Gene had given them because when they were arranging to confiscate my assets, and I told them about the money stashed abroad, they said: "Where are all your watches?"

"So Gene told you everything," I said to myself.

Prosecutions continued throughout that year and the next. In 2001, I was working in the new business I had chosen, which was building houses. I was building houses in the $800,000 to $1 million range, making decent money at it. I figure that four houses would realize a $1 million profit, which would let me buy Lynn a house again. Until the tragedy of September 11, the matter of my sentencing was a big weight hanging over my head. It was very likely that I would do serious time; the question was how much. But a few days after September 11, I got a call from Lex, telling me that the information we had provided about Osama bin Laden was now being actively pursued, and our situation had improved. Three days before the attack on the World Trade Center, the Taliban or Al Qaeda had assassinated the man we had hoped would be our contact, Ahmad Shah Massoud, the man who had become the Northern Alliance leader.

Lex had gotten a call from a boss of a new section in the FBI who wanted to talk to him about the whole Stinger deal. We had done a careful job of putting it together, using connections Lex thought he had with both sides in the Afghan War. We had provided the actual serial numbers of the Stingers, which had been available in '98, and we had passed on what we thought was an active cell phone number for bin Laden.

To our way of thinking at the time, we had provided a way to reach bin Laden that should have been important to the U.S. government. Gene had fouled the deal by raising our asking price for the Stingers from $300,000 to $3 million. Now the information was deemed important, even though the Stinger deal had not gone through. Lex, for all his other faults, was a very patriotic guy and a diehard Republican, and he was anxious to help the country any way he could—particularly if it served his purposes.

Then the entire block of defendants indicted in my case pleaded guilty, so it ended up that there was no trial after all. Most of the guilty pleas brought one to three-year sentences. I was grateful to Lex for including me in the record of the details he gave the FBI when they came to him about the Stingers and the bin Laden contacts, because that improved my case. The FBI and the prosecution wanted to suppress our involvement as much as possible even after 9/11.

My future was still in the hands of the judge. Based on remarks by Lex's lawyer, I hoped that I would be spared prison time. But there was also the risk that I could be deported. If that happened, I could possibly go back to trading, because none of the lifelong restrictions against me in the U.S. would apply out of the country.

If I received no time or a short sentence, I would continue with my real estate development business. I felt that I had the talent for creating and running a sizable business, and building homes seemed to be my best prospect. I have had to re-invent the image I had created of myself as a man who would someday be worth a great many millions of dollars. If I do acquire real wealth again, I'm going to do beneficial things with some of it, say a non-profit enterprise for children.

But I believe that in life the people who create and acquire wealth are people who have the specific abilities to do just that. That's how and why they are wealthy. There's a viewpoint that says if you take away all the wealth from the minority of society that has the most of it, in 10 or 20 years, those same people will be wealthy again. It's their nature to succeed in creating wealth.

I don't like to think of myself as being better than anyone else, and I have to acknowledge the misdeeds that put me in jeopardy of going to prison. Yet, I did actually vindicate the hope that my school teacher in Milan put in me when he gave me the $10 and told me the streets here were paved with gold. I discovered that to be true. I lived on gold streets once, and I believe I will do it again. And this time, it won't be for greed and for money. It will be for my family. The frog may be dead, unable to deal anymore with the scorpion, but I have faith that a man lives on in his place.